A Principal's Guide to Leadership in the Teaching of Writing

✦

**PROFESSIONAL DEVELOPMENT IN
THE TEACHING OF WRITING**

HELPING TEACHERS WITH UNITS OF STUDY

LUCY CALKINS ✦ LAURIE PESSAH

*first*hand
HEINEMANN

DEDICATED TO TEACHERS

*first*hand
An imprint of Heinemann
361 Hanover Street
Portsmouth, NH 03801-3912
firsthand.heinemann.com

Offices and agents throughout the world

The authors and publisher wish to thank the following for generously giving
permission to reprint Eve Merriam's "A Lazy Thought." From THERE IS NO
RHYME FOR SILVER by Eve Merriam. Copyright ©1962, 1990 by Eve Merriam.
By permission of Marian Reiner.

Cataloging-in-Publication data for this book is available
from the Library of Congress.

A Principal's Guide to Leadership in the Teaching of Writing
ISBN 13: 978-0-325-02659-9   ISBN 10: 0-325-02659-6
Principal to Principal DVD
ISBN 13: 978-0-325-02660-2   ISBN 10: 0-325-02660-2
Principal's Guide plus DVD set
ISBN 13: 978-0-325-02251-2   ISBN 10: 0-325-02251-8

Design: Jill Shaffer
Production: Eclipse Publishing Services

Printed in the United States of America on acid-free paper

13 12 11 10 09 VP 1 2 3 4 5 6

Contents

Preface   *v*

One   March:
Prioritizing Writing Instruction   *1*

Two   April:
Researching and Planning   *17*

Three   May/June:
Launching the New Initiative   *47*

Four   July/August:
Getting Ready for the Year   *71*

Five   September:
Launching Writing Workshops   *87*

Six   October:
Making and Meeting Expectations   *109*

Seven   November:
Engaging with Parents   *147*

Eight   December:
Engaging with Children   *163*

Nine   January/February:
Engaging with Teachers   *179*

Ten   Into the Future:
Building Reform into Your School's Infrastructure   *205*

References   *213*

Preface

This book will help you with the beautiful, difficult, exhilarating work of supporting schoolwide reform in the teaching of writing. The book is designed as a leadership calendar, in recognition that reform occurs in real time and that real time requires hard decisions.

In order to teach or to lead well, a person must bridge the gap between ideals and practice, between big plans and the very real work of today and tomorrow. Whereas hopes and plans can swirl around in a person's imagination, coexisting in a place where all things are possible, actions take place in real time.

Over the weekend, we can resolve to do and to be all things, but on Monday morning there will be only one hour between seven thirty and eight thirty, and that one hour will contain only sixty minutes, and in those sixty minutes and in the minutes that follow, all things will not be possible. In our dreams, we can be and do all things simultaneously. When we are imagining all that we might someday like to do and all that we hope our school will someday be, one dream does not crowd out the others. But in real time, a principal must take the whirl of coexisting dreams and turn these into a calendar of actions. And when we decide to act on Monday morning and on Tuesday, those decisions have costs. We are deciding not only *for* some things but also *against* others.

We also hope the book keeps you company during the hard work of leading school reform in teaching writing. It will bring you inside a community of practice comprised of scores of principals who have also thought, "How can I provide my teachers with the support they deserve in teaching writing?" This book will allow you to stand on the shoulders of others who have tackled the challenge of supporting whole-school reform in writing.

You will notice that the book is organized chronologically, like a calendar, and aims to support one academic year. This calendar, however, does not begin in September nor end in June, but instead begins and ends in the spring. As you know, a leader must work strategically behind the scenes well in advance of the time when a new initiative is publicly launched. In order for an innovation to actually be under way when the school doors open in September, the school leader must have already spent months researching, imagining, problem solving, bringing people aboard, working out details, building infrastructure, and developing leaders.

Of course, it is optimistic to think that a principal could *spend months* researching, imagining, and problem solving in order to institute a single schoolwide reform. A principal cannot spend months (or even days) on *any* one topic. The nature of the principal's job is that he or she will always be multitasking. The principal cannot push the pause button on the needs of the day in order to institute a significant reform. Parents don't stop banging on one's door and teachers don't stop going on maternity leaves just because the school leader wants to proactively bring about significant curricular revision! This means, of course, that a principal needs help knowing the most essential work that she can do, given the fact that there is never enough time for all the work.

Although this book is a slim one, it crystallizes all the work that the Teachers College Reading and Writing Project has done over thirty years and across thousands of schools. The book is slim because it exists alongside and is aligned with other books written for members of your school community. *Units of Study for Primary Writing*, K–2 and *Units of Study for Teaching Writing*, Grades 3–5 are for the teachers in your school. *Professional Development in the Teaching of Writing* is for the literacy coach or staff developer in the building or district. These firsthand resources are built on the premise that it may not take a *village* to teach a writer, but it certainly takes more than the principal, alone, to reform writing instruction across a school! Within these series, then, there are books and DVDs that supply others in your school with the help they need, and there will be times when we cross-reference selected pages or scenes in these other resources. More importantly, we know you and your literacy coach and your teachers and your children will be in conversation together and will weld what you learn through this work with all that you already know. Together you will outgrow all these books in ways that take you beyond anything we could possibly imagine alone. What an exciting prospect!

CHAPTER ONE

MARCH

PRIORITIZING WRITING INSTRUCTION

When the National Council of Teachers of English (NCTE) held its annual international conference in New York City in 2007, my colleagues and I brought several hundred participants to visit a score of New York City schools. Those visitors, like the thousands before them who have come to see reading and writing workshops done to scale, came away saying, "I had no idea there could be whole schools in which teachers teach reading and writing as workshops and do it so well."

THIS MONTH

- Decide if writing instruction will be your priority.

- Bring stakeholders into the decision.

- Choose a particular approach.

- Throw yourself into your chosen approach.

What the visitors may not have realized is that it is far easier to lift the level of reading and writing instruction when professional development is shared among all the members of a school community. Michael Fullan, author of dozens of books on school reform, has said that if professional study is going to make a difference in our schools, it can't just make the individual smarter; it needs to make the school smarter. He feels that in most schools, capacity is far too scattered. That is, Bill knows A, Tom knows B, but what each of them knows is not aggregated. If your school is going to make dramatic progress in supporting literacy development, the day needs to come—maybe not this year, but sometime soon—when you say to teachers, "We are all in this together. We're going to help each other learn about teaching reading and writing. None of us will do this alone, in isolation."

What a difference it makes when teachers' knowledge of good practice is shared! As Tom Sergiovanni says, "Intelligence needs to be socialized" (2004). The NCTE visitors at one school watched a teacher, Zoe, convene her twenty-eight third graders in the meeting area by saying simply, "Writers," and then scanning the room, waiting for each child to pause in what he or she was doing and to look at her. "Let's gather. Watch me," Zoe said, and then she gestured for one table of children after another to stand, push in chairs, and walk to the meeting area where they sat in assigned rug spots, opened their writer's notebooks, and started rereading the previous day's writing. Claiming her seat at the front of the meeting area, Zoe began, "Writers, today I am going to teach you *another* way the essayists angle their anecdotes to support their ideas." Zoe gestured to a chart that listed strategies she'd already taught for accomplishing this goal. "Before I teach you another strategy for angling your anecdotes, would you and your partner look at the writing you did yesterday, and for just a minute, consider which of these strategies you've already used." Before long, Zoe had taught yet one more strategy, demonstrating it with her own writing and then supporting her youngsters as they practiced the new strategy. As she sent her writers off to work on their essays, one of the visitors whispered in awe, "How long has she been teaching?"

> For too many of you, the role of principal has meant, by definition, that you work alone, as no one else within your school has a job that is even remotely like your own. But it does not need to be this way.

"Three months," I answered.

Shaking her head in disbelief, the visitor marveled, "How did she get to be so good?"

The answer, of course, lies in Zoe's community of practice. Although she is a new teacher, Zoe's methods of teaching are not new. They have, instead, gone through hundreds of drafts and benefited from the brilliance of scores of teachers. And Zoe is not alone. If you establish a schoolwide approach to teaching writing, all your teachers—not just your first-year teachers like Zoe—will benefit from standing on each other's shoulders. As Tom Sergiovanni reminds us, "The greatest asset a school has is its collective IQ" (2004).

Today it is not only *teachers* but also *school leaders* who benefit tremendously from being part of a community of practice, where methods of leadership, like methods of teaching, are articulated, revised, developed, shared, and then rearticulated, further revised, refined, and shared again.

For too many of you, the role of principal has meant, by definition, that you work alone, as no one else within your school has a job that is even remotely like your own. But it does not need to be this way. Among the schools that the Teachers College Reading and Writing Project knows best, principals are continually visiting each other's schools, working alongside each other in study groups, sharing tools for analyzing the teaching that occurs across a grade level or throughout a discipline, coauthoring vision statements, developing and refining tactics for rallying their communities, sharing strategies, and improving teaching and learning. This book can bring you into this community of practice.

DECIDE IF WRITING INSTRUCTION WILL BE YOUR PRIORITY

Reform in writing will only go well in your school if you decide that this is a priority. Few things matter more than a leader having a vision and being able to rally people around that vision. Nearly every time I speak to principals, I quote from *In Search of Excellence*. The authors, Peters and Waterman, studied promising American companies in order to discover what makes their organizations work, and they came from that research with a clear message. They say, "Let us suppose we were asked for one all-purpose bit of advice, one truth that we were able to distill from all the excellent company research. We might be tempted to say, 'Figure out your value system. Decide what your company stands for.' Clarifying the value system and breathing life into it are the greatest contributions a leader can make." They add, "The real difference between success and failure of an institution can be traced to the question of how well the organization brings out the great energies and talents of its people. What does it do to help people find common cause with each other?" (1982, 279, 291).

The call to figure out one's value system is a call to figure out one's priorities. And in the world in which we live, a world in which neither time nor money is unlimited, this means figuring out how you will invest your time, your teachers' time, and your children's time. It also means figuring out how you will invest your school's discretionary budget, meager as that may be. *If* you decide that improving writing instruction across your school is a priority, then you are deciding that there will be *time* for teachers to learn about teaching writing—not endless time, not time that isn't hard-won, but nevertheless, time that teachers will use to study together. And similarly, if improving writing is a priority, then you'll help teachers ensure that children have time to write. If writing is a schoolwide priority, then you are also deciding that there will be discretionary finances to support at least the most essential materials and professional development.

Readers, the temptation will be great to decide, "My priority will be writing, math, reading, science, vocabulary, and school environment." Of course, it is normal for a school leader to spotlight more than one curriculum area, but everything cannot be a priority. If you say that your priority is to improve instruction in half a dozen subjects, then none of your reforms will have space enough to root and grow.

You will also be tempted to say, "*This* year my priority will be improving writing instruction, and next year we'll focus on improving another subject area." Resist that temptation as well! You know that no reform that is worth anything will be accomplished within a year, and if you aren't sure of this, you need only glance over research on school change to be assured. If improving writing instruction is a priority, it needs to be a priority for at least two years. After that, wonderful writing instruction will hopefully become part and parcel of what your school is all about. Before you rally teachers from throughout your school to teach in a particular way, make sure you do not consider this direction to be in the tentative, pilot-program stage. It is fine to pilot an approach, but do your piloting with just a cluster of respected teachers as part of a prolonged, fact-finding mission. I wouldn't try to rally the whole school to participate in a pilot.

I recognize that writing instruction is not the only wise priority you could decide to pursue. But if you want to make a palpable, dramatic difference in the quality of teaching and learning across a whole school and to do so in ways that will be met with universal acclaim by parents and teachers, there are frankly few other avenues you could take that would be more promising. You'll want to be clear enough about the reasons why you've chosen to prioritize writing instruction that you can share your rationale with your teachers, your curriculum leaders, and anyone else whose energy and commitment you want to enlist.

Reasons to Prioritize Writing Instruction

✦ Writing is widely regarded as one of the basics, yet it is often given short shrift. Writing has been chronically undertaught, and it is hard to find anyone who doesn't believe that attention to writing is long overdue. When a child enters an elementary school, math and reading instruction are part of that child's bill of rights. No child will be in a class in which the teacher says, "I don't really teach math, it is not my thing," or "The kids just do math while I lead reading groups," or "We mostly do math around special occasions—Mother's Day math, Valentine's Day math." Yet, although writing is essential to success in most subjects, and although children are held accountable for their success in writing, writing often does not receive attention that corresponds to the attention given to reading and math.

- The field of teaching writing is not marked by huge debates. Those who champion skills in reading and those who champion meaning agree that children need to work through the writing process, that they profit from direct and explicit instruction and from opportunities to choose their own topics and to write about subjects they care about when possible. The different camps also agree that teachers need to assess what kids can do and can almost do, and to teach children to lift the level of their work bit by bit.

- Most teachers are eager to receive help in teaching writing, allowing professional development to proceed more smoothly. Professional development in writing can usually proceed without challenging any teacher's existing corpus of knowledge and usually does not call into question any existing program. If writing instruction in a school is problematic, usually the issue is not a problematic approach to teaching writing, but instead that writing is either not being taught at all or it is not taught in any planned, consistent way. Every teacher is expected to be an expert on teaching *reading*, so it's not always easy for teachers to assume the role of novice or learner in that area. But it is generally acceptable to be a novice when it comes to learning to teach writing well.

- When teachers engage in professional study around the teaching of writing, it is easy to coach into and supervise this work because writing is concrete and visible. Principals and literacy coaches can support and supervise staff development in writing more easily than they can support and supervise staff development in other curricular areas because improvements in student writing are visible. Reading, for example, is not as visible.

- When teachers learn methods for teaching writing, they are learning methods for teaching *anything*. The field of teaching of writing has developed some high-level and very successful methods—including methods for teaching minilessons, strategy lessons, and conferring—and these methods have tremendous potential when brought into other curricular areas.

- When students' writing improves, there are pay-offs in every area of curriculum (to do well in reading, social studies, or even science depends on the ability to write well) and on most assessments. Powerful instruction in writing is one of the best ways to help students read better. Because writing and reading are reciprocal processes, the carryover between writing development and reading development is especially strong. Improving writing skills also has carryover to other curricular areas.

✦ Teaching of writing is relevant to all learners. The writing workshop is appropriate for kids with special needs, for English language learners, for kindergartners, for adolescents, for adults. When people write, they always work at their own level. This makes the teaching of writing a powerful area for shared and yet differentiated study, one that can bring a whole school and, indeed, a whole community together.

✦ When students receive clear, systematic writing instruction, the level of their writing increases in dramatic, immediately obvious ways. After a few weeks of improved writing instruction, children will already have produced more and better writing than previously. That means you and your teachers have stories and notes and letters, and then, more powerful stories and essays and letters to admire with the whole community. This creates tremendous buy-in.

✦ When people write together, relationships strengthen. We become visible to each other. We bring our lives and our voices to the table. Everything changes as a result—within a classroom, and within a school.

The decision to make staff development in writing a priority for your school is just the first of many decisions you will need to make. For now, refrain from announcing your decision to your whole staff. You have a lot of work to do before you'll want to roll out an official announcement.

Once you have chosen to improve writing instruction across your school, then it is important for you and your literacy coach, your assistant principal, and probably a core group of teacher-leaders from your school to talk through the contours of your school's approach to teaching writing. If you have purchased this book as a part of *Professional Development in the Teaching of Writing*, you may have decided already to endorse the approach represented in that series and in the *Units of Study* books. Nevertheless, it will be important to make your decision transparent and to invite other stakeholders to join you in mulling over the contours of the particular approach to teaching writing that your school adapts.

BRING STAKEHOLDERS INTO THE DECISION

There is no one right way for a school leader to go about deciding on a school's approach to teaching writing. It is probably important, though, that you consider alternatives and invite others in on your thinking. If that decision has been made already, you will still need to discuss it with others, helping everyone become grounded in the decision and learning people's areas of concern, excitement, and hope. As part of this, you'll want to be ready to address concerns people may voice.

Advocate for Your Beliefs

A school principal is called upon to lead. Inviting others into conversations about approaches to teaching writing doesn't mean you need to withhold your own views. You are absolutely entitled to be an impassioned advocate for big beliefs that matter very much to you. It is especially important for you to wear your beliefs on your sleeve if those beliefs center on children. "It's a huge priority for me that our kids grow up knowing they are writers," you might say. "For me, it is crucial that our kids not only *write* but *love to write.*" You can be public and passionate about your beliefs without shutting down debate or silencing contrary voices.

As I mentioned earlier, although you can certainly share your predispositions about approaches to teaching writing, it is also important for you to think carefully about the ideas of others. All stakeholders will need to know they have a voice in the direction of your school; you must at least show your key people that you have considered what they have to offer on this topic. You probably will not want to convene a community meeting in order to decide on an approach towards teaching writing, as that could create a momentum that ends up taking your school in a direction you didn't expect (or want), but you will certainly want to meet one-on-one with individuals, saying to one person or another, "I've been looking at our kids' writing and thinking that, as a school, we should invest ourselves more in teaching writing. What approaches to teaching writing do you think would fit well into our school?" Or "In what ways do you think this approach to teaching writing will fit well with our school? In what ways do you think we'll be challenged?"

If a person on your staff is a strong advocate for an approach you don't want to accept or have not accepted, you can usually find a way to support that person's central message if you ask that person to help you understand his deeper rationale. "What draws you to that approach?" you can ask. "What's the key thing in it that sways you?" Almost always, the goals a person wants to advance will be goals that you, too, can support, albeit in a different way. In such a case, you might decide to tailor your approach so as to highlight a few principles that a particular stakeholder especially supports.

The bigger point here is that the leader of any organization needs to create buy-in, and it will be easier for you to rally your community around a new emphasis on the teaching of writing if key people—influential people—in the organization feel as if their voices have been heard, their priorities have been protected. Your people will be more ready to invest in a direction if they feel their opinions have been heard.

Respond to People's Concerns

You'll want to talk and think with others about the approach your school will adopt. It may help you to be able to anticipate doubts others may have about the approach described in this book and to be able to address those concerns.

"A process approach isn't aligned with the writing tests."
The most widespread reason for not electing a process approach to teaching writing comes from people who worry that this approach generally does not exactly match the requirements on high-stakes tests where students do not usually have opportunities to choose topics or to work across a sequence of days. People who reject this approach, then, generally decide instead that they want every day's writing to resemble the writing that kids will be asked to do on standardized tests.

Let me speak to this concern. First, although there are defensible choices a school leader could make regarding writing that differ from the decisions I would personally make, I do not believe the decision to emphasize one-shot, first draft writing (such as one finds on tests) instead of the writing process has merit. There is national data supporting teaching writing as a process. The National Assessment of Educational Progress (NAEP) is often referred to as "the nation's report card" because it is the only assessment given across states for decades. The 2002 NAEP data show a positive correlation at all three assessed grades (grades 4, 8, and 12) between writing scores and writing folder or portfolio use. That is, students who write often and who are given opportunities to draft and revise their writing and to collect their writing in portfolios—in short, students working in a process approach—do better on that high-stakes test than those students who do not learn within such a context.

There is no evidence to support the notion that if a school's curriculum is predominately test practice, children will do better on standardized tests. In New York City, for example, the schools that do best on standardized tests are not those that substitute test prep for a writing curriculum, but are, instead, the schools that teach a process approach. The neighboring towns that boast especially high achievements on standardized tests are also strongholds for a process approach to teaching writing. I suspect this is true in your area as well—look at the high-achieving districts and you will see that very few of them boast a curriculum that revolves around a steady diet of test prep.

You and those with whom you work may still worry over the notion that a process approach to teaching writing allows children to work for weeks on a piece of writing, a luxury they cannot have when faced with a standardized test. It may be comforting to learn that whereas some advocates of a process approach never ask students to produce on-demand, one-shot writing, my colleagues and I actually track kids' abilities over time to produce effective on-demand writing. We believe that if a writer learns to form paragraphs as part of editing, the next time that writer approaches a draft, it is important to remind the writer to use what she learned (in this case, paragraphing) at the end of the preceding cycle of work at the start of the new cycle while drafting. That is, in the process approach towards writing, represented in the *Units of Study* series, teachers explicitly teach students that what they do during revision and editing must soon move forward in their writing process, becoming part of their rehearsal and drafting. This means that over time, a writer's first draft writing becomes much more conventional, more organized, and more well written. That said, it still remains true that in a process approach to teaching writing, students are not expected to fuss and persevere over refining the details of a text until they reach the final stage of working on that piece of writing.

> In the process approach towards writing . . . teachers explicitly teach students that what they do during revision and editing must soon move forward in their writing process, becoming part of their rehearsal and drafting.

"I'm not sure these teachers can manage a process approach."
Some school leaders also reject a process approach because they claim the approach relies on particularly knowledgeable teachers. Some principals question whether their teachers "are smart enough" to orchestrate a writing workshop.

I agree that a process approach to teaching writing relies on teachers' intelligence and skills. Instead of regarding this as a drawback of the approach, however, I regard this as one of the most important reasons to adopt a process approach. The decision to adopt this approach leads a school to recruit, retain, develop and make use of teachers' intelligence and skills. If you, as the principal, worry that your teachers are not up to the task of learning to teach writing well, I urge you to visit any one of scores and scores of schools across New York City and the nation that have adopted this approach schoolwide. Visit a school that resembles your own. I suspect you will see that our strengths are not in our DNA alone—our strengths are the result of the communities of practice that form around us and help us to grow and improve our work.

"I don't think a process approach is rigorous enough to be effective."
Finally, some people who question a process approach to teaching writing do so out of the belief that a process approach to writing is somehow less rigorous than an approach that asks every writer to always produce neat, correct, conventional, one-shot texts.

A process approach allows people to work as authors do, focusing on only some aspects of writing at a time, relegating other aspects to a later point in the process. Deciding to adopt a process approach means that kids in your school will usually go through a cycle of work on each piece of writing, starting with choosing a topic and planning for the writing, then progressing to writing a rough draft followed by making consequential meaning-based revisions, and ending with, finally, editing for publication. When a school adopts a process approach to writing, this means that students' work generally spans a sequence of days, and it means that along the progression of that time, the writing that kids do will not always be as perfect as possible.

> A process approach allows people to work as authors do, focusing on only some aspects of writing at a time.

For example, a writer might say, "I'm just going to scrawl my memories of that day," and then free-write quickly, filling several pages in short order, with those several pages probably not demonstrating the writer's best penmanship or spelling. A commitment to a process approach, then, requires that a school embrace longer-term projects and accept the idea that writers relegate some concerns until later in the process of work on a piece.

To those who suppose that this approach is not rigorous, show them the work done by children in process classrooms. If you do not have schools nearby to visit, show them the videos of children on the DVDs *Seeing Possibilities* or *Big Lessons from Small Writers*. Show them the writing samples produced by the children that are found at the end of each unit of study and on the CDs that accompany each set of units in the *Units of Study* series. The children's writing will speak for itself.

CHOOSE A PARTICULAR APPROACH

As I've said, you and other stakeholders in the school will probably want to mull over various approaches to improving writing instruction in order to come together around a particular approach. Your first decision will be whether to emphasize teaching writing as a process. We've anticipated objections some might have, but the truth is that there is fairly widespread acceptance of the notion that young people need to be taught how they can use the writing process to produce effective products. Even Warriner's grammar—the traditional old school textbook I recall from my childhood—assumes a process approach to teaching writing. This means, then, that in your school kids will usually progress through a cycle of work on each piece, starting with planning and rehearsing, then progressing to writing a rough draft followed by making meaning-based revisions and leading, finally, to editing. A commitment to a process approach requires that a school embraces longer-term projects.

Will You Give Students Topic Choice?

If you, like most educators, have already decided that writing is best taught as a process, there are further decisions you'll need to make before you've determined your particular approach. Odd as it may sound, the next most fundamental decision may be this: Will the writers in your school be encouraged to choose their own topics most of the time, writing about matters they know and care about; or will you imagine that teachers are assigning whole-class topics?

It may surprise you that this is as fundamental a decision as I'm suggesting, but the truth is that the tone and feel of a writing classroom is utterly different when students are given "ownership" over their writing. This means that students can progress at their own pace, with some students spending more time on one piece or another. It means that students can write about subjects they know well, using writing as a way to bring their lives and voices into the classroom, turning youngsters into teachers on topics in which they have expertise.

Respond to People's Concerns Over Topic Choice

Topic choice is one of the pillars of a writing workshop. If you and some of your colleagues are committed to the idea of giving students topic choices most of the time, then you'll want to anticipate and be ready to respond to people who have concerns with this notion.

"Our students don't know what to write about!"

Sometimes the principal (and teachers) in a school say, "We want to teach writing process, but our kids don't know what to write about, so we give them story starters." This is a reasonable thing for teachers and a school principal to say if they have not yet received help teaching writing, because it takes a certain amount of professional development to know how to teach kids to generate their own ideas and to write with self-reliance. If teachers cling to the idea of teacher-assigned topics (even after they've received help showing children how to generate their own topics), it may be that the teachers are loathe to give up responsibility for generating interesting assignments. This may have been the only job some teachers felt comfortable doing in writing classrooms. If *students* assume responsibility for deciding on topics, then what will the *teacher* do? These hesitations should fade away once teachers receive professional development. Once teachers study the teaching of writing, they will have a repertoire of strategies for helping students select their own topics, and their resistance to allowing writers to decide on their own topics will, most of the time, dissipate.

"But I have topics I need students to write about!"

Another reason teachers may have a continued commitment to assigned topics is the teacher's decision to emphasize writing as a tool for learning across the content areas, where most of the writing that students are asked to do centers on whole-class inquiry topics. These teachers are trying to kill two birds with one stone; they want to teach writing while also teaching students to develop and display a command of a curricular unit. I believe such a decision shortchanges the teaching of writing.

There is no question that it is important for kids to write throughout the day in every discipline. It goes without saying that students need to write as part of their work in social studies, science, and reading. The debate, then, is only whether these other disciplines are the best forum for teaching kids to write well. Informed people will come to different decisions about this.

Units of Study, the firsthand series for which this book creates an administrator's foundation, is fashioned around the assumption that students learn to write best when they are working with maximum engagement. The series assumes that human beings will be especially engaged in writing if they are able to write about subjects of their own choosing, and to write about subjects that they know and care tremendously about. That is, the series is built on the premise that in general, the best forum for teaching writing skills is within a course of study in which writing itself is the designated priority. It may be that for a month or two, the wall between social studies and the writing workshop comes down and students select topics under the umbrella of a curricular subject, but the series is designed on the idea that most of the time, students will choose their own topics for writing.

> You need to decide whether your teachers will rally writers to work within a shared genre, towards somewhat shared understandings of qualities of good writing.

I can imagine a contrary argument, especially in instances in which social studies or science is taught with such depth and rigor and engagement that, in fact, students end up caring passionately about the subjects under study. The downside of embedding all the writing that students do into the content areas is that teachers may focus instruction on vocabulary and concepts of the content area, devoting less time to shoring up writing skills. That is, every decision has its advantages and disadvantages, and you will need to make informed decisions. In such a context, it is difficult for the teacher to explicitly teach the skills and strategies of effective writing, however, because much of the instruction would focus on the subject rather than on ways in which students are writers about that subject.

Will Your Teachers Rally Students Around Shared Units of Study?

If you and your teachers decide that kids will learn to write best by working mostly on topics of their own choosing, then you are ready for the next choice.

You need to decide whether your teachers will rally writers to work within shared units of study. Can you imagine writers in a classroom all working in the same genre towards somewhat shared understandings of qualities of good writing? Can you imagine them drawing upon a somewhat shared repertoire of strategies for writing well? That is, can you imagine that for at least large stretches of the school year, all the children in a particular classroom might be working on, say, short stories? Can you imagine the work within a classroom will be shared so that for a few days all the children in the classroom might be inventing, using, and sharing techniques for building tension within a story? Can you imagine your teachers planning a sequential curriculum, so that, for example, one grade might focus on teaching children to write *realistic* short stories and another grade—perhaps a higher grade—might focus on teaching them to write *fantasy* short stories?

Again, it is helpful for the school leader to be able to anticipate alternate views. In this instance, you should know that some leaders of writing process approaches advocate that any sort of imposed direction compromises the individual writer's right to make choices. Advocates of such a position argue that it is crucial that children choose not only their topic but also their genre, so that one child is apt to be working on a poem while the next child works on an essay. The people who espouse this position claim that it is vitally important for young writers to learn to follow meaning to form, and therefore need to be in a position to control decisions pertaining to the form and genre of their writing. So even when students are writing in a shared genre, these proponents believe writers' work should be as varied as possible. For example, if the teacher were to gather kids together to study a shared genre such as feature articles, the teacher's main goal would be to help students discover that feature articles come in all shapes, sizes, structures, and voices. Advocates of this position suggest that a good deal of instruction must revolve around encouraging students to immerse themselves in studies of a wide variety of texts so that each child can find a text or two that resembles the text the individual wants to write. These advocates argue that if every writer is working on something different than his or her classmates, this does not hamper instruction because qualities of good writing are shared across every genre—that details matter to a piece of writing whether it is a political cartoon or a short story—and, therefore, teachers can teach a quality of writing, knowing that it might at one point pertain to the work children do with their poems and at another time to editorials.

This was my position twenty years ago, and I still encourage teachers to devote a bit of the school year to units of study that allow students to follow their meanings to a form. That is, I imagine one month might be devoted to a unit on feature articles in which the teacher might help children learn that there is no dominant structure to feature articles, thus teaching writers to follow meaning to form. For another month, a teacher might rally students to study an author, and as part of this, children might select authors they admire so that the work one child engaged in would be utterly unlike the work of another child.

However, I would not advocate that teachers devote the bulk of the school year to writing workshops in which each child embarks on his or her own individual journey. My colleagues and I have found that teaching has much more traction when children are engaged in similar work. For example, if we teach a minilesson on developing tension in a story, it is much more likely that our teaching will have traction if everyone in the room is working on a story. Then too, if everyone in the class is involved in writing a story, we can teach not only a single lesson on story tension, but we can follow up that lesson with deeper and more rigorous work on this challenging aspect of writing fiction. That additional teaching can be developed in response to what kids are doing and what they need. It is less easy to imagine how such a line of teaching would happen if, in fact, only three members of the class were writing stories in the first place.

Although I agree that some qualities of good writing are similar across genres, I also feel confident that it is a different matter to write an essay than to write a poem. For all these reasons, I think it helps to gather kids around a shared study of the major structures/genres of writing.

There is one more reason why I encourage teachers to rally all their students to work for a time on a shared genre of writing. I believe this means that the writers in a classroom can develop a shared foundation. Once a community of writers has studied some kinds of writing and developed some writing skills, the members of that writing community can harness those skills towards more complex operations, which allow the work of one year or one month to build on preceding work. It is valuable for teachers to help kids progress somewhat sequentially along a continuum of increasingly more complex writing projects.

THROW YOURSELF INTO YOUR CHOSEN APPROACH

If you've made the commitment to prioritize the teaching of writing, to use the process approach of teaching writing, to support student choice and shared genre work, dedicate yourself fully to this path. Whatever choice you make, I recommend forgiving the little problems in order to harvest the big benefits. Another time, several years down the road, you and your colleagues will no doubt look critically at whatever it is you are doing, refining and extending your practices in ways that can address glitches and gaps.

I can promise you that if you make this decision, if your teachers use the *Units of Study* books, and if teachers make a commitment to teaching a writing workshop every day (or even just four days a week), and if they plan together and help each other, your children's writing will astonish you. Their work will become dramatically, palpably better. In countless cities and towns, it has been the stellar quality of children's work (accompanied by the enthusiasm of parents and teachers) that has brought stakeholders aboard.

If you decide to make these commitments, Laurie and I hope that this book will offer you not only advice but also companionship, helping you as a school leader to realize that although you are the only one in your school with your particular job, there are thousands of other principals who have made the similar decision to lift the level of writing instruction across their school. And you need not reinvent the wheel. Instead, you can become part of a community of practice, learning from insights and ideas gleaned from all those others who, like you, have set out to make a world of difference.

By late March, you'll want to have made these decisions. If you decide to pursue the writing workshop as supported by the Teachers College Reading and Writing Project and more specifically by the *Units of Study* books, then buckle your seatbelt and prepare for a fast-paced and exhilarating year!

"Making Schoolwide Change with the Teaching of Writing." Lucy Calkins and Laurie Pessah answer critical questions about reform in the teaching of writing.

CHAPTER TWO

APRIL

Researching and Planning

Then I was a first-year teacher at Weaver High School in the North End of Hartford, I went home every evening to a sparsely furnished duplex apartment. I owned only a single lamp, and so as I moved from one cavernous room in that apartment to the next, I carried that one table lamp with me, plugging it in wherever I settled. One evening, reading student papers in the little orb of light around me, I realized that my little pool of light within that dark apartment was a metaphor for what it felt like to be a first year teacher. It was all I could do to see three inches in front of my face.

In time, of course, I came to realize that in order to teach well, a person needs a long vision. An experienced teacher doesn't progress inch by inch through the year, planning and then experiencing one day and then the next in sequence. Instead, experienced teachers learn to approach the school year having planned the longer journey, the ongoing structures, and the evolving plotline that will last across that year and many years.

THIS MONTH

- Use one-to-one conversations to tailor your plans.

- Visit a school where writing workshops are well established.

- Learn through professional books.

- Address teachers' concerns about time.

- Staff and schedule professional development.

- Build the infrastructure for good professional development.

Whether you are teaching a class full of kids or a school full of teachers, you won't succeed if you plan just one small step at a time. You instead need to approach the work of reforming writing instruction across the school with a big vision, one that allows you to imagine the year ahead and to put in place the people, the ways of working, and the structures that can provide a lasting infrastructure to the reform.

Devote the upcoming month to the behind-the-scenes self-education that will enable you to develop a big vision for the innovations your school will tackle in the year(s) ahead. In the upcoming month, take a crash course on what it *means* for a school to adopt a process approach to writing. While taking this crash course, you'll also want to prepare for the time when you go public with your decision. The crash course, then, needs to set you up to explain and advocate for the writing process approach, to spell out the broad contours of what this will mean for your school, and to respond—in words and deeds—to people's questions and concerns.

You'll angle your research so that you emerge from the month ready to rally your teachers' enthusiasm for upcoming reforms, poised to help your teachers tackle the predictable problems they're apt to find right away, and able to outline the broad contours of the professional development you'll provide for teachers over the course of the reform.

Use One-to-One Conversations to Tailor Your Plans

When I was a new faculty member at Teachers College, Arthur Levine came aboard as president of the college, and the first thing he did was to embark on a listening campaign. He held one-to-one conversations with each and every faculty member. I will never forget my conversation. Arthur began by asking me about my childhood, my parents, and my upbringing. Then he asked how I progressed from a childhood on a farm to my current position. He asked about my dreams for myself as a faculty member at Teachers College and my hopes for New York City schools. He asked what obstacles I was encountering and what he could do in the years ahead to support me. The conversation probably took half an hour—and it created the foundational relationship that allowed me to work for *fifteen* years as a positive, upbeat member of Arthur's staff.

I've come to believe in one-to-one conversations like the one Arthur and I had at the start of our shared time together. When Carmen Fariña and Laura Kotch, two of the administrators I most respect, became superintendent and deputy superintendent of Region 8 in New York City, they held 154 personal, hour-long conversations—one with each and every school principal who was part of their community. They asked people what they felt they could contribute to the work of the district and they asked also about ways the district could help them as well.

If you hold one-to-one conversations with all or some of your people and in those conversations ask people about their experiences teaching writing, their discomforts and hopes, their strengths and potential contributions, this will no doubt help you realize that many of your colleagues are hungry for more support in the teaching of writing and that many have talents and experiences they are eager to share. And if you ask about the professional development that people have experienced in the past, learning what has worked for them and what has not worked. This, too, will help you tailor your long-range plans for reforming the teaching of writing.

Conversations usually go better if they are prescheduled so that people can prepare for them. So, write to a teacher and say, "I'm mulling over the idea of putting writing on the front burner for our school for the next few years. I'm on a listening tour related to that topic. Could you and I meet for half an hour on Wednesday to talk about your experiences related to teaching writing? I'd love to know whether you feel comfortable in this area, whether you'd like me to provide more support for you and your colleagues, and if so, what sort of support you could envision being especially helpful. Could you bring all the writing that one of your strongest writers has done this year and all the writing that one of your more average-level writers has done just so we can talk about that, too? Could you also bring record-keeping or lesson-planning notes related to what you've done on teaching writing? We won't pore over this in detail, but I think looking at it can help me understand the questions I need to ask of you and others."

> Make a point to listen well, to use body language that shows you are listening, to take extensive notes, and to ask questions that unpack what a person says.

One-to-one conversations can allow people to feel heard—or they can make people feel ignored. Make a point to listen well, to use body language that shows you are listening, to take extensive notes, and to ask questions that unpack what a person says. That is, if a teacher says, "I think we need more *standards*," then you might say, "Can you tell me what *you* mean by 'standards'?" Obviously, you already know what the term means *to you*; the idea is to make that teacher know that you want to understand what the term means to *her*.

This sort of listening will help you forge a supportive professional climate around the teaching of writing—and meanwhile, the fact that you took the time to listen will in turn make it more likely that teachers will listen to you and to your emissaries (including the literacy coach).

Most importantly, act on what you've heard! Make plans based on what teachers tell you.

Visit a School Where Writing Workshops Are Well Established

Earlier in this book, we mentioned that on the day before the 2007 National Council of Teachers of English convention, the Teachers College Reading and Writing Project took more than two hundred visitors from around the world to see a score of schools in New York City in which reading and writing workshops are well-established. Over the past two decades, New York City has hosted thousands of such visitors. District leaders from Washington, D.C., San Francisco, Miami, Albany, Chicago, Seattle, Tampa, Boston, Kansas City, and Buffalo, as well as from scores of suburbs have come, many of them returning with their principals. Sometimes I have paused to think about what it must cost these school districts to fly six or ten or twenty principals from the far corners of the country to New York City, and I have asked, "Are these visits really worth their cost?" Over and over again, I've been assured that there is nothing that makes a bigger difference than these visits.

Sheila Ford, a former principal and now director of Teachers Institute in Washington, D.C., remembered her visit as a transformational experience. "We could not believe what we saw children able to do." When Joy Gabler, who is currently Assistant Superintendent of Curriculum in Hanford, CA, visited writing workshops in New York City, she returned with new energy and a clearer vision. "I could only keep thinking, 'What are Hanford children not receiving that they should be?'"

Of course, people need not visit New York City schools. Throughout the country, there are a lot of schools that can illustrate what it means to teach writing well. On the Teachers College Reading and Writing Project website, www.rwproject.tc.columbia.edu, you will find lists of the schools that could host a visit and there are thousands we don't know that could do so also.

When you visit a school, let the principal know that you, too, are a principal and that it will help you if you get a sense of the whole school rather than just a sense of the strongest classrooms. You'll want to say things like, "Can you steer me towards a couple of primary classrooms that you think illustrate writing workshops at their best?" and then go to those rooms, looking to see the commonalities between them. Then you might ask, "Can you also steer me towards a couple of classrooms that illustrate some of the typical difficulties my teachers are likely to encounter along the way?" If possible, make these visits with the hosting principal or coach at your side, and don't be shy about asking questions to learn how the host sees a classroom. After you visit the room, ask the principal, "So what do you note in this room that seems to be working well? What makes you feel like writing is not flourishing that well here? What do you see as the impediments for this teacher? The next steps?" Then say something similar to the *teachers*, too. Ask them, "Can you point me towards a couple of your stronger writers, so that I can get a sense of the writing that represents good work to you?" Then you will also want to say, "Can you point me towards some of your struggling writers—ones who struggle in ways that seem to you to be fairly typical?"

You will learn the most from children if you sit with each one and say, "Can you give me a tour of your writer's notebook (or your writing folder)? Walk me through the work you have been doing over the past few weeks." That is, don't look simply at the work of the day, but instead try to understand the trajectory of a child's work. Notice especially the progress that each writer has made from one point in the year to another. If you put the work that a couple of children have done in front of you and look at what various children did on one day and then another, you'll quickly see which aspects of the work are classroom-sponsored and which are individually chosen.

Questions to Ask Yourself as You Visit Classrooms

When you visit classrooms outside of writing workshop time, look through several randomly selected notebooks or folders and ask:

- Are children choosing their own topics?
- Are children writing daily?
- Are children writing at home?
- Has the volume of writing increased over time?
- Is there evidence of instruction?
- Are children developing in their letter-sound correspondence knowledge?
- Are children developing in their knowledge of conventions?
- Are children engaged and self-directed?
- Are children using charts as a resource?

When you visit a classroom during a minilesson, look for the following:

- Does the minilesson seem to follow a logical sequence or architecture?
- Is the teaching point clear?
- Does the teacher model the strategy for children?

- Are children given opportunities for practice prior to leaving the meeting area?
- Is the minilesson set up as part of a repertoire of strategies?
- Are children engaged? Does the teacher adjust his or her teaching if there are signs of disengagement?

When you visit a classroom during independent writing time, look for the following:

- Are children accessing their own materials?
- Are enough routines in place that children seem able to sustain work?
- Does the teacher confer with individuals and work with small groups?
- Does the teacher have a system for observing and teaching during conferring? Does he or she record conferences?

When you visit a classroom during the teaching share that follows independent writing, look for the following:

- Do children transition to the meeting area in a timely way?
- Does the teacher see the share as an opportunity for teaching?
- Do most students have opportunity to talk about their writing?

Learn Through Professional Books

You will want to get started doing some professional reading. When I open the catalogue for Heinemann, Stenhouse, or Scholastic publishers and survey the available professional books for teachers, I often feel overwhelmed by all the options, and I expect you'll feel similarly.

Find Informants Who Can Steer You to Apt Selections

My suggestion is this: Before you grab the nearest book and begin skimming it, recall the story about the blind men and the elephant. Standing beside an elephant, one blind man set out to learn about the creature. He reached his hand out and felt the elephant's trunk. Running his hand up and down the trunk, feeling its thin circumference, the man said, "Ah, yes. I understand this creature before me. It is rather like a birch tree, tall and straight." Meanwhile a second blind man also set out to learn about this new creature, only when he reached his hand out, he felt the massive creature's broad back. Flat-handed, he circled his hand this way and that, then said, "I understand this creature. It is flat like a giant wall."

I tell this anecdote because those blind men would have been far more able to piece together a comprehensive understanding of the elephant if they'd had a guide who could say, "This is just one part of the elephant. Put your hand here, too, and you will see this other section of the creature." Similarly, if you want to quickly piece together a broad overview of the writing process approach to teaching writing, I recommend that you rely on an informant to help you select key readings and to piece those readings together so you can quickly ascertain the essentials of a writing workshop approach.

Seek counsel from trusted experts within your own community, letting those in-house experts direct your crash course in the teaching of writing. Your literacy coach (if you have one) has probably done lots of reading on methods of teaching writing and may be able to serve as your guide. Alternatively, perhaps one of the teachers at your school attended a summer institute and has been doing some professional reading ever since. That person can become your informant. In any case, ask one of your internal experts to select key sections of a couple of books for you to read. "I won't be able to read everything," you can say. "Could you come up with a short list of perhaps four 10- to 15-page selections that would be especially key for me to read? And could we set a time to talk after I've read them?" Such a request will honor the expertise of your colleague, publicly demonstrate your own dependence on professional reading, launch important conversations, and set in motion a way of learning that can last long past this particular inquiry. This is one of the first steps towards the kind of collaboration that you'll want to eventually have crystallized throughout your school.

You may not want to rely solely on the sources your colleague suggests, and so let me also function as an informant. Especially if your school will be working with the *Units of Study* books, I suggest you start by reading the handbook that introduces the *Units of Study for Teaching Writing*, Grades 3–5, *A Guide to the Writing Workshop*. This is a quick read, so you may want to read it cover to cover, but if you want to zoom in on especially key pages, start with pages 9–35 and 94–106. If you really want to grasp a lot quickly, then shift between reading about a method and watching a teacher use that method on one of two DVDs, both published by Heinemann, *Seeing Possibilities* (grades 3–5) and *Big Lessons from Small Writers* (K–2).

Read, Rehearsing Conversations with Diverse Constituents

One decision, then, will involve the texts you decide to read—and it is very important to make that decision with care. But I also want to talk with you about the way you approach the texts. I heard somewhere that dragonflies

SELECTED READINGS ON THE WRITING WORKSHOP

A Guide to the Writing Workshop by Lucy Calkins

This 111 page book, part of the *Units of Study for Teaching Writing*, grades 3-5 set, introduces key methods for teaching writing and provides an overview of curriculum in a writing workshop. Although the focus is on grades 3–5, it is applicable to all grades.

Nuts and Bolts of Primary Writing by Lucy Calkins

If you have just read *A Guide to the Writing Workshop*, you will only need to read pages 8–18 and 22–51 of this book. These pages describe writing development in young children and show how teachers of primary classrooms can support their children as writers. It comes in the set *Units of Study for Teaching Primary Writing: A Yearlong Curriculum.*

Improving Schools from Within by Roland Barth

This book is not a new book, but it's a good one. It focuses on leadership rather than on teaching writing and emphasizes the importance of encouraging collegiality.

Change Forces by Michael Fullan

Michael Fullan's books synthesize research on large-scale, schoolwide reform. They are all provocative and important.

Expecting the Unexpected by Donald Murray

Donald Murray is regarded as "the father of writing process approaches to teaching writing." This is a compilation of articles. Any of them will be useful to you and your teachers.

see through multifaceted eyes, taking in the world through a mosaic of little lenses. You will need dragonfly eyes!

If you can take in key texts on teaching writing through the eyes of your various constituents, you can ready yourself for the various responses those ideas will evoke in your community. For example, if you read about the time required for a writing workshop and see this through the eyes of your teachers, chances are you'll anticipate your colleagues' protests—and this will allow you to consider your response. Then, too, as you read about the stages in the writing process, you may imagine certain parents within your

A School Leader's Guide to Excellence: Collaborating Our Way to Better Schools by Carmen Fariña and Laurie Kotch

> This book will be indispensable to you. It is a treasure trove of ideas for creating a school characterized by professional study and rich collegial relationships. There are chapters filled with help on supervision, working with parents, and the like.

Seeing Possibilities by Lucy Calkins et al

> This DVD contains approximately twenty snippets of teaching from writing workshops at grades 3–5. Teachers across your school will rely upon this resource continually, and you'll use it when you lead professional development.

Big Lessons from Small Writers by Lucy Calkins et al

> Like *Seeing Possibilities*, this DVD contains approximately twenty snippets of teaching, this time from K–1 classrooms. Watching even just five minutes of this will help you imagine kindergarten and first grade children working with independence through the writing process.

Writing Workshop: The Essential Guide by Ralph Fletcher and JoAnn Portalupi

> This book could help teachers understand the broad ideas behind a writing workshop. Teachers new to writing workshop will find tips at the end of each chapter helpful.

community reacting in certain ways to the ideas in these passages; again, this will allow you to plan your response. In these ways, your reading can help you rehearse your responses to the concerns of the different people in your community.

While you read, remember that very soon you will convene your faculty to let your teachers know that the teaching of writing will be a schoolwide focus for the coming year. Soon after you convey this message to your faculty, you'll convey it also to your students' parents. As you read, then, flag sections of the texts that you may want to incorporate into your remarks.

More importantly, notice how the authors of the texts demonstrate ways to let people understand reforms in writing. For example, when you read *Guide to the Writing Workshop*, notice that I talk only briefly about the importance of giving children *voice* before I emphasize the importance of also teaching children *skills*. I deliberately emphasize the need for explicit instruction in expository as well as narrative writing. As you read my overview of writing instruction, notice how I assuage worries. I know some readers worry that I might be one of those theorists who advocates immersing kids in wonderful literature in lieu of explicit instruction, who stresses "creative" writing but overlooks spelling, who teaches poetry and yet doesn't teach essays and reports, who wants to empower kids without equipping them with skills. Although the teaching of writing may be especially important to *you* because it is child-centered and developmentally appropriate, be sure to present a balanced view of writing instruction. Be sure your representation resonates also for constituents whose priorities differ from yours.

Read, Planning How You'll Unroll Your New Curriculum

As you read, you will also want to think about ways in which a writing process approach to teaching builds on work that is already faring well in your school. Think of the lessons involving writing that you have seen in your school, the writing that teachers have celebrated on bulletin boards, the homework assignments teachers have given. Think about ways in which all that existing writing is similar to what you find in the professional literature on teaching writing. Take a walk through your school. If you look closely at the writing on display, you can see the teaching that preceded that writing. Perhaps you will find there are classes in which children already choose their own topics. It will help you to locate ways the teaching of writing described in the professional reading seems like a natural extension of good work that is already underway in your school. Instead of presenting your plan for a schoolwide commitment to writing as a referendum on what teachers have already been doing, this will allow you to characterize the new work as a natural next step, as a way to extend the good work that teachers have already demonstrated.

Read, Gleaning an Overview of What the Future Holds

Skim parts of the books. You may be fascinated with the details of writing development and instruction, but especially at this early stage in the reform effort, it is not important for you to be in a position to teach the fine points of revision to a class full of second graders! You *do*, however, need to be able to imagine what writing workshops will look like at all the grade levels across your school. You need to envision what it means to teach writing well in kindergarten, in first grade, in all the grades. How will the writing workshops that you aim to establish be similar and different across the grades?

As you read, think about the fact that you will need to provision teachers with the professional development, supplies, time, and supervision they need. For example, when you watch classroom scenarios on the DVDs, do so with an eye towards the resources your teachers will need in order to lead effective writing workshops. Think, "What materials do these classrooms have that my rooms will need?" You'll be gratified to see that the teaching of writing is an inexpensive enterprise, one that requires very little provisioning, but you will definitely want to provide teachers with the limited materials that make teaching writing easier (more on this later).

You will also want to identify the big challenges that you and your teachers will confront once you have suggested that the school place a new emphasis on the teaching of writing. What demands will this approach place on your people? Some of those challenges will be idiosyncratic ones, unique to your particular school, but many of them will be challenges that principals before you have also encountered. The upcoming section will help you address the challenge of finding time for writing. It will especially help you plan ways to provide your teachers with first-class staff development.

Address Teachers' Concerns About Time

Your decision to spotlight the teaching of writing will place new demands on an already overcrowded curriculum. Teachers will be expected to support a level of writing productivity that exceeds anything most teachers have ever known. Allington's research has shown that in exemplary teachers' classrooms, kids write ten times more than they do in other classrooms—and your goal will be for all your teachers to become exemplary teachers of writing. In Allington's research, children in an exemplary teachers' *first grade* classroom, for example, wrote an average of four pages a day (and read thirty-six books a week, three times each). In contrast, in the classrooms of teachers who were identified by principals as solid, average teachers, first graders wrote an average of three sentences a day. Therefore, improving the teaching of writing will start with and center around increasing both the time allotted for writing and the volume of writing (Teachers College, 12/6/06).

Bring the Issue of Time Out from the Shadows

Teachers know that one of the biggest problems in American schools today is inflation—inflation of the curriculum, with everyone adding and multiplying all that a teacher is expected to "cover." Writing workshop isn't something that can be wedged into the seams of an already crowded curriculum. You will play a critical role, therefore, in helping teachers determine where they will get the requisite time to lead a daily writing workshop.

Questions regarding time are enormously important because what human beings do with time is what we do with our lives. Although I suggest that you, as the school's leader, avoid micromanaging every minute of teachers' days, I also don't think it is wise for you to circumvent conversations about how teachers schedule their days. You'll want to sympathize with teachers who are frightened to admit they cannot find time to teach, say, the expected twenty minutes of vocabulary every day. Of course, this example is just one case in point; this situation can occur around all sorts of subject areas, multiplying that feeling. Roland Barth, the founder of Harvard's famous Principal's Center and author of a score of books on school leadership and change, including *Run School Run*, has said that the healthiness of a school's climate is directly related to the number of non-discussables in that school. He describes these non-discussables as the elephants in the room that everyone sees but no one discusses, except in the parking lot, the lavatory, or at home with our spouses and partners. "These are the big huge issues that we're gifted and talented at tiptoeing around," he says (Teachers College, 11/07/07).

> One of the biggest problems in American schools today is inflation of the curriculum . . . . Writing workshop isn't something that can be wedged into the seams of an already crowded curriculum.

In far too many schools, the inflated curriculum has created a gigantic non-discussable. Most teachers know they are not covering all they are expected to cover, and most believe that no one in the school is doing so. They believe that the expectations are impossible. Therefore, when you (or others in positions of power) say that you expect teachers to spend this or that amount of time on a subject, these instructions sometimes roll off teachers as if they were made of Teflon.

It is problematic if all, or even just some, of your teachers ignore your curriculum requests. Of course, some of the time you may not really care. Perhaps it was the district that made that announcement about vocabulary instruction and you actually believe that vocabulary is best tucked into a rigorous discipline-based curriculum (as research suggests). But there will be other times when you very much care, when it is crucial to you that your staff follow your instructions. You do not want the culture of your school to be such that you say, "Let's put a spotlight on writing and begin to give writing the same amount of time as we give to reading and math. Let's devote an hour a day to writing," and teachers nod yes but don't do it. Nor do you want to start creeping around, checking up on every teacher's use of every moment. Doing so, and especially doing so without addressing the larger problem, will only create a climate of deceit and feelings of shame, guilt, and defensiveness. My suggestion, then, is that you acknowledge that it will never be easy to decide how to make best use of time and you create a culture of transparency around this important topic.

Instead of talking to teachers first and most about the need to shoehorn writing into the overcrowded curriculum, I'd launch schoolwide work on the topic of time, keeping this as far from the writing initiative as possible. Work with your teachers around the challenge to make good use of time, and be up-front about time-related decisions before you add new stress to the issue by talking about adding time for writing.

Working on this general topic at least a few weeks (if not longer) before you add new stress to the issue by talking about the teaching of writing. The fact that teachers feel the curriculum is overcrowded and the fact that they are sometimes not up-front about how they spend time is a separate issue from the fact that teachers find it hard to add writing workshops into their overcrowded day. If you lump the two issues together, you let the teaching of writing carry more than its share of the stress.

It is crucial that any school principal be willing to put teachers' concerns about the overcrowded curriculum at the center of the table and study the real, true facts of the situation. Barth says that school leaders would be wise to bring the conversations that are now occurring in the parking lot and the bathrooms out from the shadows. Start this inquiry with the assumption that the data you find will change you, it will affect you, and you will alter some of the messages you have given teachers. Start with this assumption because you can also assume that the data you find will challenge teachers, and you want that data to change teachers as well. As Ralph Peterson once said to me, "We cannot affect another person if we are not willing to be affected by that person." If you expect this inquiry to change you and are prepared to let this be public—to say to teachers, "I'm realizing that I need to change what I have been asking"—then you are in a better position to also, in the end, say to teachers, "I hope this information is changing you."

So gather real, true data. How much time are teachers really spending in various aspects of teaching? What corners are teachers cutting? Involve others in gathering data. If you do this, you will find that it is not remotely possible that teachers on your staff can do all that they have been asked to do. Do the arithmetic yourself, or sit with your literacy coach or a teacher and ask that person to help you do the arithmetic. You will probably see that teachers in your school can't possibly jump through all the hoops they've been given and that even your very best teachers are ignoring a fair percentage of the time requirements. They must!

Be Prepared to Offer Solutions

One big issue to resolve is how much time needs to be devoted to teaching skills *out of* context and how much time can be devoted to helping children learn skills *in* context. Take the teaching of reading, for example. One could list all the isolated skills that might appear on a list of state standards or that might show up on a standardized test: synthesizing, inferring, predicting, monitoring for sense, finding main ideas, determining importance, learning high-frequency words, understanding synonyms, using context clues to understand vocabulary, and the like. These are all words that people use to describe what skilled readers do. They are skills that beginning readers need to develop over time. But if children are deeply engaged in rigorous, thoughtful reading, and if they are making sense of text as they read and talk and write in response to that reading, aren't they developing skills that constitute that reading? Why do teachers need to cancel *reading time* to talk about one of these skills and to administer skill-builder worksheets on that skill? If a school decides to "drill down" to isolated skills, the principal and teachers need first to resolve the question of whether these reading skills even exist in isolation. How is it possible to teach a reader to synthesize without also teaching inference and monitoring for sense? That is, is it really true that those skills *can* exist in isolation?

> Gather real, true data. . . . If you do this, you will find that it is not remotely possible that teachers on your staff can do all that they have been asked to do.

As your school looks at the crowded curriculum, my hope is that you will see that skills that are worth teaching are important because they are integral to reading well and to writing well, and most of those skills are strengthened through rigorous engagement in reading and writing. One place to start, then, is to examine students' work to see whether the skills that teachers feel pressured to teach *out* of context are, in fact, being learned *in* context. It may be that you and teachers can look over lists of skills (such as any list of state standards) and agree that dozens of these skills are being developed within the context of rich, rigorous reading and writing workshops. If you cross some items off the "must cover" list, you will be in a good position to say to teachers, "I also need you to make some changes."

The first change I would insist on is a new honesty and openness. If I were a school principal, I'd put that into operation by asking each teacher to begin by making a commitment to post a flow-of-the-day chart detailing the day's agenda for children, and I'd ask teachers to stay inside the confines of that chart. That is, if math is supposed to begin at 11:00, a teacher needs to worry if it is 11:10 and math has not started. Children benefit from working inside predictable time structures. They can see they have half an hour to finish an allotted amount of math and can work to accomplish the goal within that structure. Teachers, too, need to make cutting decisions. Perhaps a teacher decides to add a second example to embellish a minilesson, but the teacher needs to bear in mind that the decision has a cost. She is taking time from something else—perhaps she'd rather make a different choice.

The second change I'd ask is that teachers be willing to consider ways they could save time—and invest the time they save. Before engaging in this talk, you may want to research the different ways in which teachers in your school already use time. If you and other administrators in the school set out to collect some data on this, you'll soon find that some teachers have a great deal more instructional time in their day than do other teachers. Look especially for how different teachers handle transitions during the day or at the start and end of the day. For example, one year, Anna Marie Carillo, the principal of PS 116 in New York City, investigated how teachers across the school handled the final moments of the day. For two weeks, Anna Marie and her leadership team made a point to stop by as many classrooms as they could during the final half hour of the day. What they found was that in some classrooms, packing up began a full twenty minutes before the end of the day. These teachers gave kids long stretches of time to copy down the evening's homework (rather than expecting them to do this on the run throughout the day). Some teachers had elaborate procedures for passing out the papers that kids would need for their homework. Some called one table at a time to the coat rack and had the whole class poised on the edges of their seats with coats and backpacks in hand well before the buzzer signaled the end of the day. Meanwhile, in other rooms, children worked right up until that end-of-the-day buzzer, and the going-home rituals all occurred in a flash as kids gathered their stuff and traipsed from the room.

Principals have also noticed similar differences in the teachers' use of morning time and in the transitions preceding and following lunch and special assemblies. For example, in many NYC schools, teachers meet their students in the auditorium or the gym at the start of the day and walk the line of children to the classrooms. Some teachers stop half a dozen times en route to be sure stragglers keep up with the line. These teachers also tend to ask the entire class to wait outside the classroom door and then send only a cluster of kids at a time into the room to hang up their coats and settle at their desks. This means that for these teachers, a full ten minutes of the day was spent simply crossing the threshold of the classroom. Now if morning transitions are prolonged in that fashion, this eats up valuable minutes. Of course, a school principal may want to work with teachers needing help with these transitions without attaching this supervision to the addition of a writing workshop, making it less likely that teachers approach the teaching of writing feeling as if this subject will be one that gets them into trouble.

It will be important for you to help teachers examine ways in which they could save minutes here and there across the day, but in order for teachers to devote an hour a day to a writing workshop, some hard decisions will need to be made.

Ways Schools Make Time for Writing Instruction

✦ Consolidate social studies and science into thematic studies. Some schools decide that reading, writing, and arithmetic are so essential to every other subject that they make these subjects priorities, consolidating the time spent on other subjects. For example, they decide that children will study social studies and science in just one hour a day of "thematic studies." Sometimes the topic during thematic studies time is primarily a social studies topic, sometimes it is primarily a science topic, and often the one topic—say, water—has ramifications in both disciplines.

✦ Vary the schedule across the year. Some schools decide that for one or two months of the year, children's *reading* will revolve around a social studies or science topic, and for another month or two, children's *writing* will do the same. In this way, there are portions of the year when either reading time or writing time is merged with social studies or science time. This may not alter the flow of every day, but it does allow for portions of the year when a teacher has more time flexibility. These portions of the year tend to provide the teacher with time to do more with vocabulary and spelling (allowing the teacher to devote less time to these subjects earlier in the year), as well as more with social studies and science.

✦ Devote three hours a day to the language arts block. Some schools decide that penmanship, spelling, and vocabulary are all well served by writing, so they constrain the amount of time teachers spend teaching those other language arts subjects to give writing its due. Generally this means that a teacher spends an hour a day teaching reading, plus twenty minutes a day on phonics, word study, and spelling, and time also on reading aloud and on whole-class discussions on the read-aloud book. Language arts instruction, then, consumes three hours on most days, with one hour of this time reserved for writing. This means, of course, that the teacher does not lead guided reading groups outside of reading instruction. Small-group instruction in reading occurs within the reading workshop itself and after and before school for children with special needs but does not consume instructional time that has been set aside for writing.

✦ Teach each subject four times per week. Some schools decide that every subject (yes, even math) can be taught four times a week without disrupting the momentum of that subject.

✦ Reduce other writing times. Some schools find that before adopting a workshop approach to writing, writing was tucked throughout the curriculum, with writing activities inserted into reading, spelling, and social studies. At least for a time, as teachers spotlight the writing workshop itself as the primary forum for teaching writing, they will probably want to bypass the writing assignments within the reading textbook and to cut down on much of the other free-floating writing that students were doing so that now most of the writing is done within a writing workshop. This, of course, frees up lots of bits of time, although it doesn't open up a free hour every day.

✦ Uproot "weeds." Some schools take this opportunity to help teachers do something that Douglas Reeves calls weeding the garden. In order for there to be space for new plants to grow—that is, for writing to flourish— a person needs to pull out the weeds. Assure teachers that you will do your part in "weeding the garden," taking away some of the things that take up their instructional time. Reeves suggests that principals ask teachers to consider all the little riffraff that fills the day, the week, the year, much of it imposed from above. Reeves encourages principals to create a joint exercise in which each person, in turn, proposes a way to weed the garden. "I propose getting rid of the fifth grade state reports," one person says. "I propose we stop the endless PA announcements," another says. "I think we can cancel the St. Patrick's Day party," and so on. Of course, deleting these items will require more conversation, but that conversation needs to begin with the assumption that one cannot add onto the curriculum without also subtracting from it (Teachers College, 11/6/06).

Staff and Schedule Professional Development

Chances are good that as you read about the teaching of writing, you'll find yourself thinking that your teachers will need help learning how to teach writing well. It is very likely that none of your teachers have taken a single graduate level course in the teaching of writing and that they also feel insecure as writers themselves. So listen to your instincts!

Michael Fullan has pointed out that it takes capacity in order to build capacity. I agree. In order to develop your teachers' knowledge and skills, it is crucial that they have the opportunity to learn from at least one person (if not many people) who have more advanced skills than they have in teaching writing.

> To develop your teachers' knowledge and skills, it is crucial that they have the opportunity to learn from at least one person (if not many people) who have more advanced skills than they have in teaching writing.

You have three choices. You can rely on an outside expert, you can develop your own internal expert(s), or you can do a combination of these. If possible, I recommend the latter course. Over the past thirty years, I have witnessed hundreds and hundreds of schools that have lifted themselves out of the quagmire in the teaching of writing with relatively small amounts of help from an outside consultant. You may ask, is it possible for a school to make these improvements without hiring an outside consultant at all? The answer is *absolutely*. But it *does* take capacity to develop capacity, and so your school will not want to circumvent the need to learn from people with expertise. It's just that the needed expertise may come from within as well as from without—perhaps it lies in a couple of classroom teachers, in a reading specialist, in a literacy coach, in an assistant principal, in you, in outside consultants, or in some other combination of people.

Secure and Schedule an Outside Consultant

There are a number of centers of expertise in teaching writing that you can contact in order to find someone who can work with your school as an outside consultant.

The Teachers College Reading and Writing Project has a staff of approximately seventy full-time staff developers, each of whom works not only with local but also with distant schools. The Project refers to distant districts as our "affiliated districts" and leaders from these far-flung places have coalesced into an informal support network, providing each other with support. Leaders from the Project's affiliated schools convene once a year for a three-day conference in New York City. During that conference, these people visit NYC schools together, pool their own area of expertise, and learn from whatever is especially new at the Project. Mostly, though, affiliated districts learn from the staff developers with whom they work closely, for these individuals travel to the affiliated school and provide professional development there. There is always a wait-list for Project services. Interested schools can contact us via our website rwproject.tc.columbia.edu. (Click the link "Join the Project.")

Professional organizations also provide names of consultants. The National Council of Teachers of English, for example, functions as a clearinghouse for consultants with expertise in reading and in writing. You can access information by visiting their website at www.ncte.org/profdev.

In addition, schools wishing to secure services from an expert in the teaching of writing may want to contact the publisher of books that are especially important to that school. Sometimes the author of one of those books might be available as a consultant. Heinemann, for example, has an outreach department that connects their authors to interested schools. You may access contact information by visiting the website http://pd.heinemann.com/. Sometimes authors who are especially in demand send colleagues to do the professional development that they themselves cannot do.

My advice as you proceed is this: Be cautious. I would not contract with a consultant for long-term work without visiting (or sending someone you trust to visit) a school in which that person has worked extensively. And before you hire a consultant, I'd check that person's references. I cannot tell you how often someone says to me, "I work with one of your people," and I say, "Oh, who is that?" and then the person mentions the name of someone

I knew only in passing thirty years ago. If you do not feel confident about an outside consultant, you'd be far wiser to develop expertise from within rather than securing it from without.

I do not recommend you bring a potpourri of experts into your building, as teachers will be confused by the slight differences between one person's message and another's and, therefore, not feel confident in engaging in the work. Having said this, let me also caution that most outside experts are stronger at either primary level or upper elementary/middle school level work, so you may want to secure one outside staff developer for your K–2 teachers and one for your 3–5/8 teachers, doing your best to make sure the two are in sync with one another pedagogically.

A few words of advice around securing an outside expert to act as a consultant for your district: You will find that it is not easy to locate someone who can do this job well. Experienced and skilled staff developers in writing are in extremely high demand. If you hope to secure such a person for the year ahead, don't wait to reserve some dates.

Let's assume you do contact someone to function as an outside consultant. Are there preferable ways for that person to work? This entire book will provide you with detailed help on this topic, but for now, let me lay out a few issues to consider.

First, make sure that if you are hiring an outside expert for your district, you do not sprinkle the consultant's eight days throughout the district so that eight schools in your district each receive one day of support. Such a schedule would mean the district as a whole learns only one day's content. This would literally leave everyone at square one. Instead, concentrate those days in one or two schools.

Next, decide whether you are going to support teachers throughout the entire school in rethinking the teaching of writing, or whether you will support a smaller group of interested teachers, bringing others aboard the following year or even just six months later. The amount of expertise you'll need will increase based on the number of teachers involved. If it's an entire city that will be reforming the teaching of writing, this is an altogether different proposition than if it's a dozen interested teachers within a single school! Be judicious. If you can secure an outside expert in whom you have tremendous confidence, but if he or she can only come to your school for four, two-day visits throughout the year (and if you do not have someone internally in your school who can provide additional support), then you'd be wise to launch professional development in the teaching of writing with only a dozen or so interested teachers. Of course, you'll also invite your administrative team to participate. The good news is that the following year, you will have people within your school with the necessary expertise to help newcomers; this means that during the second year, you could bring everyone in the school aboard.

In general, those of us who work at the Teachers College Reading and Writing Project think it is ideal if an outside staff developer works with a school for a few days before the start of the year, and then returns for a day or two of continued work at regular intervals throughout the year. During those return visits, the staff developer will certainly lead inservice courses for the participating teachers. It is also crucial that the staff developer work approximately half the time within classrooms, teaching all the children in "lab site classrooms" while as many as a dozen teachers from similar grade levels participate. The adage "A picture is worth a thousand words" is true when referring to staff development—the opportunity to watch a skilled teacher of writing as he or she works with kids gives teachers a deeper understanding of methods of teaching writing than those teachers could possibly glean from courses alone.

> It is ideal if an outside staff developer works with a school for a few days before the start of the year, and then returns for a day or two at regular intervals throughout the year.

It is important that the *participating* teachers actually *participate*. Be sure that the teachers who attend the professional development make a commitment to participating in all of it across the year (if an outside expert comes ten days, this means the expert will be part of in-class work as well as courses of study on each of those ten days). More importantly, make sure these people agree to participate also in the professional development that is supported by in-house expertise (to be described later) and, above all, that they commit to leading daily writing workshops in their classrooms.

Ideally, staff developers work with kindergarten teachers separately. First and second grade teachers can often be supported simultaneously, as can teachers in grades three through eight. But grade-level differentiation is ideal.

Once you have secured an expert or two, be sure to reserve specific dates in advance. Think now about whether you want to bring the person in for your district's Superintendent's Conference Day or for Election Day. Securing teachers' time to learn is not easy, so it helps to take advantage of the times when teachers will be able to study together. If you don't establish specific dates now, you risk finding that other schools get onto the outside expert's schedule before you do and that the person is available only on Halloween, the two days before winter holiday, during your testing season, and for the last week of the year! If possible, secure at least three days in a row in the summer, choosing a stretch of time when your chances of convening teachers are good. Then bring the expert back for two days as early as possible in September and two days as early as possible in October. Then sprinkle the remaining dates across the year, perhaps one every two months, ideally in a recognizable pattern such as the last Wednesday of every month.

Another suggestion: Invest time and attention in your outside expert(s). Nurture the relationship between you and that person. It may seem to you that you will be paying the consultant a fortune and that money, alone, should cement the relationship, but many school leaders rely on outside consultants as colleagues and confidantes, and such a relationship will provide you with support while also assuring that the consultant goes the extra mile for your teachers. A consultant who becomes personally invested in you and your school will bestow on you and yours all sorts of long-distance generosity.

The professional development I've described can provide a wonderful context in which your in-house literacy coach can work. And when a school is lucky enough to have people on staff who are experts or who are willing to develop expertise in the teaching of writing, then those internal experts can provide support to the school. Now let's discuss the in-house expertise that you will want to develop, cherish, and use well.

Develop In-House Expertise

Across the nation, thousands of schools are establishing positions for literacy coaches. Research is increasingly clear that the best way to help all students prosper is to raise the level of classroom instruction. Every struggling reader and writer is created by a classroom that can't meet that child's needs. Schools *can* produce classroom teachers who in turn produce kids who can *all* read and write on grade level—schools do this by investing in professional development (Allington, 2002). As I mentioned earlier, Allington found in his research that in the classrooms of exemplary teachers, kids read and write ten times more than in other classrooms. The average fourth grade *exemplary* teacher brought kids up two grade levels in reading and writing, while the *average* teacher (described by school principals as a solid teacher) produced an average of five months' growth in children. More and more, research is showing that we, as a nation, *do* know how to educate kids so they become skilled readers and writers. The secret—the only secret—lies in providing those kids with skilled teachers. This realization is the reason schools are increasingly identifying a person who can help teachers teach well, developing that person's skills and setting that person up to lift the level of teaching across a school.

You may wonder about the credentials that a person needs in order to be an effective literacy coach. Must this be someone with advanced certification? Is the training for a literacy coach different from the training for a reading specialist? The answer to this differs from state to state, school to school. At Teachers College, for example, I direct an MA program, the Literacy Specialist Program, for certified and experienced teachers who want to develop skills in teaching reading and writing and in leading staff development. Not all graduate schools of education offer programs such as this one, however, nor is such certification essential. I've known fabulous literacy coaches who have taught for ten years and those who have taught for five years. I've known fabulous coaches with advanced degrees in teaching reading and writing and those who are self-taught. Literacy coaches need a certain kind of personality as well as advanced knowledge. They need to be able to work well with teachers, children, and with you. They need deep reserves of energy and dedication.

> Literacy coaches need a certain kind of personality as well as advanced knowledge. They need to be able to work well with teachers, children, and with you.

If you do not already have a literacy coach and you are considering creating such a position in future years, you might keep this to yourself while providing a couple of teachers whom you regard as candidates for the position with extra support in teaching reading and writing. Watch how these teachers take to the education you provide them. Set them up to serve as mentors for novice teachers, and watch closely. You'll find that some people seem natural at the role of teacher-of-teachers and others do not. In general, I tend to find that the people who push to the front of the line, saying, "Oh, I could definitely be wonderful in such a role. After all, I know so much!" tend to not be well accepted by their peers, and those who instead say, "I don't feel ready for such a role. I have so much still to learn," will fare better.

I have been speaking as if in-house expertise needs to come from a literacy coach, and this is far from the case. You could redesign the job description so that a person who is currently providing remedial help to some children assumes responsibility for in-house professional development. This person might, in the future, devote two mornings to supporting the teaching of writing. You could locate a master K–2 teacher and a master 3–5 teacher and organize your staff so that those teachers have access to additional specialists and do not teach for full days. Perhaps these teachers do not teach math, thus gaining a free hour each day to support writing instruction across the grades. Or perhaps two afternoons a week, the children in those classrooms study with a thematic study specialist. This would mean that the classroom teacher would have no responsibility for social studies or science and could instead work with other classrooms. Perhaps you hire a retired teacher to return to work half time as an in-house, part-time coach for the teaching of writing.

If you take the time to consider a whole range of different alternatives and do so before you have staffed your school for the year ahead, you can probably find ways to tweak everyone's load so that one or two people on your staff have some release time to support colleagues in the teaching of writing. The bigger challenge is to be sure this person has the requisite expertise and can walk the requisite tightrope of being both a colleague and a mentor to other teachers. The series with which this book is aligned, *Professional Development in the Teaching of Writing*, is designed to help literacy coaches develop the expertise they need to support teachers using *Units of Study* in writing.

The important thing is that you envision the big picture of how staff development will proceed in your school during the year ahead so that you can sketch this out in broad strokes to your teachers, positioning any in-house experts and outside consultants in ways that are likely to pay off.

BUILD THE INFRASTRUCTURE FOR GOOD PROFESSIONAL DEVELOPMENT

You can have the most gifted literacy coach or staff developer in the world, and yet that person may be utterly ineffective if you do not also create structures within which your *teachers* will learn how to teach writing. I cannot tell you how many coaches and staff developers waste time begging teachers for the chance to stop into classrooms to help out a bit! You'd never teach children by sending them off to do whatever they choose to do and then sending an expert teacher to mosey among them, say, on the playground, trying to catch them in the act of reading so as to insert a little tip! Instead, if you want to teach children to read, the first step is to create the structures within which that learning will happen. You convene a class of children, you bring them together in a place, a classroom, and you encourage the teacher to set aside time for shared work in the subject on hand (in this example, it would be for shared work on reading).

You need to provide at least as much structure in order for teachers to learn from a literacy coach or a staff developer. And moreover, neither the staff developer nor the coach can be the one to create those structures. It is not the coach's job to say to teachers, "There will be a course that lasts six sessions" and to describe the parameters for involvement. That must be the job of the principal.

For the time being, of course, you are not inviting anyone into any course. That will come soon, after you announce the new initiative. But for now, you need to think ahead about the structures you'll create to support staff development.

As you do this thinking, here is the crucial idea. One important goal for the organized, formal staff development will be that it helps create a professional learning community characterized by teachers studying together on their own. This means you need to establish structures that can be lasting ones and that can bring teachers together in day-to-day ways to learn together within the normal context of their teaching.

Establish Cohorts of Teachers Who Are in Sync with Each Other

There is one especially important structure that you can put into place, one that I believe has unparalleled power to support both the work that your staff developer/literacy coach does, while also helping establish a professional learning community within your school. This is it: I strongly suggest that your teachers work in collaborative groups (ideally, these will be grade-level cohorts) and teach a shared sequence of units of study in the teaching of writing.

There are few decisions that you and your teachers can make that are more important than the decision that classrooms will travel in sync through a year-long curriculum in the teaching of writing. This decision means that classrooms in your school will not function as separate islands, but instead that teachers and children can rely on each other for support. One teacher can invent a way to abbreviate and simplify a minilesson from one of the *Units of Study* books—and then share this with colleagues. Another teacher can find a mentor text that fits perfectly into a unit of study—and share this with colleagues. Teachers can bring their student work to a meeting and talk together about how they can respond to the predictable problems that kids across all the classes are encountering.

What teachers are expected to know how to do is too complex these days for teachers to close their classroom doors and teach in isolation. If one teacher has special knowledge in teaching math, that teacher's teaching needs to be transparent enough and public enough that other teachers working at the same grade level can borrow on her expertise, teaching math in sync with the math expert. And if no one has expertise in math, one teacher could spend extra time studying division, another studying fractions, so that teachers can cumulate their knowledge.

If teachers across a grade level (or sometimes across two grade levels) teach in sync with each other, then the more experienced teachers can support the less experienced, the community can participate in shared planning and shared inquiries, the literacy coach or staff developer can be helpful in ways that have impact across classrooms.

For the schools with which the Teachers College Reading and Writing Project works, teaching in sync means, first of all, that all teachers embrace the image of a writing curriculum as a sequence of roughly month-long units of study. In the late spring of every year, cohorts of teachers meet to plan the writing curricular calendar for the upcoming year.

> It is crucial that teachers who agree to travel in sync through shared units of study have common prep periods and common lunch hours . . . to plan together and to support each other.

Teachers bring out a blank calendar, and on each month, they write the title of that month's unit of study. In some schools, one teacher signs up to be the facilitator for each unit, and during the summer that teacher does extra reading on the unit(s) she will coordinate. If your school will be leaning on the Heinemann *Units of Study* series, then presumably your teachers will want to follow the sequence laid out in those books. They will also read to invent some of their own units, and these can be inserted into the sequence of these books. After holding tight for a year to the course that is set in the published *Units of Study*, grade-level groups of teachers will probably decide to diverge somewhat from that course. Still, it will be important that the classrooms across that grade level continue to work in sync with each other.

Obviously if you decide that teachers will be teaching units of study in sync with each other and if you make that choice because you believe that shared planning will be helpful to them, it follows that you will need to find ways to allocate more time for grade-level planning work. It is crucial that teachers who agree to travel in sync through shared units of study have common prep periods and common lunch hours so they can use at least their prep periods (you can't enforce that they also use their shared lunch periods) to plan together and to support each other. If you provide even just a bit of time at the start of the year for these cohorts to become accustomed to leaning on each other, then you will see this often creates relationships that are so sustaining and important that teachers will devote endless hours of their own time to shared planning and reflection. So by all means, go the extra mile to make it likely that your teachers come together in study groups that work for them.

I discuss this in greater detail during the chapter describing the work you will do this summer to build a schedule. For now the important thing is that you weigh whether you will put new emphasis on teachers teaching in sync with each other and whether the cohort groupings you imagine in your school will be comprised of all the teachers across a grade level. When you unroll the new writing initiative, be sure to help teachers imagine what it will look like; as part of that, you may want to mention the image of grade levels teaching a shared sequence of writing units of study. If you mention that teachers at a grade level will be working in close alliances with each other, some teachers may be prompted to seek your counsel, asking whether you'd consider allowing them to change their grade level. Listen carefully to these requests. The composition of a grade-level grouping matters tremendously. You can alter the tenor of your entire school by making some careful revisions in your roster. As you do so, here are a few principles to keep in mind:

Principles to Keep in Mind While Establishing Grade-Level Cohorts

✦ Be sure to distribute leadership so there is someone at each grade level who can rise to the role (official or unofficial) of grade leader. Be sure you don't negate the person's leadership power through the combination of people. That is, you not only need to put a leader in place, you also need to put followers in place.

✦ If you want teachers whose methods of teaching seem especially entrenched to rethink their teaching, you might move them to a very different grade level. Now the teachers can no longer rely on the old plans. They can be learners at new grade levels without losing their dignity; although seasoned teachers, they are not experienced with this particular grade level.

✦ Whenever possible, say *yes* to teachers who want to loop with their class. Usually it makes sense to announce this to the entire school: "I've come to believe that knowing kids well makes our teaching immeasurably more efficient and powerful so if any of you want to loop with your class, see me and I will make the alterations in other people's loads so that you can do this." If you make this announcement to all your teachers, fair and square, then the fact that some end up suffering the consequences of others' decisions will seem a bit less unfair. You can count on the fact that only strong and child-centered teachers will take you up on the offer.

✦ Think about where you need special strength. Among the principals I know best, many believe that third grade is a turning point and that if third grade is poorly taught, this has especially powerful negative effects. You may pinpoint other areas that merit particular attention.

✦ Don't take kindergarten lightly. Lots of schools have children entering first grade who are already well on the road to success as readers and writers. What a difference that makes! In kindergarten, children develop a concept of school and of themselves as people who do school. You cannot afford for kindergarten to be poorly taught.

So far, I have emphasized the structure of grade-level cohorts teaching shared units of study. This structure will be revisited often throughout this book. For now, let me stress that you need not only to create cohorts of teachers who teach in sync with each other but also to create courses of study for your teachers.

Plan Ongoing Study in the Teaching of Writing

I think it is tremendously important that you and your literacy coach (or your outside staff developer or your lead teacher) devise an overall plan for courses of study that will be offered in your school to support the teaching of writing. You will want to be able to say to teachers, "This is the professional development that we will offer. If you would like to participate, these are the requisites." That is, you can't under any circumstances expect staff development in writing will go well if teachers are invited to stop by a course on a whim, participating one day and not another. Instead, you need to think of this professional development as similar to a university course. People can sign up if they are interested. Those who come aboard essentially agree to the contract. (You can say, "I know more of you are interested than we can possibly support, so this first course will be for those who can commit to the following conditions.")

You can't set the conditions without also considering the rewards. That is, what will you give teachers who participate? If you, yourself, will be a front row learner in this course, then one compensation is the chance to study shoulder to shoulder with you. Few goodies could possibly be of more value. Perhaps you'll also give teachers who participate substitute teacher coverage so they can work with colleagues for two hours, once a week, for six weeks in a row. In the lonely profession of teaching, the chance to study with colleagues can be a great treat. Perhaps you will also provide those who participate with materials—special folders, a short stack of especially chosen books, the *Units of Study* books from Heinemann. You'll decide what the benefits will be. Just make sure that they come as part and parcel of the professional development, even if that means you need to keep some teachers' materials in storage for a few months, unbeknownst to them.

Later in this book, I'll discuss professional study in more detail. But for now, let me simply make one other point. The professional study needs to involve shared work in a classroom, in what we call *lab sites,* as well as shared participation in *study groups* outside the classroom. I recommend that a cohort of teachers (such as all the teachers across one or two grade levels) join together to study from an expert teacher within a lab site classroom. That classroom can belong to anyone at the grade—there is nothing special about the room that is the lab site; in fact, this tends to alternate every month or so. What is special is that teachers learn alongside each other in the presence of kids and do so in a predictable, scheduled way such as meeting for one lab site a week for six weeks at a time (punctuated by some stretches of time where they may not convene in lab site classrooms).

The challenge of building an infrastructure to support professional development is not a small one. You'll need to learn a lot, and this will involve conversations, visits to other schools, and professional reading. Then, too, you'll need to create the structures that allow your teachers to learn a lot. This will mean creating cohort groups of teachers who teach in sync with each other and giving those cohort groups time to plan together. At the same time, you'll want to organize and schedule ongoing professional development. Planning for change is an ambitious undertaking!

DVD

Principal to
Principal

"Setting the Stage for Change." Principals talk about beginning the process of change by looking at their own needs and resources.

CHAPTER THREE

MAY/JUNE
LAUNCHING THE NEW INITIATIVE

Very soon, you will announce your school's new emphasis on writing. Up to this point, you will have kept your cards close to your chest—you haven't wanted word to leak out until you were ready for the whole-school and whole-community discussion. There is a bit more work that you need to do in order to be ready to announce the new initiative.

I can see you arching your eyebrows and peering at me over the page of this book. I can anticipate that you want to remind me that you *are* the principal of a school, after all, and frankly, you didn't get to this position without knowing how to announce a new initiative. I can hear you saying, "Thank you very much for your concern, Lucy, but really I think I'll skip the pages about how one can go about rehearsing for a little announcement at a faculty meeting. I'm pretty capable of doing that."

But hear me out. You and I both know that every year, school leaders make all sorts of proclamations about how the school will embark on this or that new initiative. Many schools are characterized by a constant stream of new programs, new initiatives. Parents always want to hear that districts are on the cusp of new research. Publishers flood teachers with brochures announcing the New, NEW, NEWEST materials. Superintendents seem to want to embark on a new initiative every year. And frankly, the constant frenzy to adopt new programs is exhausting.

As principal, you have been on the receiving end of this constant frenzy to adopt yet one more panacea. As you read this, put yourself back in the room where a district leader has taken the floor and announced yet another new program, another cure-all, another new plan. As you read this, for an

THESE MONTHS

- Decide whether the new reform will be mandated or voluntary.

- Rally your teachers to invest in the new reform.

- Roll out your vision.

- Do preliminary work in a few classrooms.

- Demonstrate your willingness to be a public learner.

- Work with your literacy coach.

- Plan summer study opportunities.

instant relive that moment. You are sitting in the chair, the superintendent or some other big shot takes the floor, and out comes the news of the new initiative: "In the year ahead, we're going to adopt this new program . . ."

Relive your physical response to the news.

My hunch is you feel flattened by the weight of yet one more new initiative. I suspect you are rolling your eyes at the rhetoric. You are thinking, "Here we go again" and whispering a prayer, "Spare me . . ."

I can promise you that if you are not careful (and frankly, even if you *are* careful), many of your teachers will respond to your announcement that the school will embark on a new writing initiative with the same heaviness, the same cynicism that you have felt when your superintendent announced new initiatives. Think of the new initiatives that have come and gone across your teachers' lives. Go into the school's storeroom or the teachers' closet and look at the layers of materials that are there. You could do an archeological dig through those materials, and as you dig through layer after layer of new materials, you'll reconstruct the sad history of the school's efforts to reform curriculum.

The problem is that all those failed initiatives have left a legacy. They have taught teachers that new initiatives come and go, and few of them amount to much. Seymour Sarason has written eloquently about this in *The Culture of the School and the Problem of Change.* Discussing the implementation of new math, Sarason points out that as teachers implemented new math, they stretched it, tweaked it, chopped it, twisted it—all in an effort to make it practical, to make it their own. The problem is that in the process of adapting new math to fit into (rather than to challenge) the teachers' assumptions of the norms of American education, pretty soon *new math* looked very much like *old math.* Sarason points out that this is what happens all too often in American schools, which is why the norms of American classrooms have not changed very much since colonial America. "The more things change, the more they remain the same," he writes (1971, 58).

> Your goal will be to convey the message that this new initiative is more than just another turn in the merry-go-round of reform.

When you announce the new initiative in writing, your goal will be to break through teachers' cynicism about new initiatives and to push past some of their very reasonable resistance. Your goal will be to convey the message that this new initiative is more than just another turn in the merry-go-round of reform, that it is different, that it is more. Because the truth is that the writing initiative is nothing without your teachers' energy. Their energy will be the wind in the sails of this new initiative, and you cannot take that energy, that trust, for granted.

So yes, I know that you already know how to announce new initiatives to your staff. I am asking for you to consider that the task before you is an enormous one and that it merits your attention.

Decide Whether the New Reform Will Be Mandated or Voluntary

First, you need to at least begin deciding how the rollout will progress. The biggest question to consider is one of scale. That is, will you launch the new initiative by asking for volunteers and working only with those who step forward, or will you essentially mandate this for the whole school? Before you leap to answer this question, let me remind you that either option can be done well or poorly. There is no right and wrong answer to this question. For example, one could certainly argue that a teacher needs to be treated as a professional and be able to make professional decisions and that a new initiative is far more apt to succeed if teachers are eager and enthusiastic. Why would a principal not want to invite rather than mandate participation?

But it is important for a leader to train herself to imagine options other than the one that springs first to her mind. There *are* reasons why a wise, principled principal could decide to mandate that every teacher in the school participate in the school's writing initiative. For example, if you believe that writing is an essential skill, it no doubt follows that your entire faculty should participate in the learning opportunities you are constructing and that the school as a whole should work in a learning community to make the teaching of writing into a vital part of each child's education.

I do have a strong opinion. After supporting school reform in writing for thirty years, I believe that there is no question but that in the end, you want your whole school to participate in a shared approach to teaching writing. That approach will not be exactly the same as the approach you initiate now. Obviously, stakeholders in your school will shape the school's evolving approach to teaching writing. The approach, too, will become stronger over time in response to new demands and new knowledge. But yes, I believe that you should say to teachers, "All of us in this school will participate in this approach towards teaching writing. This will be a schoolwide initiative." The question for me is only whether the new initiative will be launched as a schoolwide approach or whether, for now, it will be launched only in the classrooms of a few interested teachers with the other teachers set to come aboard in the following year.

In the literacy coach's guide with *Professional Development in the Teaching of Writing*, I brainstorm the advantages and disadvantages of each way of proceeding. Mull these over so that when you do announce the new initiative, you can push either towards whole-school involvement from the start or towards starting with a smaller group of interested trailblazers.

Let's imagine you would like to involve your whole school from the start. The next thing you will need to decide is whether you will, therefore, announce the professional development in the teaching of writing as an immediate mandate or first try to rally the whole school at the risk that you might not get everyone aboard. If you decide to work towards the goal of involving the whole school without mandating the reform, you might still plan to begin your announcement by saying this initiative will *eventually* involve the whole school. Then you might say that you are moving heaven and earth to help teachers be able to do so. You could then describe the plan for the upcoming year, leaving teachers with a choice. "I know a lot of you will be really eager to join me in this exciting endeavor, and I can't wait to work closely with those of you who are willing to participate. Think about whether you can come on board, and let me know. I'm aware that some of you may think this is too much for you just yet and will want to wait another year before starting."

> You will need to decide whether you will . . . announce the professional development in the teaching of writing as an immediate mandate or first try to rally the whole school at the risk that you might not get everyone aboard.

If you choose this way, it may happen that there are only a few resistors, and you could always go to those people afterwards, saying to them that interest was so great that you have decided that in fact you'd like everyone to come aboard from the start. That way, most teachers will participate through choice, and only a few will experience the initiative as a mandate.

It may be that someone above you has mandated the writing workshop for your school and for the district. This happened to Laurie and me—New York City's Chancellor went to PS 172, a Teachers College Reading and Writing Project stronghold, and announced, "The literacy curriculum in this school will be the literacy curriculum for New York City." It was a new challenge for us to work under such a broad mandate, so I solicited advice from other educators.

Jon Gillette, a professor at Yale, said, "Lucy, the key thing is this. When an approach has been mandated, it is tempting to take that as a signal that you needn't worry too much about creating buy-in, or about inspiring and motivating people. But, in fact, the opposite is true. If an approach has been mandated, then you really need to shovel on the coals, to light the fires. Inspiration becomes *more* important, not *less* important, once an approach has been mandated."

RALLY YOUR TEACHERS TO INVEST IN THE NEW REFORM

Tom Sergiovanni has on several occasions spoken to gatherings of principals at Teachers College. Each time he has urged us to remember that the form of leadership that will serve us best is *idea-based* leadership. Some people rely on *personality-based* leadership, hoping that they will be powerful enough, charismatic enough, well loved enough to rally people to follow their lead. But principals who rely on personality-based leadership are always vulnerable. You take a wrong step, you lose face, and you find your followers will be fickle. It is far more effective for a principal to rally people around enduring ideas and principles (Teachers College, 10/20/04).

Carmen Fariña and Laura Kotch, coauthors of *A School Leader's Guide to Excellence: Collaborating Our Way to Better Schools*, begin their book with an entire chapter titled, "Formulate and Communicate Your Vision." They write, "Formulating a vision and communicating it clearly and understandably provides a framework for making commonsense decisions, large and small. While every member of the community need not always agree, everyone understands that there is a plan of action that is thoughtful, cohesive, and aligned with the school's needs and mission" (2008, 4).

Take time to think about ways to inspire your teachers. Inspiration will bring teachers the energy and commitment they need to take this work on fully and with happy hearts.

You will invite them to join you in the cause of learning more about the teaching of writing. To do this, you need to become a little bit of a preacher, a rabbi, and a guru. You need to be willing to hoist the flag, the standard, and to call, "Come this way." You need to gather your congregation and say, "I have a dream. I have a dream that one day . . ."

Rise to the Challenge of Being an Inspirational Leader

There are no rules for how to rally people to care about reform in writing, but there are a few strategies that have proven effective in leading change.

Tell stories about yourself and your people.

One way to inspire your teachers is to rely on a personal story, perhaps from your own childhood. I encourage you to sit with a blank sheet of paper in front of you and jot down some thoughts. See if this progression of questions helps you recall a moment in your life that you could "storytell" to your teachers and parents, using that moment to frame your call-to-work:

- When in your life did writing especially matter to you? Be specific.
- When in your life was writing one of the worst things in the world? When did you really hate it?
- What was it about that first time that made you care about writing?
- What was it about the other time that made you resist writing? How can you create conditions in your school so that kids have more opportunities to care about writing and fewer instances when writing is the last thing they want to do?

Howard Gardner, in his book *Leading Minds*, points out that directly or indirectly, leaders fashion stories, principally stories of identity. Gardner advises leaders: tell stories about yourself, your group, and do so in ways that allow you to talk about where you and your people came from, where you are headed, what you fear, what you dream (1995, ix).

If you can ground your school's unfolding plotline in your own life story, then you embody the story, as many of the world's greatest leaders have done. Think of Eleanor Roosevelt, who told *and embodied* the story of how an ordinary person can do extraordinary things. She once said, "I do believe that even a few people who want to understand, to help, to do the right thing for a greater number of people, can help." Think of Martin Luther King, whose life story matches his message, for he demonstrated what he meant when he called people to rise against the pain of oppression, holding onto "the beloved community."

Create a mantra and repeat it often.

Carmen Fariña and Laura Kotch encourage you to take the time to crystallize your ideas and your goals into a short list of three or four values and to turn these into a mantra. They suggest that alliteration helps, as in, for example, the goals of *equity, energy, expectations, ensemble* (2008, 11). One principal may decide to say to teachers and parents, "Our approach to writing will emphasize *skills, structure*, and *significance*." Another principal will convey a similar message differently, perhaps saying, "Our approach to writing is going to be based on *time, topics* that matter, and *techniques* that writers use," or "This year, we're going to revise both writing and our teaching of writing, and we will do so by studying models and mentors." Carmen and Laura emphasize that, whatever words you decide to use, it will be important for you to say the same thing over and over and to say the message to one constituency after another so that you demonstrate the consistency of your message and enlist support from all your stakeholders. Of course, a list of terms alone doesn't translate into a talk, and you will want to gather illustrative examples of each of your core principles.

Clarify and share your vision.
It is not essential for you to use alliteration to package your vision into a mantra. But it is essential for you to have a set of core beliefs, a vision. Fullan writes, "Working on vision means examining, and making explicit to ourselves, why we came into teaching. Asking, 'What difference am I trying to make personally?' . . . The reasons are there, but possibly buried under other demands . . . It is time to make them front and center." He adds, "I cannot stress enough that personal purpose and vision are the starting agenda. It comes from within. It gives meaning to work" (Teachers College, 1/24/07). You need not only to define a vision but also to articulate it often to everyone.

Roll Out Your Vision

When you talk to your staff about your plans for a new emphasis on the teaching of writing, I suspect that you'll want to convey to them the following:

This initiative is not business as usual for you.
Serve chocolate-covered strawberries. Put a tablecloth under the coffee pot. You might even begin by saying, "I hope the strawberries and the table-cloth helped to convey to you that today is a special event and that today's meeting will not be business as usual."

You will want to convey that you have tremendous interest in a deep, real investment in the teaching of writing. You are confident that this reform will yield benefits in dramatic and important ways that include but go far beyond simply improving the quality of writing throughout the school.

Remember, your goal is to give the writing initiative a big push out of the gate. Your hope is that the teaching of writing will do more than improve writing instruction across the school. Your hope is that this one initiative will lift the level of your professional learning community, invigorate and revitalize the school, help teachers develop stronger teaching methods in general, create new and more powerful relationships between teachers and kids and among the staff as a whole. Literally, you are hoping for whole-school reform and more. In thousands of schools, the teaching of writing has made a world of difference. It can do this in your school. But in order for it to make a big difference, you will need to convey to teachers that this new initiative is not just business as usual.

For example, you might say, "I need everyone's full attention because I want to talk to you about something that I have been mulling over for a long time. I've come to the decision that the time is right for our school to make a dramatic step forward, to take up a really crucial mission, and today I want to take some time to share my thoughts with you about the mission."

This initiative will build on the school's strengths.

Your commitment to this new initiative comes from a desire to capitalize on teachers' strengths rather than to repair their weaknesses. You know the new work will extend what many of them are already doing. For example, you might say, "I know this approach to teaching writing is an especially challenging one. It is the sort of approach that colleges embrace and that one sees in the leading prep schools across the country. So for the past month, I have been visiting your classrooms and talking with you, just trying out in my mind whether I think we are ready for an undertaking like this. And what I have come to realize is that in many ways, we are halfway there already. Already in this school, I see teachers pulling in close to really listen deeply to kids—and that listening is at the core of teaching writing. Already in this school, I see teachers planning teaching together and helping each other teach well—and that collaboration, too, is at the core of this effort to improve writing."

This initiative is not an experiment.

A word of caution: Laurie and I would not recommend that you tell teachers that you will be testing a "pilot program." This suggests the approach towards teaching writing is one that is still untested. That's far from the truth! Then, too, it suggests that you are not yet convinced this is an important direction for the school. Such a statement could invite those who are resistant to this proposed change (or any change) to fight against reform in writing. Even if the announcement that you would be piloting a writing workshop didn't ignite opposition, it would certainly signal to teachers that they'd be wise to stand back, arms folded, waiting to see if this initiative will actually take hold. Given that in American education schools take on and discard new initiatives at a terrific clip, teachers who hear that this will be a pilot are within reason to not take the initiative too seriously. Our bigger point is this: Your staff needs you to be a spokesperson. And you need to rally people through passion and conviction, not through mandates.

You are personally committed to this initiative.
You will be involved in implementing this initiative. Those who volunteer to come aboard will receive your support and will be working shoulder-to-shoulder with you as well as with other school leaders. For example, you might say, "I think one reason I am so excited about this is that I have been longing to get more involved in curriculum and teaching, and I see this as a vehicle for me to learn alongside you. I'm so ready to explore new approaches to teaching together. So I'm hoping some of you will be willing to let me learn from you and your kids."

The initiative requires long-term commitment.
Because so many people are apt to be interested in reforming the teaching of writing, those receiving the first staff development need to be ready and willing to commit to following through. If you believe more people will express interest than can be supported, you will want to lay out conditions for involvement. For example, you might say, "I suspect that most of you will want to be involved right from the start rather than waiting to become involved later in the year or next year. We may not have the capacity to provide all interested people with staff development, so I am going to ask you to think about whether you are willing to commit to this endeavor. It will mean not only participating in the staff development at least once a week for the first two months of the year, but also making a commitment to actually teaching writing at least four days a week during those first two months. Then at that point, we can all reassess, and if you'd like, you'd have the chance to sign up for continued study (or not)."

Professional development is part of the initiative.

People will receive support for learning about the teaching of writing. For example, you might say, "I've been researching to learn about the support I can provide so we learn to teach writing really well, and I've got a variety of ideas that I'd like to run past those of you who will be participating. For now, the important thing to know is that this will be a schoolwide priority. And that means that I will move mountains to be sure that all of us receive the help we need in order to do this well. I am, for example, contemplating the idea of a summer institute (and if we do that, those who attend will receive per session pay for coming), and I am also thinking about ways we can bring in a national expert and also use in-house talent. I see this effort to improve the teaching of writing as a way for us to come together as a school in a professional learning community."

This initiative is about the kids.

You may say that you have come to believe that some things are so essential for kids that they deserve to be part of every kid's bill of rights. You might say that you cannot imagine leading a school that doesn't say to every family, "We promise that your child will receive the education that he or she is entitled to receive. Just as this means that math will be taught every day (whether or not the teacher "feels like it"), so, too, will writing be taught every day. And just as math is taught in a planned and sequential way, so, too, will writing be taught in a planned and sequential way."

In the end, you'll do everything right and some teachers will still roll their eyes and say, "Here we go again." If you want to sway teachers from feelings of, "Oh no, one more thing" and "How are we possibly going to fit yet more into the school day?" the best strategy is to own those reservations. You might try telling the story of your journey towards embracing the idea of this new initiative, and tell the story in a way that allows your listeners to identify with you. "A few months ago when I first realized it might be time for this school to take on really significant work in the teaching of writing, my first response was, 'Oh my God, one more thing?' I thought about our overcrowded curriculum, where we already race from one thing to another to another and I thought, 'No way!'"

Then proceed to account for the step-by-step evolution of your own feelings, telling the story of your journey in ways that you hope will say to teachers, "I hope you, too, progress through this journey. I had the same reservations as you, but then I thought . . . , I realized . . . , I noticed . . . ,

I imagined . . . , and now I'm very clear that this could be a life-giving option for all of us."

Remember as you talk with teachers that the message is going to get lost in the messenger. Just as you can respond to a child's work in a manner that helps teachers to respond similarly, so, too, you can respond to the prospect of reform in writing in ways that set the tone for teachers' responses. Make this personal. Be truthful. Be real. That, more than anything, will mean this is not just one more mandated innovation.

Finally, shift to talking about specifics soon after announcing your plan. The power of the idea lies in the implementation details. Let people know you have thought very carefully about how this will unroll.

Do Preliminary Work in a Few Classrooms

Because you will probably not be able to bring all your teachers on school visits to show them schools where writing workshops are going wonderfully, developing sites within your own school can be a way to help all your teachers develop that crucial big-picture image of what's possible.

After announcing the writing initiative, invite a small group of interested people to join you in putting the new ideas into practice right away, before the official launch in September. Of course, the phrase "join you" is a bit of a euphemism. You won't be able to devote an hour a day to teaching writing. But you *will* be able to stop by a classroom for a couple of twenty-minute visits each week, and in that time, you can demonstrate your eagerness to learn about the teaching of writing. And if you recruit especially energetic teachers to give this a go during the final months of the school year, those teachers will get a leg up on the fall. Try to choose teachers who are influential in the social structure of the building, people who could, with some support, help other teachers.

Even if you are not able to spend a lot of time in the classrooms that are starting this work, make maximum use of the time you do spend there. Harvest lots of stories from even fleeting moments there, and then tell lots of teachers those stories. Invite them to stop by the classrooms to talk to the children about their writing. Even over a short period of time, growth in writing will be very visible and dramatic. After just a few weeks, teachers will be able to see that growth. Nothing is more convincing than growth in kids' work!

For lots of reasons (including the pressures on your time), it is important to involve others from your administrative staff in this initial launch. That will allow you to devote a bit less of your own personal time to the work and will, meanwhile, help you develop a small leadership team that can support staff development in the year ahead. If you are lucky enough to have an assistant principal, involve that person in this learning adventure. These reforms will influence every subject area and will provide teachers with a new repertoire of methods for teaching. It cannot be schoolwide without *everyone*.

If you do not already have a leadership council, you'll probably want to establish one during the upcoming year and meet regularly with them. Presumably your council will include your assistant principal, your guidance counselor, your in-house literacy coach, your outside staff developer, a parent leader, a couple of teacher-leaders, and other people who you believe can assist you in the school's mission. If you anticipate forming this team in a few months, it can help to lay the groundwork for it right now. You may, for example, try to include your guidance counselor or your special education teachers in this work even at this early stage, simply as a way to test out which of these people will be part of your core leadership team.

Of course, one of the most important people involved in this exploratory learning will be your literacy coach (or the person who will assume the responsibilities of a literacy coach). Especially if your coach has never used the *Units of Study* books, it is imperative that the coach be given a chance to work with those books and a classroom of kids before the start of the new year. That way your coach will be one step ahead of the teachers by September. So by all means, give the literacy coach a classroom or two and set that person up to co-teach the writing workshop work suggested by the first book in the *Units of Study* series.

> Even just a little bit of personal involvement from you will energize the teachers who agree to be your advance guard.

I also suggest you team up with a classroom teacher or two and try your hand at doing some of the teaching that you'll ask your teachers to do in the fall. This will allow you to learn firsthand about the joys and the problems your staff will encounter in the year ahead. Meanwhile, even just a little bit of personal involvement from you will energize the teachers who agree to be your advance guard.

There are countless advantages to this plan. You and a few especially trusted colleagues will have a low-pressure place to try out the methods before they go to scale in the fall. You'll be able to experiment and to learn from mistakes, to develop a repertoire of techniques. The fact that you'll be working in just a small cohort of classes will mean that any missteps will not take the whole school off course.

Demonstrate Your Willingness to Be a Public Learner

Perhaps the most important reason to do some preliminary work in a few classrooms is that this will allow you to demonstrate your stance to others in the school. Once work has started in these few classroom, invite teachers to join you in the learning. Try saying something like this to teachers who are not part of your advance guard: "Eliza (substitute your coach's name) and I are having a terrific time learning from Becky's kids. Their work is mind-boggling. I don't really know what I'm doing yet as a writing teacher, but Eliza's giving me lots of pointers. If any of you want to peek in on what we're doing, let me know and I'll get you coverage."

There are some important things to notice about a comment like this. First, this isn't self-promotional. You aren't claiming that you and the class-rooms are models of perfection for teachers to emulate. Instead, you are describing the classroom as a learning laboratory. Teachers would rather be invited into the ground level of experimentation and development than be asked to robotically emulate. Then, too, notice that you've described your-self as a student of the coach. Your coach will need your support if she is going to be able to instruct teachers, and you definitely want her doing this!

When teachers do come by and visit, be sure that you demonstrate your learning posture. Say to the coach, "Can I try my hand at conferring with a kid and get some pointers?" Be sure that you remind the coach that you will want her to actually critique your work and show you how you could have done it even better (she will be hesitant to publicly critique you unless you give her full permission). If you welcome feedback from her, think of the message you will send!

When teachers join you in the classroom, show them ways in which you are (and are not) relying on the *Units of Study* books. If you are holding onto the book as a bit of a lifeline (for the time being), then you help teachers realize that they, too, will have that sort of support. In this way, you make it much more likely that teachers will begin reading the books now. You make professional study into something respectable.

Roland Barth has often spoken to Teachers College Reading and Writing Project principals. In a recent keynote, he argued that schools must be places where everyone's learning curve is as high as it can be. To Barth, the principal's primary role must be to be the "lead learner" in a school, the per-son who exemplifies the joys of learning. Barth paused in his keynote to ask the principals who had convened around him to jot down times when their learning curves were especially high and to record topics on which they'd done a lot of learning recently. Once everyone had done this, Barth said, "Now I have a second question. Who knows about the learning you have been doing?" He went on to ask, 'Do the parents of your students know about your learning? Do the teachers know about your learning? Do the kids?" Barth's point was that for a school principal to model what it means to be an eager, reflective, open, and responsive learner and to do so in ways that create a contagious energy around professional learning, that principal needs to make his learning life public. "Wear your learning on your sleeve," Barth said. "Tell everyone about it" (Teachers College, 11/07/07).

> When you ask teachers to dedicate themselves to learning about the teaching of writing, you are asking not only that teachers focus on teaching writing but also that they be learners.

Following Barth's advice is crucial for principals who want to create a culture of professional study in a school. Consider this. When you ask teachers to dedicate themselves to learning about the teaching of writing, you are asking not only that teachers focus on teaching writing but also that they be learners. Most of us, as adults, like to do things we are already good at doing. We don't usually spend a lot of time anymore doing things that are new and hard for us. We especially don't tend to do those things publicly.

Reading researcher Kylene Beers recently pointed out to a group of principals that it is not easy for any of us to be public learners. "I gave up tennis for just this reason. How many times can you call out 'Sorry' when your ball lobs into the other court before you start to feel humiliated?" Kylene said. Then she asked the principals who had gathered, "Think about something you do poorly. Now imagine doing that one hundred and eighty days a year, six to eight hours a day in front of those who matter the most to you. Isn't this what we ask struggling readers to do—to show up, day after day, and make their struggles visible?" (Teachers College, 1/30/07). Questions such as these can help you consider what you will be asking your teachers to do. When you say, "All of us are going to participate in a rigorous professional development program aimed at making us more skilled as teachers of writing," you are asking your teachers to become public learners.

From the start, then, it is essential that you are the lead learner in the area of teaching writing and that you go public about that learning. Try your hand at exactly what you'll ask teachers to do. If your school will be using the Heinemann *Units of Study* series, try out the first unit in that series. Remember that as you, your assistant principal, your literacy coach (if you have one), and your advance guard of teachers try your hands at using the *Units of Study* books to teach writing, it is important that you all deliberately demonstrate the sort of learning you hope teachers will do in the fall. For example, by carrying these books around with you and saying, "I'm just starting the first of these books; it's got me rethinking so many things," or "This book makes me uncomfortable. It is making me realize that I never really gave all that much thought to the teaching of writing," you will dignify the learning life and make it honorable to be a novice, a learner. If you are a public and open learner, your learning life can be contagious. Others will join in your public inquiry, and they'll be more willing to make this joint journey when they are learning *with* you, rather than later, *from* you.

Although you will learn from the *Units of Study* books and from your colleagues, the most important learning you can do is that which involves pulling close to youngsters, listening to what they are trying to do as they write, hearing their sense of what good writing entails, and looking at their work. Chances are good that you will come from those interactions feeling all the more convinced that children deserve help in writing.

Work with Your Literacy Coach

No literacy coach can have a big effect on a school if the principal is not engaged with that person. When the Teachers College Reading and Writing Project works with a school (we tend to do this for twenty to twenty-five days a year), a prerequisite is that the school principal and every other administrator attend a portion of every day's professional development. We have created this policy because we have found that if administrators are not involved in professional development, that work is apt to be no more than footprints in the sand.

Clear the Air If Necessary

You and your literacy coach may be fast friends, and learning together may be the norm for you two, but it could be that you and the literacy coach have some long-buried difficulties, leading to tensions that are just under the surface. These difficulties are sometimes the elephant in the room, the non-discussables. If that is the case, remember Roland Barth's counsel. These undiscussed topics can be toxic to a workplace. Consider whether you and the literacy coach could perhaps go behind closed doors and try to improve your relationship. If you decide to do so, here are a few suggestions that might help.

Suggestions for Clearing the Air with Your Coach (or Anyone)

✦ Ask permission for the conversation and give the other person a sense for the time frame and the ultimate goals of the conversation. For example, "Can you and I take fifteen minutes or so to see if we can address some tensions that I've been feeling, and I suspect you have as well, so that we can put these behind us and get in sync?"

✦ Take ownership for your part in the tension rather than simply blaming the other person. As often as not, if you take ownership for your part, the other person is able to do the same.

✦ Keep in mind that you cannot change the other person, you can only change yourself. For example, "Earlier this year when I asked you to do X, I may have been mistaken, but at the time it seemed to me that you did Y. I should have checked my perception of this with you, as I may have been wrong, plus you probably had really good reasons, but it made me feel like my leadership was being challenged. So I began a mental list of Times When You Challenge My Leadership. As I tell you this now, I realize this was silly of me, because in life it is inevitable that people will challenge a leader, and I should have been able to take that in stride and carry on with the job, or else talk to you about it . . ."

✦ Shift from looking backwards to looking forwards. Set goals, plan next steps.

✦ If the two of you have problems to discuss, then do so. But after they've been put on the table, the conversation needs to turn towards next steps. "We have spent time talking about problems; now let's try to find solutions. What can we do to make things better?"

✦ Ask for the other person's input. "What positive steps forward do you think we can take from here?"

✦ Use email only to communicate a meeting time or to give someone a compliment, not for communicating important interpersonal messages.

After your conversation, be sure to act on what you've learned or de-cided or planned.

Be Your Coach's First Student

It is especially important that you set up opportunities for your literacy coach (and/or for any other in-house people who will be supporting your teachers in the fall) to demonstrate methods of teaching writing to you. Your coach needs practice doing this and needs feedback as well.

Make appointments for the coach to teach you. Say something like this, "Later this week on Friday morning, I'll have some time to spend with you and Maria in her classroom and to perhaps visit other classrooms, too. When we are working together, could you demonstrate the different parts of a minilesson for me and set me up to get better at seeing what is and isn't working in minilessons as I observe them? Maybe a few days after that, you could set me up to give a minilesson." The coach will prepare for those opportunities, and in this way you'll mobilize your coach's learning life. By creating appointments for the coach to teach you, you also allow yourself to scaffold and guide the coach. As your coach teaches you, you'll want to give feedback that helps the coach be better at teaching adults.

Giving Feedback to Your Coach

Ask yourself, "What is this person doing well that I can support?"
If you are anything like me, you'll probably find that your mind fills with suggestions and critiques, and therefore you'll need to discipline your observations so that you are in a position to talk at some length about what the person you are observing has done well. In order to find something significant to compliment, you might ask yourself, "What does this person seem to be aiming to accomplish?" The coach may be kind to everyone and you could remark on this, but if this is a long-standing part of your coach's character, you'll also want to try to notice the new and challenging work the coach is attempting to do so you support her newest growth. For example, you may find that the coach has made a big effort to pace her minilesson well. If pacing will be one of the big things you will compliment, try enlarging the power of the compliment by seeing if there are several instances of effective pacing. Did she encourage kids to come quickly to the meeting area? Did she speak in a quick, brisk manner? You earn the right to critique someone if you first see and name what that person has done well.

Help the coach teach teachers, not just kids.
Teaching *kids* is probably what comes most naturally to your coach. Your job is to be sure she frames that teaching so that adult learners can extrapolate

transferable principles. For example, before she launches into the mini-lesson, does she talk to you in front of the children, giving you an overview of what you will watch for? She should! If I were the coach, I might say something such as, "You will see in time that every minilesson has the same four components. Minilessons begin with the teacher situating the minilesson in a context—naming what the kids have already been doing or have already learned. Then, secondly, the teacher names what he or she is going to teach. That's the teaching point—it is a sentence or two that crystallizes what the whole minilesson will be about. The teaching point could be called the goal. Usually this is what a teacher writes on charts that hang in the room. So watch me teach the first portion of this minilesson—watch how I situate the minilesson for the kids and then name the teaching point." Of course, the coach needn't frame her teaching in exactly that way, but she does need to remember to teach you as well as the kids.

The important thing is to notice whether she alternates between teaching you and teaching the kids. If she doesn't—if she simply teaches the kids and hopes you extrapolate principles from what you see—talk with her about this and suggest that she can rely on the books *Professional Development in the Teaching of Writing* we have written for her in order to learn some ways of explicitly teaching adults at the same time she is teaching kids.

Support the coach in adapting the minilessons.
The coach will probably draw on one of the minilessons in the *Units of Study* books. Ask her if she can point out to you which minilesson she is using as her foundation, and then hold that minilesson open before you as the coach teaches the minilesson, noticing the extent to which she adapts it. You should see that the coach uses her own personal stories in her version of the minilesson. If I've written about the day my dog Tucker was lost, you wouldn't expect Tucker to reappear in the coach's minilesson!

Notice, too, whether the coach abbreviates the lessons from the grades 3–5 books. They're rich enough that teachers can rely on these lessons not just one year but over successive years, but they are sometimes too rich. If I've given three examples, the coach may only give one. If I've tucked in four or five pointers, the coach may only tuck in two of these. The coach's reduction of the minilesson should preserve the form of it—that is, it would be a problem if the coach's minilesson contained only the first half of the minilesson and not the second half of it, thus leaving off two of the predictable parts of a minilesson.

Notice, too, whether the coach adapts the teaching plan to draw in the particular kids before her. Does she mention their names, their stories, their work, when appropriate? Does she seem to notice when their attention is waning and liven up her teaching just a bit to draw them in? Does she seem to notice when children are confused and adapt what she is saying so that her content makes sense to her students?

If you see the coach making the minilesson from the *Units of Study* books her own and tailoring it to work with these kids, applaud this. If you do not see any of this, let the coach know that doing these things seems to you (and to me) to be crucial.

Finally, notice what helps and hinders you as a learner, and talk about this with the coach.
You need your coach to be deeply invested in your learning and ready to move mountains to help you maximize your learning. As part of this, the coach should be able to take cues from you (and from her other adult students) so that she is as helpful as possible. For example, after you have watched the coach give a minilesson, you'll probably feel as if you have only just begun to grasp the essential components of a minilesson. You may find you are not ready to learn about a whole new topic. So you might say to the coach, "I feel as if I am just barely grasping the structure of a minilesson. I'm wondering if I should learn more about minilessons before even trying to learn about conferring." If you were to say this to the coach, ideally she would take your learning needs into account and tailor the rest of your time together accordingly.

Your request to continue thinking about minilessons rather than to shift towards conferring need not derail all the coach's plans. For example, if kids were dispersing to write, you and the coach could still travel among the kids, talking with individuals. But the focus of your conversations could be on ways in which looking at student work can fill you with ideas for a future minilesson. The important thing is that a coach needs to attend to her students' learning lives—and now you and the other educators are her students.

Help All Your Teachers Learn from the Coach

Experienced teachers are often resistant to learning from a coach who is also a colleague. Schools can be competitive places and it often seems that if one member of the staff is considered superior in any way, the whole school gangs up on the "star." You'll need to think carefully about the norms of your community, considering how you can figure out a way to help teachers feel okay about learning from a colleague.

Tips for Helping Your Teachers Learn from a Coach or Lead Teacher

✦ Make it clear that you insist that the coach actually teaches teachers. Be sure that you present the coach as someone acting at your request. "I've asked (the coach) to teach me and the rest of us about . . ." or "I'm trying to convince (the coach) that she needs to give me feedback about how I could do this better." Otherwise, it may seem as though the coach has taken it upon himself to critique his colleagues— an approach often harder to swallow by those being taught.

✦ Give the coach extra information. She earns the right to step forward if she has insider information and materials to share. If possible, give the coach access to knowledge on teaching writing that others don't yet have so that when she steps forward to teach or share what she's learned, other teachers can recognize and accept the coach's expertise a bit more easily.

✦ Demonstrate your enthusiasm for learning from the coach. If you are excited to learn from the coach, this will make it easier for others to do likewise. It helps if you are the one to spotlight the coach's or lead teacher's expertise. Principals, as I talk about demonstrating to teachers that you are learning from the coach, I need to add a caveat. The truth is, this needs to be more than just show. You need to be sure that you *do* have a coach who knows a great deal more than you do, even about the teaching of reading and writing, and whose skills and knowledge are ad-mirable to you. If you are not convinced that your coach has that sort of knowledge, then send the coach out for staff development—even if this means setting the coach up to intern in another school for three weeks.

✦ Remind the coach that any of us can give suggestions in ways that debilitate and ways that help. It's important for both you and the coach to learn how to say difficult things to teachers in ways that can be heard. So work together on how you can couch critiques. For example, instead of saying, "Your minilessons need to be more compelling. Here are some ideas I came up with for doing that," your coach might say, "I've been trying to make my minilessons more compelling and lively. I reread the *Units of Study* books and found some tips that have helped me—I'd be happy to share them if anyone wants."

✦ Distribute leadership opportunities to others in addition to the coach. Think about the teachers who are especially apt to resist learning from the coach or from mentor teachers. The issue is probably one of pride and dignity. Can you find ways for these other people to play parallel leadership roles in another subject? Could you ask one of these teachers to lead a task force on math? To work over the summer helping you write a grant application? Can you find ways to publicly appreciate these people's strengths?

PLAN SUMMER STUDY OPPORTUNITIES

The work I've described so far in this chapter is the essential work you'll need to accomplish in May—or whenever you launch your school's work with writing. If your calendar is truly in sync with this book—if this *is* May—then you'll want to try to accomplish one more thing: plan summer study for your teachers. Summers can provide critically important opportunities for teachers to write together, to plan teaching together, and to develop skills in teaching writing. A year from now, you will almost certainly want to plan for a weeklong in-house summer writing institute, and you will probably also try to send your lead teachers and your literacy coach to one of the intensive summer institutes that are offered elsewhere during the summer. These summer institutes offer teacher-leaders and literacy coaches an invaluable way to develop their capacities so they, in turn, can help your teachers outgrow themselves.

For now, then, the only question for you to consider is whether at this early stage of your school's work in writing, you'll want to send key people to a distant summer writing institute or would it be wiser to schedule your own homegrown institute? The question really comes down to one of capacity because if you can possibility do so, it would prove worthwhile both to send your key people to a superb summer institute and to lead a similar institute at home.

Institutes Away from Home

The Teachers College Reading and Writing Project always leads two summer writing institutes at Teachers College, Columbia University in New York City, each involving approximately 1,000 educators. People come from all corners of the globe. Last year, for example, our July Writing Institute participants came from 48 states and 49 countries. However, we always receive many more applications that we can accept.

There are other options. Every summer, the University of New Hampshire leads an institute on the teaching of writing. Also, staff members from the

Teachers College Reading and Writing Project lead local institutes in towns and cities dotting the country, and these are sometimes open to people from other districts.

What a difference it can make if all or many of your teachers can spend time in the summer writing alongside each other, forging a close intimate writing community, learning about the teaching of writing from firsthand experience writing, and beginning to grasp the big picture of the *Units of Study* books. If you do have the chance to provide your teachers with this sort of an opportunity, I encourage you, too, to attend the institute as a participant. Work on your own writing alongside your teachers.

Homegrown Institutes

The demand for professional development in writing is far greater than the opportunities for such study. This means that you cannot count on being able to send your teacher-leaders to summer institutes. You may want to consider bringing an outside consultant to your district to lead on-site summer staff development. If you can secure the right person, a summer institute will prove a magical experience for all who participate.

Let me describe the homegrown summer institutes that staff members from the Teachers College Reading and Writing Project often colead with leaders from schools. If you decide to provide such an offering to your teachers, you'll be able to borrow or adapt this template if you choose to do so.

- We generally separate teachers by grade level so that at the very least, K–2 teachers study together and teachers of grades 3–5 (or 3–8) study together. If we are able to do so, we also create a separate kindergarten section.
- Usually teachers spend half the day in large group sessions learning methods for teaching writing and half the day in small groups (usually no more than twenty people) working on their own writing and on practicing and refining methods of teaching writing. For example, sixty K–2 teachers might meet with one staff developer in the morning to learn methods for teaching K–2 writing and then divide into three smaller sections in the afternoon, while meanwhile a similarly large group of grade 3–5 teachers follows the reverse schedule, meeting in small groups in the morning and convening as a larger group in the afternoon.
- We tend to begin an institute on day one by helping people think about the bottom lines of teaching writing and about the ongoing structures

and the essential methods of teaching that last across the year. The upper grade teachers spend a day or two learning about units of study in narrative writing, then a day or two learning about units of study in expository writing, meanwhile working across the week on a single piece of narrative writing.

- The primary teachers tend to learn first about launching a writing workshop in a kindergarten or first grade classroom and then progress chronologically throughout the year and along a developmental continuum. That is, after learning about the ongoing structures and methods for teaching writing, these teachers might learn about the first days and weeks in a kindergarten or first grade unit of study and then learn how those units might unroll a year or two later as children cycle back to do more advanced narrative work. Similarly, these teachers would learn about simple and more advanced informational writing.

- Primary teachers often write a set of pieces that they can use within minilessons and conferences to demonstrate to kids the sort of writing they hope children will do. They use a narrative continuum or rubric to guide them to write a series of progressively more complex pieces.

If your literacy coach or some of your teachers are knowledgeable about teaching writing, you might ask them to lead an institute for your staff. If you are unsure that people will follow their lead, then I'd keep the institute brief. Be sure that you are a front row participant or a coleader, and be sure that the bulk of the time in the institute is reserved for teachers to read and write together and to watch relevant sections of the DVDs you might use, such as *Big Lessons from Small Writers*, *Seeing Possibilities*, Carl Anderson's *Strategic Writing Conferences*, or others. Also, you may need to find a way to pay teachers for their participation during vacation hours. Some people provide teachers with a stipend for participating; some allow the institute to count as inservice credit hours.

Although I am enthusiastic about the benefits of holding a homegrown institute, this book and this series are based on the assumption that you may well not be able to pull this off during your school's first summer. That is, I've written the books for literacy coaches describing how they might launch writing workshops, assuming they'd have not had the chance to teach teachers for a week during the summer. Obviously, it could be that your school can manage this. If so, alter the coaching books accordingly, and feel pleased with your lot!

Professional Reading for Teachers

Even if you decide not to provide a summer institute for your teachers this year, you'll want to make it as likely as possible that teachers spend time over the summer doing some professional reading, and high on your list of preferred reading will be the *Units of Study* books that teachers will rely on in September. If you want teachers to read these books *over* the summer, lure them to begin reading the books *before* the summer. Following are some ways that principals have made it likely that teachers will begin this professional reading before the school year is over.

Convene your teachers in a study group. Give each teacher the first book in the appropriate *Units of Study* series (K–2 or 3–5). Tell them that you have been giving yourself the minilessons in the first unit and show them how they can do the same. Teach them a condensed version of the first mini-lesson and show them the writing you did. Nudge them to do a bit of similar work, giving them five minutes for abbreviated writing. Do the same for the second minilesson. Then suggest that teachers can grasp the flow of the entire first unit if each of them presents one of the subsequent sessions in a similar way. Give teachers four to five minutes to prepare and then circle the room while each teacher presents a crystallized minilesson in sequence. If you have time to do this with a second book, you might select the fiction book, as it is an especially intriguing yet comprehensible book. If you help teachers grasp the gist of even just one unit of study, however, you'll show them the sort of payoff they'll get from reading these books. Tell teachers that over the summer, you hope they do this for themselves. Schedule the first meeting at the start of the school year as a time to share summer writing with each other.

Alternatively, ask teachers to read Sessions I, II, and III of the *Launching the Writing Workshop* book and to come to a breakfast or lunch meeting (you provide the food) to discuss what interested them in these sessions. Steer the conversation in such a way that teachers look across the sessions to note the replicable features that are applicable to all three sessions. At the meeting, print out a bit of the DVD, a homework assignment or two from these sessions, and show teachers related snippets from the DVD, *Seeing Possibilities*.

"Creating Buy-In." Principals promote building a collaborative learning culture across the whole school.

CHAPTER FOUR

JULY/AUGUST

GETTING READY FOR THE YEAR

When Georgia Heard, author of *For the Good of the Earth and the Sun* and other books on teaching poetry, was a staff developer with the Teachers College Reading and Writing Project, she was also a student of poet laureate Stanley Kunitz. At one point, Georgia went to her mentor and said to the great man, "I want to be a poet. What should I do with my life so that I can become a poet?"

Stanley Kunitz looked Georgia in the eyes and said, "Go be a rock hound, a pastry chef, a star gazer, a bird watcher. Become a classroom teacher, a disc jockey. You'll find your metaphor in the rocks, the croissant, the stars, and the kids. You'll find your metaphor and your messages in the whole of your life."

I remind myself of Kunitz's advice every summer when I walk away from my staff and my students, from the schedules that need to be organized, the piles that need to be sorted, the emails that need to be answered.

You, also, need to walk away from your work and spend time with whatever it is that you love. You need this because leading a school is one of the most demanding jobs imaginable, and to do the job well, you need great reserves of patience, optimism, commitment, and trust. To do the job well, you need emotional intelligence. And none of us can be emotionally healthy unless we take care of ourselves.

THESE MONTHS

- Mine your vacation for metaphor and messages.

- Draft and revise possible schedules for your staff.

- Get to the brass tacks of scheduling.

- Gather gifts and supplies for rewarding teachers' professionalism.

- Help teachers set up classrooms to support workshop learning.

MINE YOUR VACATION FOR METAPHOR AND MESSAGES

As you spend time with your family and friends, see if you can bring the writer's double consciousness to those experiences. See if you can both live and also think about your living, mining your experiences for the insights they can yield. For example, I've recently lived through medical scares revolving around my mother, who has always been the all-strong Rock of Gibraltar in our family. She's okay now, but for a time, she was barraged with one medical crisis after another. During that difficult time, I watched her curl into a ball and become passive and withdrawn from her own life. Watching this, I realized that I sometimes underestimate how absolutely essential it is to protect a person's sense of personal agency, of self-determination.

> Because I am a person who writes, I step back from the roller coaster of life and think, "So what am I learning?"

There are children in our schools who, like my mother during those awful weeks when it seemed she was slipping into dependence and passivity, are at risk of giving up on themselves.

During the interval when my mother's health was bad, it became absolutely clear to me that there are ways we can protect a person's dignity and sense of personal agency. For example, the doctors all said my mother had lost too much weight and needed to eat. When she returned home from the hospital and could only shuffle about the house, I'd get a yogurt out for her and one for me, too, and I'd put hers within her reach, along with a spoon, and then I'd sit nearby eating my yogurt. But I couldn't feed my mother as if she were a baby bird! No matter how nutritious that yogurt might have been, its advantages weren't so great that it made sense for me to treat my mother as if she needed to be spoon fed.

And when I took my mother to the eye doctor, I remember how he picked up Mum's charts, glanced at (and then past) her, and then looked over to me—sitting in the far corner—and said, "What medications has she been on?"

There was no way I would answer such a question! Parlaying the question back to my mother, I said, "Mom, what medication have you been on?" Sick as she was at that moment, *she* was the authority on that matter. Under any circumstance, it would have been ridiculous for the eye doctor to direct his question to me, but this was all the more true in our case because my mother is a physician. I don't begin to know all the various names for one medication and another, and certainly there was no way that I'd engage in a conversation about my mother's medications as if she were an inert object to be discussed in the third person.

Because I am a person who writes, I step back from the roller coaster of life and think, "So what am I learning?" I leave my parents' home and I sit with the page in front of me. For a moment, I zoom in on little everyday moments, such as the encounter with that eye doctor. Then I write these episodes in all their detail, supplying exact quotes even when I do not recall every word a person actually said. Then I skip a line, indent, and write what the vignette makes me realize. I write, "This makes me think . . ." Writing allows me to learn from even difficult periods of my life. It allowed me to come from that experience with my mother convinced that people can either shore up or reduce a person's sense of personal agency, of self-determination. A small act such as when I redirected that eye doctor's question can turn out to not be so small; it is not a little thing to resist the world's tendency to make people into passive victims. It is not a little thing to be reminded that nothing matters more than a person's verve towards life, a person's initiative and personal power.

My experiences with my mom have given me a way to talk and think about truths that pertain to teaching. People listen to my personal stories with open hearts, thinking of their own moms. They are with me. And then I tell them that sometimes when I teach kids, I am like that eye doctor.

I encourage you, too, to try your hand at writing. Write for yourself, not just as a model for your teachers. Yes, if you do some personal writing over the summer, it will, in fact, give you an incredible resource to draw upon when you work with teachers and kids in the fall, but the real reason to write is that doing so will help you. There is something profound about not only experiencing one's own life, but also pausing to reexperience it.

Long, long ago cave men put stories of hunts and journeys on stony cave walls, and then they stood before those murals and recalled those hunts, those journeys. As they relived those experiences, they learned from them. This is how we human beings became intelligent. Writing is a fundamental part of the human experience, and you'll discover this for yourself over the summer if you give yourself some time with a writer's notebook and a pen.

Gather Resources that Will Support Writing Reform

Birds gather stuff from here and there in order to make nests for themselves. You, too, will want to collect the stuff that can help you and your teachers create the richly literate culture you dream of. Cut clippings from the paper, save the poem that you like. When you were a teacher, you collected for your classroom; now you'll collect for your school—but the stance toward what could otherwise be viewed as roadside garbage is the same. You'll probably recall that when you were first teaching, everything you did became grist for your teaching mill. You went to a concert and saved the program to show a few of your young songwriters. You saw that a big bin of nectarines was on sale at the grocery store and contemplated buying them for indoor snack. This summer, try to remember that your teachers need you to inspire, channel, rally.

Live like a magnet, then. Collect picture books, poems, and anecdotes that you may be able to use on those occasions when you convene your people and try to be inspirational. For example, principals across New York City have found that Kevin Henkes' picture book *Chrysanthemum* can be a metaphor for the need to know children as individuals. Carmen Fariña used this story as an invitation to talk to her PS 6 teachers about how important it is to be sensitive to all the diverse children in our classrooms. She also shared the book *I Love You Like Crazy Cakes* by Rose Lewis with her staff because it conveyed to her teachers (and later, when she was Deputy Chancellor, to her principals and superintendents) the appreciation she felt for their humane, nurturing efforts on behalf of kids. Below is a list of a few resources I recommend you find, keeping them on hand to draw upon as needed during the school year:

- Peter Reynold's picture book *Ish* tells the story of a boy who wants to be an artist but is eternally dissatisfied with everything he does, wadding up one drawing after another. His little sister scavenges through the trash can, retrieving discarded drafts, and creates a display of these. In the end, the artist learns to glory in his own approximations, drawing things that are fish-ish, happy-ish. This book celebrates reading-writing connections but more importantly, it encourages people to rejoice in their own and each other's rough draft efforts.
- All of Byrd Baylor's picture books carry important messages, but one in particular, *I'm in Charge of Celebration*, seems especially essential. The narrator of this story realizes that if she pauses to really look at all that is around her, she will see reasons everywhere to celebrate. The narrator says, "Last year/I gave myself/One hundred and eight/Celebrations/Beside the ones/That they close schools for./I cannot get by/With only a few." Of course teachers (and principals) need to be reminded to pause, to really see the miracles in the mundane, and to say, "This matters."
- *Ira Sleeps Over* by Bernard Waber is the story of a little boy who struggles over whether he can bring his teddy bear with him when he sleeps over at his friend's house. Finally, in the middle of the night, he hears his friend creeping about and realizes that his friend, too, has his own version of a teddy bear. The story can be used to encourage teachers in a school to be open and vulnerable within the community of a school, willing to let each other know that none of us are as self-sufficient and all-confident as it might appear.

• *Miss Rumphius* by Barbara Cooney is a beautiful story that celebrates a woman who does something to make this world a more beautiful place.

DRAFT AND REVISE POSSIBLE SCHEDULES FOR YOUR STAFF

Some principals vacation in July and work in August, and others do the reverse. I hope you can vacation first (if only by giving yourself a mini-vacation to clear your head) so that when it comes time to plan the school's schedules for the year ahead, you approach this job with great wells of energy and ambition. I'm convinced that if you've had a chance to walk along an empty beach as the sun sets or to sit for long hours in a cafe with a loved one, you'll return to school accustomed to finding majesty and meaning in the smallest moments of your life. This consciousness will help you approach the task of scheduling your school.

My sons have both flown the coop, and so I recently altered my teaching schedule at Columbia University so that one evening a week, my husband and I are both home together (before now, our goal was always maximum coverage to achieve maximum supervision, so we arranged our schedules so we were home on *different* nights). Even this one tiny decision—to free my Wednesday nights so John and I overlap for an evening, midweek—has made a dramatic difference in the rhythms of my time. How important it is that you schedule your own and other people's lives with great care! You need to do this work fully aware that when you plan for people's schedules, you plan for their lives and their communities. What could matter more?

When working on a task of this importance, it is always wise to delay closure. A plan will spring to mind early on in the process, and you'll want to studiously avoid seizing upon that plan and then simply plowing ahead, executing it. Force yourself to remember that there is not just one way to schedule your school. Deliberately refrain from seizing on the obvious plan. Push yourself to conceive of alternatives, and keep an open mind.

Developing a schedule for your entire school is never an easy job, and this summer the challenge will be more complicated because you'll want to be sure cohorts of teachers can participate in professional development together. This will require that you synchronize the prep times and ideally, the lunch times for teachers within each cohort. Before thinking through the details of how you can do this, let's reflect on priorities you'll want to keep in mind.

Schedule in Ways that Support Collegiality

Roland Barth has pointed out that the finest professional development program in a school exists when teachers are engaged in collegial relationships with each other (Teachers College, 11/07/07). The teaching of writing can provide the forum for collegiality—but, of course, this won't happen without your attention. Too often, relationships among teachers are not at all collegial. Very often, in fact, teachers exist alongside each other like two-year-olds engaged in parallel play—say, in the sand box. Typically, two-year-olds talk all the time but never to each other. One has a pail, another a shovel, but at no point do they share toys. Teachers sometimes function in similar ways.

But it doesn't need to be this way. Professional development in writing can give you an opportunity to help your school become a place where everyone's learning is off the charts—and the first step is for you to organize schedules so that it is possible for cohorts of teachers to convene often. As you begin to plan your schedule, consider Barth's advice: "Collegiality is the presence of four specific behaviors, as follows: Adults in schools *talk about practice*. These conversations about teaching and learning are frequent, continuous, concrete, and precise. Adults in schools *observe each other* engaged in the practice of teaching and administration . . . Adults engage together in *work on the curriculum* by planning, designing, researching, and evaluating curriculum. Finally, adults in schools *teach each other* what they know about teaching, learning, and leading" (Barth 1990, 31). How can we schedule to support these four behaviors?

> Professional development in writing can give you an opportunity to help your school become a place where everyone's learning is off the charts.

For starts, as I've mentioned earlier, it will be crucial for you to be sure that teachers who will teach *Units of Study* in sync with each other have time to plan, assess, and learn together. Then, too, if you are hoping to use the teaching of writing as an opportunity to help your teachers develop closer and more collegial relationships, then you must remember that if you bring in an outside staff developer for a curtailed amount of time, your whole goal will be for teachers to work with that one outside expert and with each other *in ways that continue long after the outside expert has gone*. The scheduling you do for that outside staff developer should not only involve the isolated days when the staff developer will be on-site. You cannot say to yourself, "The work with a consultant will only involve six days, and I'll schedule each of those days in an idiosyncratic fashion when the time comes." Instead, try to schedule the outside staff developer in such a way that an inside expert can eventually step into the role initially played by this outside expert. Your goal will be for the outside expert to nudge teachers to come together in study groups. So organize teachers' schedules so that it will be easy for them to work together on a regular basis.

Schedule Different Staff Development Formats

Before you can schedule professional development and ongoing teacher collaboration, it will help to imagine how the upcoming year might unroll. I recommend at least four formats for writing staff development. These are the formats for staff development we describe and use in *Professional Development in the Teaching of Writing*:

Collaborative planning: Often teachers across a grade level will coplan the teaching that they will do in sync with each other. This planning may occur during prep periods, or teachers may do it before and after school or at home via email.

Small study groups: For at least sixty minutes each week and preferably for more time, teachers will convene in study groups. These study groups will usually bring together the same teachers who worked in the lab site classroom, but the groups may also be more inclusive. These study groups will usually be led by the person who also led the in-class lab site work, but they may be led by a lead teacher or an administrator. Members of a study group spend some time doing the same writing work that they'll ask children to do, and they generally spend time looking at student work through a shared lens.

Lab site work: Often—for sixty minutes once a week throughout the year or for four- to six-week intervals punctuating the year—cohorts of two to eight teachers will work either with an outside staff developer, your literacy coach, a lead teacher or, if need be, with each other inside one teacher's classroom with that teacher's class. This one class will be referred to as the lab site.

Whole-school professional development: From time to time, the whole school will study an aspect of the teaching of writing together. This may occur during faculty meetings, professional development days, or on other occasions. This professional development may be led by the literacy coach in concert with you and lead teachers, or it may be led by an outside staff developer.

You may worry that this is more professional development time than you can imagine providing, and I'd caution you to reconsider this, remembering that your goals for writing professional development extend far beyond writing itself. But if you are convinced you simply do not have the time to free teachers this much, then at least try to free teachers this much during the start of the year. This time together will help teachers launch effective writing classrooms and will provide them with the supportive relationships that they'll need. When you subsidize teachers' time so they learn together, you make it vastly more likely that they will learn together outside the bounds of that time.

GET TO THE BRASS TACKS OF SCHEDULING

When teachers study together in cohorts, this means that more teachers are able to participate in the same staff development, creating a bigger drumroll around that professional development and also creating a shared conversation. And most importantly, these teachers develop a sense of camaraderie among themselves and become accustomed to helping each other learn.

Schedule Common Preps and Study Groups

It will not be difficult for you to imagine ways to free teachers for common prep periods—this is probably your usual practice. How important it is, though, to align scheduled prep periods so that all the teachers across a cohort (usually a grade level) have a common prep period! As you go to this effort, remind yourself that it may be important for you to be transparent with your teachers about the reasons for this schedule. Remind your teachers that the purpose of *prep* periods is preparation, and let them know you believe common planning is crucial. Of course, each school has its own mores, and you will need to work with (and around) these, too.

As we discuss in more detail during Chapter 6, when you are scheduling common prep times, it is wise to consider ways you can give teachers opportunities to extend these periods of time. For example, you might schedule a prep period immediately before or immediately after lunch. If the music, art or other prep teacher (not the classroom teacher) handles the transition between his or her special class and lunch, the classroom teachers whose children are with those specialists will be able to begin some shared work during their common prep period. They then can extend that work over their lunchtime without needing to disperse while each teacher collects his or her class from the specialist and takes the children to their next destination.

Similarly, you can extend the length of a prep period if it is at the end of the school day as long as it is the specialist teacher (and not the classroom teacher) who then releases the children to go home. You may want to decide on a cohort or two of teachers that would be apt to take advantage of this sort of timing, scheduling their classes into specials right before or after lunch and before the end of the day.

Bear in mind that the culture of most schools is such that it must be you, the principal, who initiates the request for the specialist to take children to their buses at the end of the day. Policies such as these may not be wildly popular with your specialists. For this reason, if you decide to initiate these policies, avoid linking them to the reforms in writing (or you'll garner unnecessary ill will around those reforms).

Schedule Lab Site Work

Scheduling for common prep times will probably not be new for you, but it may be new and challenging to also make a schedule that will support stretches of time in which most, but not all, the classes of children at a grade level are otherwise occupied so those teachers can participate in lab site work. You may wonder if it wouldn't be more effective for your in-house coach to work with teachers individually, rather than work with cohorts of teachers in a single lab site classroom. Certainly this would be easier to schedule. Laurie and I, however, strongly encourage you to pull teachers together for one hour a week of shared work in classrooms and to do this for at least several four- to six-week stretches of the year. We have found that if the coach works one-to-one in a sequence of classrooms, she tends to function simply as another set of hands in those classrooms, teaching side-by-side with the classroom teacher. This has benefits for the kids on that one day, of course, but if your goal is for the coach to demonstrate to teachers in a way that sets them up to practice similar work with increasing independence, it is much more likely to be achieved if the coach is teaching a group of educators.

Here are some ways that principals go about scheduling cohorts of teachers to work together in shared lab sites:

Ideas for Scheduling So Teachers Can Study Together

✦ Some principals organize the schedule so that specialist teachers work with most but not all classrooms at a grade during the time slot that is normally reserved for the lab site. That is, three specialist teachers might be scheduled to work with the four third grade classrooms at the very start of every Friday morning. The three specialist teachers, then, free up three third grade teachers to work alongside the literacy coach and the fourth third grade teacher in that fourth teacher's classroom. As the year progresses, the room that is designated as the lab site switches (although it may not be that every classroom becomes a lab site).

✦ Some principals secure roving substitute teachers for the days when teachers study together in lab site classrooms. That is, if for the next six weeks, the three fourth and three fifth grade teachers will all work together in one 9:00–10:00 lab site, there may be five roving substitute teachers in the school on those days, freeing up three or four of these six teachers. One of their rooms will be used for a lab site, and the school may be able to cover one or two of the other classrooms, reducing the number of roving substitute teachers who will be needed. Then those roving substitute teachers can progress to different grade levels, again freeing up almost all the teachers at those grade levels.

✦ Some principals make sure that student teachers go through the due process so that it is legal for them to be the only adult in the classroom. Student teachers are then able to lead classrooms while teachers attend lab sites.

✦ Some principals convince a specialist teacher to work with larger-than-usual gatherings of children. For example, some schools have a spectacular music teacher, and this one teacher is able to convene four classrooms in a large room—say, the auditorium—for a mass class that frees up prep periods.

Schedule Your Literacy Coach

While you are scheduling your teachers, you will also want to devise a schedule for your literacy coach, if you have one. To do so, you'll need to spend some time together. You and the coach may not work out all the specific details of a schedule in the summer, but you do need to agree on a general plan, and the summer is a good time for aligning expectations. It may be that the coach's job description entails working alongside you during the summer, but even if it doesn't, invite him or her to join you for chunks of time. The two of you need to become accustomed to working closely together in support of your new writing initiative. Following are some suggestions for scheduling the coach's time.

Ideas for Scheduling So Coaches Can Best Support Teachers

✦ The coach's work with teachers will be much more powerful if it is predictable. This will allow the coach and teachers to establish a rhythm of working together, and it will make it likely that shared work can extend what has gone before and set the stage for what will come next. It is crucial that you set aside regular, predictable times for the coach to work with teachers, for example, from nine to one o'clock on Mondays, Wednesdays, and Fridays.

✦ Be sure to schedule some sacrosanct time for the coach to work with teachers. This time needs to be prescheduled, and it is very important that everyone respect the schedule and the shared work. Nothing should interfere with this time. Make sure you yourself don't make an exception. If, for example, the coach is scheduled to lead lab sites with the K–2 teachers on Tuesday mornings, resist the temptation to jettison this work during the last week in October because you need the coach to help you cover classes. Instead, schedule some flex time when you can call on the coach to lend a hand in the needs of the day. Remember that you set the tone for everyone else's response to your coach's time. The more confidence you have in your coach's staff development, the more sacrosanct time you will set aside.

✦ The coach's job is not to *replace* but to *enable* teachers. If the coach works too often with any one class, the teacher will end up stepping back and the coach will step forward, assuming a position almost as the classroom teacher (or the writing teacher) in that room. If the coach was recently a star teacher, it will be especially important for you to help her realize that her job now is to *make the classroom teacher into that star teacher*. The coach's schedule will help shape her role. Make sure she does not work with any teacher more than two days a week at the very most.

✦ Shared work in classrooms is only one way for the coach to support teachers. It is also important for the coach to work with teachers away from kids, helping teachers plan minilessons, study student work, anticipate conferences and small groups, and so forth.

✦ The coach can help teachers not only by working directly with them, but also by enabling teachers to work with each other. For example, the coach might take over a lead teacher's classroom for an hour a day at the start of every Wednesday for a month, freeing that lead teacher up to mentor another teacher. Such a use of the coach's time could end up helping not only the apprentice but also the mentor teacher.

GATHER GIFTS AND SUPPLIES FOR REWARDING TEACHERS' PROFESSIONALISM

I opened this book by telling you that just before the 2007 annual conference for the National Council of Teachers of English, my colleagues and I brought several hundred educators from across the country to visit scores of New York City schools. What I did not tell you was that after those visits were over, I wrote to the principals and told them that the Project had located one of New York City's finest pastry shops and bought an enormous sheet cake for each host school, which could arrive on any day the principal selected. Over the years, my colleagues and I have invented all sorts of imaginative gifts. We've given every teacher in a school a hardbound copy of Peter Reynold's book, *Ish*; we've given teachers' gift cards to neighborhood bookstores; we've even given a school a machine that turns pages into posters.

Gifts matter. Think about a time when you received an unexpected gift. Think of a gift that came with a personal note of thanks attached. Neither teachers nor principals receive enough gifts. The work we all do for children is endless, taxing, and sometimes, thankless. I strongly encourage you to look creatively at your budget and see if you can tweak it so that you will be in a position to lavish your teachers with gifts that convey your appreciation and support.

You may be shaking your head in doubt, wondering if I have any idea how restricted you are when it comes to budget. Perhaps you have money only for the bare bones—for a limited number of books and supplies per classroom, and that's it. Here is my suggestion: Purchase those books and those supplies with care and store them somewhere. Instead of leaving a tower of thirty books inside each classroom door, squirrel the books away. Then when a cluster of teachers joins you in a breakfast think tank to discuss a schoolwide way to record writing conferences, end the meeting with a little speech about how grateful you are that these teachers gave their own time to this cause, and give each teacher a copy of a carefully selected book. If you have set aside not only books but other materials as well, use these supplies in similar ways. Perhaps you decide to visit all your kindergartners to check that writing workshops are well underway. After these visits, write a note telling your kindergarten teachers that you were blown away by the courage and inventiveness and energy of their young writers, and tell them you couldn't resist getting them some supplies, supplies that you hope keep enthusiasm for writing sky-high. Then, enclosed with your letter, send along a tiny bit of the supplies you would otherwise have doled out on the first day of the year!

Of course, it is important that you are not the only person to give teachers supplies. Your literacy coach will need all the support he or she can get, so by all means give your coach a key to the secret supply closet. This way, when the literacy coach wants to lure teachers to do some of their own writing and knows they're not going to be head over heels in love with this plan, the coach can buy their compliance by giving each one a beautifully wrapped, extra-special writer's notebook.

The CD-ROMs in *Units of Study* list supplies linked to specific units. You may want to purchase those supplies for your writing teachers. Most materials carry instructional messages with them, and these materials become more valuable when they are embedded into instruction. For example, I'd recommend giving a first grade classroom some extra staplers and scissors when the class is embarking on a unit of study on revision; I'd give students a tape recorder or two when they are about to write poetry; and I'd give them a stack of all-about nonfiction books when they are embarking on a unit on all-about writing.

We recommend you purchase materials for teachers as well as for children, and we recommend that you embed these materials into instruction (in this case, professional development instruction). A few of these materials need to be given to teachers up front, when you share with teacher's the fact that the school as a whole is embarking on a crucially important shared study. Follow up your talk with a gift of three-ring binders with dividers already in place. Tell teachers you hope they store any papers related to that study in these binders. From this day on, whenever you distribute papers that you hope teachers will save in their binders, be sure the papers are three-hole punched. Make a similar binder for yourself, and use yours as a model. Carry it with you, and remind teachers often that they, too, need to bring their binders to meetings and professional development opportunities.

Along with other materials, you will need to purchase professional books for teachers. Presumably, given that you are reading this book, you will have already decided to equip each of your teachers with a box of *Units of Study* books. You may want to purchase a different book on the qualities of good writing for each teacher, with the intention that the coach will give these out at some point and will ask each teacher to read and mark up her book and to share from it (teachers can then exchange books). If you decide to do this, here is a list of books I especially recommend:

Books Recommended for Teachers of Grades 3–5

Writing Down the Bones by Natalie Goldberg
A Writer Teaches Writing by Donald Murray
On Writing Well by William K. Zinsser
Bird by Bird by Anne Lamott
Inventing the Truth by Russell Baker et al.
Elements of Style by William Strunk Jr. and E.B. White
The Power of Grammar by Mary Ehrenworth and Vicki Vinton
What a Writer Needs by Ralph Fletcher
*The Writing Workshop: Working Through the Hard Parts (And They're
    All Hard Parts)* by Katie Wood Ray
Writing a Life by Katherine Bomer

Books Recommended for Teachers of Grades K–2

One to One: The Art of Conferring with Young Writers by Lucy Calkins,
    Amanda Hartman, and Zoe Ryder White
Writing Workshop: The Essential Guide by Ralph Fletcher and
    JoAnn Portalupi
About the Authors: Writing Workshop with Our Youngest Writers
    by Katie Wood Ray
Don't Forget to Share: The Crucial Last Step in the Writing Workshop
    by Leah Mermelstein
*Second Grade Writers: Units of Study to Help Children Focus on
    Audience and Purpose* by Stephanie Parsons
A Quick Guide to Teaching Persuasive Writing by Sarah Picard Taylor
A Quick Guide to Boosting English Acquisition in Choice Time
    by Cheryl Tyler and Alison Porcelli

It is important to avoid deluging teachers with far more materials than they could possibly hope to study and use. The most important materials, for now, will be the *Units of Study* books themselves, which you or the coach can help teachers become acquainted with.

Help Teachers Set Up Classrooms to Support Workshop Learning

The new school year is about to begin. The schedule is in place. The bus routes are finalized. The painters have washed their last paint brush. Soon teachers will be coming to set up their classrooms. You still have the last teacher to hire. Before you know it, children will be arriving in droves, refreshed from the summer and ready for the new school year to begin. But wait! I have one more suggestion. Roll up your sleeves and help teachers arrange their classrooms to support workshop teaching. It will be much easier to do this now before children are in the room.

Of course, you won't want to assume control of the arrangement of teachers' classrooms, but you can give well-timed suggestions, and you can especially do so if you've rolled up your sleeves and pitched in to unpack, scrub, arrange, and the rest.

Organize furniture to support collaboration.
How we arrange the furniture in our homes says so much about what we believe is important. If we situate the chairs in our living room in a cluster next to the sofa, we are giving a message that conversation is important. We want our guests to talk to each other. If, on the other hand, we position chairs in a corner, angled towards the television, then we are not thinking so much about potential conversations.

How we situate the furniture in our classrooms gives similar messages. In writing workshop classrooms, teachers usually arrange desks in clusters. Teachers who are not accustomed to this arrangement might be worried that children will talk too much and, therefore, might want to wait before they try it. Encourage teachers to accept the challenge. Assure them that you know that this will not be a problem and that you are sure children will rise to the occasion, as will the teachers.

Set up areas for group, partner, and independent work.
Encourage your teachers to turn one corner of the room into a meeting area. In this space, teachers will be able to gather children's attention more easily if children sit in close proximity to each other, the teacher, and an easel. In addition, children need places in which they can sustain independent work or talk with a partner. Take some time to think about traffic patterns so that children can move easily from area to area.

Set up wall space and easels for teaching.

Suggest that teachers set up an easel and chart paper at the front of the group meeting area to use during direct instruction. They'll collect the teaching points on cumulative charts that will serve to remind writers of all they learned on previous days. This is crucial in a workshop because one day's teaching is meant to affect not only that day's work but every day's work.

Just as charts provide instructional support for children, word walls can do the same. Word walls contain a manageable number of high-frequency words, written in large enough print for students to read from their writing areas. As students become adept at spelling high-frequency words correctly, new words can replace known words.

Teachers will also set aside wall space for displaying children's writing. Some teachers title these displays "Celebrate Work in Progress," thereby ensuring that parents won't question less than perfect spelling.

Supply writing centers with tools of the trade.

Make sure you have given teachers the supplies they need—appropriate paper, staplers, date stamps, tape—to set up a writing center. Perhaps you will want to order a container with a shelf for each of several kinds of paper. In any case, you want to be sure the supplies are organized so that children can access them on their own.

Arrange the classroom library to support reading and writing.

In most classrooms, teachers convene children in a space that doubles as a library as well as a meeting area. Classroom libraries are essential. Children will only be able to write well if they are given lots of opportunities to read wonderful literature. In addition to using the library space to provide a place where children can browse for and find books, many teachers use it to display books that can serve as mentor texts for the writing workshop.

Now it's time to walk your building and help teachers put any final touches in place. You might want to surprise teachers with one of those presents you've planned—a tub of books that are mentor texts for the first unit of study or some other helpful materials.

The rooms are ready. Your teachers are ready. It will be a great year!

"Promoting Professional Development" suggests kinds of support structures you might put in place for your teachers.

CHAPTER FIVE

SEPTEMBER
LAUNCHING WRITING WORKSHOPS

Hold your hat! The year will soon be upon you. I once had a duplicating machine that contained a flashing light. I'd press *Go* and the machine would flash, "Not ready. Not ready. Not ready." At the start of every school year, I always feel as if I need one of those lights to signal, "Not ready. Not ready."

But of course, the parents and teachers and kids will come, ready or not. Suddenly, there will be demands placed on your every minute. If you are anything like the principals I know best, you'll enter school in the morning, leave school in the evening, and feel as if the entire day was spent putting out fires. There will be one crisis, then another, then another. You'll have no time to breathe.

That's life for a principal. Don't be surprised. Expect that your time will not be your own. That's how the start of the year will always be for everyone in your position.

THIS MONTH

- **Reflect on your own leadership style.**

- **Participate in launching writing workshops.**

- **Observe writing workshops to celebrate specific practices.**

- **Talk with teachers about what you've observed.**

REFLECT ON YOUR OWN LEADERSHIP STYLE

The problem is that for far too many people, the craziness lasts not just for the first few days of school. For far too many people, this becomes the norm. And because you are always frantically busy, you can convince yourself that this sort of running from one crisis to another is what it means to lead a school. You can convince yourself that you are busy enough and needed enough that you must be doing your job well.

But pause for a moment and think about it. Think about the teachers who lead their classrooms especially well. Conjure up images of those classrooms. Are the especially effective teachers the ones who cannot take three steps without youngsters tugging at their trouser legs to ask for one thing or another? Are the especially effective classroom teachers the ones who seem to rush from one crisis to another? I doubt it. And the same is true for school principals.

So give yourself a test, and use it to think about your leadership style:

- Do you find that each day is utterly unique, and that you have very few patterns that persist from one day to a next? Do you find that on most days you devote most of your time to simply meeting the needs of the day as each need becomes pressing?
- Do you find that the parents of your students are very needy and that they're pressing their various concerns onto you, often at inconvenient times?
- Do you find that your teachers are very needy and that they, too, are always pressing their various concerns onto you, often at inconvenient times?
- Do you find that you are chronically in a state of trying to catch up, to dig out of a hole, and that you are almost never ready for whatever will come around the next bend until it is literally upon you?
- Do you find that when you delegate responsibilities, other people generally let you down, and as often as not, you end up doing the work you expected they'd do?

If you have answered *yes* to any or all of these questions, then you may want to use the new year as an occasion to draw a line in the sand for yourself as a leader and to resolve to work towards new habits. Although I am not a principal and, therefore, my constituents are different from yours, I am pretty sure that, alas, my answer to my own version of these questions would need to be *yes, yes, yes*. Despite this, I still fancy myself to be a fairly effective leader (so all is not lost if you are in as much trouble as I'm in). But I think it is important for us to at least be aware when our leadership has flaws. If you have answered *yes* to the questions I posed you, like me you need to give yourself a problematic report card. Let me go through the questions one at a time.

If every day seems utterly unique, you need to create predictable structures.

If you answered the questions in number one with a particularly resounding yes, think about creating predictable routines to anchor your time. It is very common for a leader to feel as if every day is unique and unpredictable, but what this really means is that we are lurching from one crisis to another.

Because our schedules are always created on the spur of the moment, this means that people around us can't plan for the work we do together. They can't anticipate and plan for our shared work. Instead, we're always collaring one person after another, dragging that person into our space, addressing some topic or another, and then rushing to call on another unsuspecting soul.

How much more powerful it would be if we scheduled ourselves so that during our first morning in the office each week (usually Mondays, but sometimes Tuesdays) we met with our assistant principal. It would be better still, if during these meetings we always addressed four topics (including the needs of the week, presumably) and we always heard the assistant principal's report on an item or two that were her responsibility. Then too, rather than popping unexpectedly into a meeting of second grade teachers, for example, how much more powerful that visit would be if those teachers could anticipate that we'd attend their first meeting of the month. They could save items for discussion, plan on addressing concerns, and so forth. Of course, convening regular meetings with the assistant principal at the start of each week and holding weekly scheduled meetings with cohorts of teachers won't alone provide structure to a principal's time, but it's a beginning.

If parents are always interrupting at inconvenient times, try proactively establishing a system of communication.
Many of the principals with whom I work closely have found that if they are always on call for parents, then parents come by with any fleeting question or concern, often bringing issues to the principal that could just as well have been directed elsewhere. These principals have found that it helps to set up somewhat formal procedures in order to give parents access to them. For example, in some schools parents must fill out a form in duplicate, stating the reason for the requested meeting and citing whether they have already brought the concern to someone else (e.g., to the classroom teacher). Then the school secretary calls the parent and schedules a five-minute appointment with the principal (unless the concern should be taken elsewhere).

Principals say that simply requiring parents to fill out the form dramatically reduces the number of requests. Sometimes when a parent must put the request into black and white, the parent rethinks whether the request is really all that necessary. These forms also allow the school secretary to triage requests. Sometimes the secretary can read the parent's summary of the issue and convey to the parent that, actually, the parent needs to talk with someone else. This structure also helps parents realize that the principal's time is precious and limited. If the parent usurps too much time, this cuts into another parent's time (the secretary needs to appear in the doorway to say, "Your next appointment is here."). Appointments need to be scheduled back-to-back for just this purpose. Then, too, when these conversations are scheduled, the principal is able to prepare for them. If the topic of conversation is a disagreement between a parent and a teacher, and the parent has already addressed concerns directly with the teacher, then the principal can do his homework in preparation for the meeting.

The principals I know best do not only schedule one-to-one meetings with parents, they also schedule a great many opportunities for parent education. Laurie and I discuss these in more detail later in the book.

If teachers are always interrupting at inconvenient times, try establishing systems of communication with them also.

Principals and teachers work shoulder to shoulder, interacting informally all the time. As important as these interactions are, there is still a place for one-to-one appointments. The principals I know best tend to post office hours, and teachers sign up, individually or in small groups, for appointments. The principal may cut out the middleman and simply post times on her door, inviting teachers to sign up for any open 15-minute slot, or the principal can work through the secretary. In addition, many principals find it important to schedule one-to-one conversations with each teacher towards the start of the year and again at a later time during the year. I wrote about these one-to-one conversations earlier, but mention them again now as September is a great time for them.

If you find yourself chronically behind, distribute leadership by enabling others to share your load.

Earlier I asked you to consider whether you find yourself chronically behind and whether you find that delegating responsibilities inevitably backfires on you. These two questions relate to each other, of course. You and I will be chronically behind and always working to dig ourselves out if we find that we are the only ones who can accomplish anything. The problem is we end up lumbering down the highway of time like a slow-moving snowplow, with everyone else needing to follow slowly in our tracks. The only way to ease the congestion is for us to work with others in ways that enable, not disable, and that help them get their jobs done well. I've had a lot of people over a lot of years advise me how to do this.

Suggestions for Successful Delegation

✦ Be explicit about what you want the person to take on. State your goal clearly and give the person some time to determine how to reach it.

✦ Ask the person who will take on a responsibility to sketch out a plan for proceeding and to run that plan past you for input. Don't feel as if you need to do all the work of coming up with a plan.

✦ Ask the person to suggest a timetable (which you can agree with or alter). Make sure the timetable builds in time for the person to do some remedial work if necessary (so you don't end up doing it yourself). Once clear dates are established, make sure they're honored.

✦ If you do not concur with everything the person has done, weigh carefully whether your reservations are weighty enough that you need to register them. Some will be, in which case try to name these in ways that allow the person to learn from them. Some of your reservations will simply derive from the fact that you would have done the job a bit differently, as will always be the case. Let these go!

✦ Bear in mind that you are not being a good leader if you do all the work yourself. If you find yourself feeling virtuous because you've shouldered the whole load, rethink this. If you want smart, strong people to enjoy working alongside you, these people need opportunities to engage in substantive leadership work, and if you hog all these opportunities, your people will not flourish alongside you!

I once paid large sums of money to hire a leadership coach for myself. Every week, my coach and I spoke on the phone for half an hour. I learned a lot from that work, including how important it is for a leader to have a confidante who helps us lead well. If you have such a person in your life, encourage that person to ask you questions like these:

• What goals do you have for your school, say, in the next 3–5 years?
• What can you do now to work toward those goals?
• What obstacles might get in your way?
• What positive steps could you take to tackle those obstacles?

Participate in Launching Writing Workshops

Picture how it will go. Five teachers (let's say) meet with the literacy coach in one of the teacher's lab site classroom, and these five teachers plus the coach colead a writing workshop with those kids. The kids write up a storm!

Then the four visiting teachers return to their own classrooms with instructions to teach the very same lesson to their own kids, only without any added teachers for help. And then all five teachers (the lab site teacher included) are given guidance by the literacy coach in a small study group or in collaborative prep time, and together the group plans ways to continue teaching a writing workshop every day during the week, until the group reconvenes the next week with the literacy coach in the lab site classroom.

At this second visit to the lab site classroom, the coach will again help the group of teachers take the same kids further into writing. The teachers will again go back to their own classrooms and take their own children further into writing in similar ways to the way the literacy coach did in the lab site classroom. During the small study group, everyone will share stories of the problems they've encountered while teaching writing on their own and will plan for the upcoming week.

You won't be surprised to hear me say that it is quite a trick getting the teachers to actually launch writing workshops in their own classrooms! And yet, as you can see, if some teachers do this and others don't, the more hesitant teachers will get more and more out of step with their colleagues, and their problems—and hesitancy—will compound.

Once you launch the writing workshop in your school and provide structured professional development to support it, you need to move heaven and earth to make it as likely as possible that all your teachers actually launch writing workshops in their classrooms, devoting close to an hour a day to teaching writing. Very few things are more important than this. You are apt to think that teachers may need a bit of breathing space right now, that it is not a good idea to rush them towards leading writing workshops. You may say to yourself, "Each teacher will come to the idea of leading a writing workshop when she is ready." This may be true, but the fact is this: If your more hesitant teachers hang back from launching their own writing workshops while bolder teachers take this on, then your teachers will be out of sync with each other, and the very ones who most need support and companionship around the teaching of writing will be left to work all alone without the advantages of professional support aligned to their teaching. If a coach or a staff developer is working with a cohort of your teachers (as we recommend), then you need to personally make sure that each of the members of that cohort actually gets started teaching writing and continues to teach writing every day.

Reinforce the Daily Teaching of Writing

Talk up the fact that it is crucial for every teacher to teach writing every day. Perhaps you and your assistant principal and the coach can spread out, stopping in the classrooms to lend a hand. You can describe this as "lending a hand," but, of course, you'd also be giving teachers the nudge they need. It is impossible to overemphasize the importance of helping all your teachers get themselves mobilized to teach writing. Once teachers have launched writing workshops, there are other predictable problems, but none of these other problems will require your help as urgently as this one.

You can also make it likely that teachers are teaching writing every day if you schedule study groups and ask teachers to bring their children's writing notebooks (grades 3–5) or their writing folders (grades K–2) to those meetings. Set these meetings up well in advance so they serve as a nudge for teachers to get their kids launched, rather than as a "gotcha." Position this as support, saying something like, "Let's all bring our kids' writing to the grade-level meeting on Friday of this week, and we'll help each other see what the

> Talk up the fact that it is crucial for every teacher to teach writing every day.

kids' work is telling us." Be prepared in a situation such as this for one teacher to arrive without writing in hand. Send that teacher back to his classroom (or offer to run the errand for him). Otherwise, you will inadvertently convey that your requests to bring student work can be easily circumvented. Of course, the teacher who does not bring children's writing may be one who hasn't actually started the writing workshop in his class, so in the end, you'll need to join him soon to help him support his kids' writing.

One way or another, you are sure to find that some teachers are not teaching writing workshops. There will be all sorts of reasons for this. Listen, but then convey that you can't live with the idea of one group of kids not having a chance to grow as writers. Blame your need for every class to spend time each day writing on your commitment to the kids—that rationale is hard to refute.

Of course, if a teacher conveys to you that this mandate is hard for her, offer maximum support. Say, "What can I do that will help you teach a writing workshop?" and then be prepared to meet the teacher's requests if you possibly can. You'll find that once the teacher has launched a writing workshop and once her kids have momentum as writers, she won't be apt to need support in order to maintain momentum.

Visit Classrooms to Celebrate Writing Workshop

Once workshops are launched, your visits will be crucial. During these early weeks of the school year, you will definitely want to stop by classrooms to see that writing workshops are in full swing. You can let teachers know this will be your priority. "This week, I want to visit your rooms while you are teaching writing. Can you send me your schedule for the week?" You need not schedule any particular visiting time nor stay long, but let teachers know that wild horses couldn't keep you from wanting to watch youngsters write.

When you visit a writing workshop, you'll want to have in mind some of the important things to watch for and celebrate. In order to offer the best possible feedback to teachers whose classrooms you visit, it helps to keep a mental list of concrete things to notice and suggest. I hope the rest of this chapter will help equip you to do this. It is probably more important, however, for you to remember that you are extremely powerful. You can intervene in ways that lift teachers' spirits and launch them in deep learning, or you can intervene in ways that dispirit teachers and lead them to literally or figuratively leave their positions. Let me talk a bit about the actual classroom visits themselves.

Imagine How Your Classroom Visit Can Go

Most of the principals with whom we work most closely pop in and out of classrooms frequently, so these classroom visits are not part of their formal supervision of a teacher. A principal will let teachers know that during the upcoming week he plans to stop into rooms to help out during writing workshops, and the principal will acquire teachers' schedules for teaching writing (if the principal doesn't already know this). But the visits themselves are not formally scheduled. And remember, as Doug Reeves says, "Exemplary leaders make it their mission to catch teachers doing something right" (2006b, 58).

Usually a principal will have a plan for which rooms to visit. Perhaps on one given day, Anthony, principal of PS 199 in Queens, will aim to visit all the first grade classrooms and some of the second grade classrooms during their writing time. Let's imagine that in this school, those two grade levels all schedule writing at the start of the day, right after morning meeting.

Starting at 8:50, then, Anthony will walk among the classrooms, noticing who has and who has not yet switched from the meeting time to writing workshop. He watches one teacher convene her class and begin her mini-lesson. He slips into the hall to look in on another minilesson but discovers that Janet is still leading her morning meeting. She is already ten minutes behind the posted flow-of-the-day schedule, and he notes this. He moves on and catches the bulk of a second teacher's minilesson, noticing ways in which it is similar to and different from the first teacher's. He stays in this second room to watch the all-important transition from minilesson time to writing, noticing how kids get themselves started on writing. He works with a table of writers himself, briefly, and takes note of the work that a few writers at that table have obviously done on the preceding days.

Anthony moves to yet a third classroom, signaling a greeting to the teacher, who catches his eye. The children here are all writing (or sitting over their work). He first sits himself on the meeting area carpet in this room so that he can survey the scene before entering into it. Two children are talking together nearby, so he listens to their conversation. He spies an empty chair at a nearby table and goes to that chair, and from this new perspective, he is able to see what the youngsters around the table are doing. He is a bit confused over what is going on, so he says to one child, "Can you tell me about what you guys are doing in writing right now?" When the child uses writing workshop terminology, Anthony presses to understand the child's interpretation. "What do you mean you are 'stretching the words out'?" he asks. "Can you show me what you mean?"

Anthony finishes this conversation and joins the teacher who is talking with a child. She looks up and he signals, "Carry on." She finishes the conversation, and he gives her a compliment. "There was such intimacy in that interaction. I think he felt like the king of the world." Then he says, "Can you coach me a bit? Can we look at a child's work, and can you help me know what I could teach the kid, if I had time to do it?" They talk together about a child's work. Anthony signals that he needs to run to yet one more room, and the teacher, too, can tell her kids need some help sustaining writing.

Anthony now enters the fourth classroom, the room that got a late start on writing that day. He notices the teacher has a supervisory pose; in that instant, at least, she seems to be teaching from standing above the room, calling out to kids. Anthony joins a table full of writers and begins a conversation with one of them. "What have you been working on as a writer?" he asks, and soon the youngster is giving Anthony a tour of his writing folder. Anthony wonders if the teacher assigned this child's topics, so he asks another nearby child, "Can I look at your writing?" and when Anthony looks between the two collections of student work, he confirms his hypothesis.

In just over an hour, then, Anthony has slipped in and out of four writing workshops. You may think he has collected just fragmentary information on each of those rooms, which is true, but he has already gleaned the gist of how those four teachers are faring as teachers of writing he has demonstrated his commitment to writing to those teachers and to the school, and he has far more in mind that he could say to those teachers than any of them will be able to hear.

Pointers for Successful Classroom Visits

✦ You'll want your teachers to become accustomed to you making frequent, brief, unscheduled, informal visits to their classrooms. Tell teachers in general that you'll be popping in and out of rooms in an effort to help and to learn, but don't schedule your visits with any precision.

✦ Have a plan in mind for the classrooms you'll visit—usually this will mean visiting all the classrooms on a particular grade level. Looking at these rooms alongside each other will help you see patterns and will also help you see inconsistencies.

✦ Slip unobtrusively into classrooms. Teachers and children should be so accustomed to your visits that they look up, note your presence, and then return to work. If children stop work because you've arrived, signal for them to keep going, let them know you're just watching for a time, and do that.

✦ Don't always go directly to the teacher. If writing time is under way and kids are writing and the teacher is working with one writer or a small group, you'll diminish pressure on the teacher if you do not immediately shadow her. Instead, sit in the meeting area, or find an empty seat in the midst of the kids' work spaces.

✦ Look around for a bit before launching into a conversation with one writer or another. This way, when you do begin a conversation, you will already have a sense of the child with whom you'll talk. Does this seem to be an especially gung ho writer? An especially struggling writer?

✦ When you talk with one child, talk quietly so that others around you continue to work. If others pause in their work to listen, you'll probably want to use nonverbal cues to signal that they need to get back to their own papers. Meanwhile, start a conversation with the one child by asking, "What are you working on as a writer?" In time, you will see children become very skilled at answering that question. For now, kids will probably tell you their topic and show you their writing.

✦ While listening to one child talk, you can also glean a lot about the classroom environment, the rituals that are in place in a classroom, and children's abilities to carry on as writers with independence. You can also watch from afar and ascertain a great deal about the teacher's teaching. Listen to the one child, and meanwhile gather data about the classroom as a whole. If you look with specific questions in mind, you will notice a lot more.

✦ Shift between observing and helping in the class. Help a child or two, but don't get so consumed with an intense one-to-one interaction that you lose your ability to see what's going on and to ascertain patterns.

✦ At some point, speak to the classroom teacher quietly. Be sure to say something supportive in this brief interaction. Later you can have a longer conversation and make some suggestions. If you are not sure what exactly to say, you are always wise to talk about what you noticed one child doing as a writer. Remember that if you want the teacher to find beauty and majesty and humor in children's work, you may need to mentor her in this, so be appreciative of a particular child. Your appreciation will be more powerful if it is specific. Quote something the child said or wrote, in all its detail.

✦ Make sure that in an least one of the classrooms, you solicit the teacher's help learning to teach writing. You may not actually get that help right then and there—you can ask for the teacher to help you later—but do continue your stance as a public learner. Ralph Peterson, author of *Life in a Crowded Place*, once said to me, "You cannot affect another person if you are not willing to be affected by that person." If you will want to make some suggestions to the teacher, you will make it much easier for that teacher to learn from you if you have also demonstrated that you are willing to learn from that teacher. So at the very least, say something like this: "When I watched Brian, I realize I have no idea how to help him. Later, can we catch a moment and can you give me some pointers on how you'd go about helping him?"

Observe Writing Workshops
to Celebrate Specific Practices

When you visit a writing workshop, you'll want to know some of the important things to watch for and celebrate. One of the best ways to become skilled at observing writing workshops is this. Ask your literacy coach which teachers are leading effective writing workshops, and visit two or three of those classrooms during writing time. Then learn which teachers are leading especially troubled workshops, and visit those classrooms during writing time. You'll see and feel the difference, and this sense will help you learn qualities that make for effective writing workshops. If you are not sure that any of your teachers are on track yet, then observe the scenes of classroom teaching on the DVDs and contrast them with your classrooms (although remember those scenes are from unusually effective writing workshops). It can also help to be given lists of things to celebrate. If you notice and support the very things that the coach has emphasized, for example, this empowers the coach and the coaching, making a world of difference. Here are some of the things that you will probably see your teachers gesturing towards doing, things you can watch for and support.

Notice and Support Workshop Management Structures

Even the transitional moments before a writing workshop begins matter. Look for the classroom management structures the teacher has put in place to make the workshop run successfully.

Is the teacher attending to the way kids gather?

Does the teacher seem to care about *how kids gather* for the minilesson? The kids may still not have smooth transitions, but the fact that the teacher is attentive to them will be something to celebrate. Does he support kids who walk quickly and quietly to the meeting area, perhaps by giving one a meaningful thumbs-up gesture, perhaps by saying to another, "I like that you are coming quickly and quietly." (You can join him in some nonverbal gestures of support.) If kids are not gathering quickly and quietly, does the teacher ask kids to try the transition again, and this time does he clearly remind kids of his expectations in ways that attempt to raise the standards?

Is the teacher attending to organizing kids in learning partnerships?

Has the teacher taught kids that they have specific rug spots, and has he done the work necessary so they are sitting next to longtime partners? If so, this suggests the teacher is putting structures into place that will serve the workshop well.

Is the teacher teaching towards independence?

What can kids already do with automaticity? This will be something to watch over time. If the teacher takes time to remind kids to push in their chairs at the start of September, later in the month you should see that the teacher simply compliments them for doing so or assumes they will. Does the teacher use compliments and/or nonverbal signals to support very specific actions that he sees kids taking?

Does the teacher strive for focused attention from the children?

Does the teacher use an attention-getting device, such as perhaps the single word "Writers" to secure kids' attention? Does the teacher then wait silently, giving the classroom a 360-degree scan while he makes sure that every child has frozen in the midst of what she is doing and given the teacher her eyes? If the teacher resumes talking before he has the full attention of the class, signal for him to wait even longer until he has everyone's full attention. If one or two children are wiggling or whispering, a hand on a child's shoulder or a nonverbal signal (such as a shush gesture) can help.

Above all, is there evidence that the teacher and/or the kids seem upbeat about the upcoming writing workshop, and is there a sense of urgency ("We don't want to waste a precious minute") to this time?

Notice and Support Effective Minilessons

During the minilesson, you'll be looking for the focus, clarity, and effectiveness with which the teacher makes his teaching point.

Is it easy to learn from the minilesson?

Listening to the minilesson, do you find that you are able to learn from it? Does it make sense to you? Is the teaching point clear? Is it presented in a way that all children can understand and remember?

Is the minilesson brief—approximately ten minutes long—saving maximum time for writing?

If kids try to intervene with lots of questions and comments, does the teacher convey that this is not the ideal time for interruptions, and does she carry on without losing momentum? When teachers are taught traditional teaching methods, they're often taught to *elicit* information from children, leading to teaching that contains lots of little questions. In minilessons, on the other hand, a teacher hopes to take a few minutes to explicitly *teach* kids something. The clearest and most efficient way to do so is to talk to them. Generally, then, in an efficient and clear minilesson, the teacher will not ask questions of kids and will especially not ask known-answer questions (questions for which the teacher has the answer). If the teacher refrains from asking questions and instead speaks to kids in a straightforward manner, support this.

Has the teacher tailored the minilesson so it is responsive to this particular class of children?

Often when an approach is new to teachers, they will rely heavily on a model, staying close to the lesson in the *Units of Study* book. It isn't ideal for teachers to read aloud sections of a minilesson (or entire minilessons), nor is it a crisis if some do. Be sure to encourage teachers to move away from this as they gain confidence. Usually the teacher's adaptations will involve bringing in the teacher's own true-life stories, referencing his own students by name, shortening the upper grade minilessons and elongating the K–2 ones, and paraphrasing rather than reading aloud at least most of the printed minilessons.

Do the teacher's actions show that he notices and cares that kids are involved and engaged in the minilesson?

Is the minilesson delivered *quickly and in a lively tone* of voice, so that it is *compelling* enough for kids to be at least somewhat engaged? When kids' attention seems to drift, look to see that the teacher adjusts teaching to capture attention, even if these adjustments do not totally succeed. Does the teacher sit before the group, leaning in to talk with some earnestness and intensity, *referencing work that has been written* (or that he writes extremely quickly) on chart paper? The minilesson should feel a bit like a huddle before the football game.

Do the children seem to understand how a minilesson usually goes?

In other words, do they understand minilessons in general, enough so that when the teacher wants to begin, they grow silent, and while the teacher talks, few interrupt, and when the teacher wants kids to "turn and talk" they can do this (and then come back from doing this) efficiently?

Does the teacher transition smoothly from the minilesson to the writing time?

Listen for the teacher to remind kids that writers have choices today and cite several alternatives. This shows he is using the minilesson as a way to introduce a strategy or writing tool to be used when the need arises for the writer, rather than as an assignment for today's work. Does the teacher disperse one cluster of kids and then enjoin those who are still with him on the rug in the meeting area to admire the way the first group is getting started on their writing (thus reminding those children of his hopes) before dispersing the second group? This may not be the teacher's system for handling transitions; the important thing is that the teacher seems to notice and care about this time and that he is explicitly teaching kids ways to meet his expectations.

Notice and Support Independence and Stamina in Writing

Writing time is your opportunity to observe young writers at work.

Has the teacher set up systems so children can get materials and get started on their own immediately?

Do children seem to have a system for securing the tools they need in order to write, freeing the teacher up from having to dole out paper and pens? Are many of the children able to generate their own ideas for writing? It is likely that many still need the teacher to give them a jump start, but see if the teacher is working towards showing them how to start themselves.

Is writing happening daily?

Is there evidence in the children's folders (if these are K–2 kids) or their notebooks (if these are writers in grades 3–5) that the children wrote yesterday, and the day before, and the day before?

Is there evidence in the children's writing that they are already growing as writers?

(See the October and December chapters for discussion of how kindergarten children, first graders, second graders, and children in grades 3–5 should probably be growing as writers.) Charts hanging in the classroom should suggest what the teacher has been teaching. Can you see evidence in the children's work that they have been trying to do some of what the charts suggest the teacher has been teaching them to do? If there are no charts, you can ask a child, "What has your teacher been teaching you to do as a writer?" and then you and the child, together, can look for evidence of that.

Does the teacher move from one area of the classroom to another so that her presence is felt everywhere?

Does the teacher bring along a chair or crouch down or in some other manner work at eye level with children rather than standing above the class, supervising, as one might see recess monitors supervising during playground time?

Is there evidence that the teacher is teaching kids strategies for carrying on with their work with some independence?

You should see that kids can finish one piece of writing and start another without checking with the teacher. Similarly, kids should be able to get help from each other, spell unfamiliar words, and so on, without relying on the teacher's help. Is there evidence that the teacher is trying to put rituals and structures into place so that kids do not constantly interrupt the teacher's conferences? Ideally if a child needs help, she will stand nearby, listening in as the teacher teaches someone else, and ask for help only when the teacher has completed the conference.

Does the children's stamina for writing become stronger over time?

After a period of time in which children are all writing, the room will probably begin to stir, as if many children feel they are done. If children seem to you to run out of steam as writers, see whether the teacher seems attentive to this and whether he does something to keep them writing a bit longer. One of the most effective ways to do this is to interrupt the whole class, talk to them for a minute (usually giving them new goals), and then set things up so that each child confers with her partner for a few minutes. Usually this break gives kids new direction and energy for writing, and the teacher is able to push the class to write a bit longer.

Do the children have energy for writing and commitment to their topics?

In a good writing classroom, many kids want to write. When a teacher teaches really well, kids' energy for writing goes up, not down. This is a goal worth working towards. How many kids are in fact writing during this writing time? Be ready to celebrate the fact that many kids are actually putting pen to paper. Plan on making similar counts in other classrooms and later in the year in this classroom.

Notice and Support End-of-Workshop Methods

Finally, look at the way the teacher brings the community of writers together and brings the writing workshop to a constructive and positive conclusion.

Does the teacher have a system for students to reconvene quickly in the meeting place and to bring any necessary materials?

Do the children simply know that at a certain pre-arranged time they need to come back to the rug? Does the teacher ring a bell or make the lights flicker? Do children move efficiently through this transition time?

Does the teacher use this time not only to celebrate students' work but also to teach?

Does the teacher restate the teaching point of the minilesson or add a layer of complexity to it, depending on the students' needs? Does he offer tips for ways to use the strategy, illustrated by some of the children's work processes from the work time? If the teacher mainly uses the time to support children in sharing the work they've done, does he stop the sharing process at an appropriate time, reminding everyone that other children will share on other days?

Does the teacher successfully make the transition from talking about one child's good work towards showing how this pertains to other children, other pieces, other days? Do children seem to understand that they can use the strategy illustrated in the share on any piece of writing on any future day, as needed?

Does the teacher have strategies for keeping students engaged?

If teachers ask children to share with a partner, are youngsters listening to each other in ways that suggest engagement? Are the children facing each other and asking each other questions? If you hear silence or uncomfortable giggles, you'll know that the children aren't yet used to working with each other.

Does the teacher have strategies (including the use of the attention-getting device) for getting and holding students' attention? Does he use these strategies effectively? Does he wait until there is a respectful attentiveness in the room before teaching or supporting a child in sharing?

Talk with Teachers About What You've Observed

At some point following your visit to a teacher's classroom, you will need to offer him some feedback. Decide a good time and place for this. There are a few circumstances under which you might give feedback to the teacher at the end of your visit, but more often, especially at this point in the year, you'll probably need to talk outside the classroom at a later time.

Remember advice that has helped you.

Before you talk with a teacher, it is helpful to think about times in your own life when a person in power worked with you, interacting with you in ways that enabled (or disabled) you. Think about what you hoped such a person would do to help you. Think of your minister, your rabbi, your priest. Think of your exercise coach, your barber, your piano teacher. When has another person—someone you regard as more of an expert and who has power over you—watched you work and then intervened in ways that made you feel more powerful, more equipped, more ready to outgrow yourself? Let that memory be your guide as you work with the teacher in question.

Look for important patterns and next steps.

To prepare for this conversation, stand back from all the minutia you saw, all the details you gathered, and think, "What are the really big things that this person is doing well, things that I want him to continue to do and to lean into even more? What were some specific instances that I saw of the teacher doing these things? Why is this good thing really important and deeply personal?

Think, too, "Of all that I want to suggest for this person, what are the biggest next steps or new tactics or new goals that I can get behind? What do I think is well within this teacher's reach that might make a big difference to the classroom? How could I help him reach for these next steps? What sort of support might he need (if any), and how could I make sure the person receives this help?

Ask the teacher how she thought the classroom time went.

When you talk to the teacher about what you observed in his classroom, it helps to follow the guidelines that coaches will teach teachers to use when conferring with children. Teachers will learn that conferences begin with research, and so, too, you will want to begin your conversations with teachers by asking for their input. "How did you think that minilesson was going?"

you can ask, or "So what were your insights or thoughts about that table of kids that you and I worked with together?"

Starting like this has many advantages. First, you can glean a lot about the teacher's readiness for feedback just by watching how he begins the conversation. You can hear, too, whether the teacher felt the sampling you took of one day's writing workshop was indicative of how things tend to go in the class. In fact, you will probably want to come right out and ask that question: "Was what I saw typical of how things tend to go during writing time?" The teacher may protest that no, usually the kids are light years better than they were during the visit, and you may or may not entirely trust this, but at least you'll know that the teacher wishes the kids had been better during the visit. A teacher's assessment of what you observed can say as much as your observation does!

Ask follow-up questions to help you understand.

Remember that when teachers talk to you about their teaching, they will use words that you may need to unpack. For example, a teacher might say, "They were bad during the minilesson." You may well agree, but you do not really know the grounds for that teacher's assessment, so you will want to ask for more specifics. "What bothered you especially about the way they acted?" you could ask. All of this talk will give teachers the opportunity to beat you to the job of pointing out areas for improvement, and that will prove enormously helpful.

Offer the Teacher Compliments

Even if the teacher critiques himself and his kids, don't be lured into beginning the conversation by joining in the critique. Instead, discipline yourself to first give the teacher some heartfelt compliments about the teaching. You can give compliments that teachers will dismiss, or you can give compliments that teachers will remember for decades. Try for the latter, remembering that you can compliment even mediocre teaching extremely well.

One way to give compliments that matter is to look at what precisely this teacher has done that you want to support. Retell the action in all its detail. Don't gloss over it in generalizations. If the teacher looked a child in his eyes as he talked, and even after he finished talking, held his eyes for an instant or two longer, making deep contact, then don't simply say, "I liked how you paid attention to kids." Instead, provide the evidence. "When you were talking to Ramon, I watched you looking intently at him as you talked. Even after you finished talking, you held his gaze for a minute longer." Then describe the effect of his action, again using very precise words to name exactly what it was about the action that seemed effective. "There was something so tender and intimate about the way you looked at him. It felt like you were fully present for him." Take a step back and think, "How in the world of today, in the context of our culture, in the life of this teacher and this child, does this action seem to you to be emblematic of something deeply good? Then try to name that, choosing just one particular reason why this teacher's way is so important. "In this world when everyone is making us hurry, hurry, hurry, when kids are reduced to test scores, it is so huge to me that you take the time to really see each child and to help each child feel really seen." Resist the impulse to list all the good qualities, but do try to say a lot about the power of what the teacher has done.

Another meaningful compliment is one that acknowledges a strategy or behavior mastered by children that is memorable in a teacher's classroom. Again, remember to be precise. Instead of saying, "Your children are well behaved," name the action the children demonstrate (and the implicit teaching the teacher has done to effect this): "It's clear that routines are a priority in your class. Children know how to leave the meeting area, get their materials, and begin work immediately."

Finally, give compliments that offer some next steps. "Congratulations! I've noticed that you have worked on making sure that your minilessons have all the parts—the connection, the teaching, the active engagement, and the link. Last time I was in your room you didn't include the active engagement, and it's evident you've been working with the coach on that. As you get more seasoned doing this, it will be interesting for you to time the active engagement, to notice when you see kids understanding, and to make it a little shorter."

Offer the Teachers Suggestions for Improvement

Of course, in addition to compliments you will want to give teachers help. Try to think of one or two major principles that you believe could help the teacher and a couple of small specific examples for each of those principles. That is, refrain from giving the teacher a laundry list of seventeen suggestions for ways to improve. Instead, decide what the really big messages are you want to convey—choosing just one or two big ideas. Perhaps you think the teacher would be wise to help kids work with greater independence (that's almost always a big suggestion that will help at this time of the year). If so, spend a bit of time rallying the teacher around that big idea. "With so many kids in the class, it will help you to set each of them up to carry on with as much independence as possible, freeing yourself to teach." Then think of specific examples, telling the teacher just enough to allow him to generate yet more suggestions for himself. "Take access to materials. The class will go more smoothly if you find a way to leave paper and pencils and staplers out for the kids so they aren't lining up to ask you for supplies." Then try a second example. "And topic choice, too. I noticed that you spent a long time helping two or three kids come up with topics. Pull away those scaffolds. Maybe just bring a group over to the chart of strategies for generating narrative writing, and suggest they help each other use those strategies to come up with topics."

My bigger point is that you will, no doubt, come from an observation with countless topics that you could give teachers. Instead of sharing them all, choose a couple of especially important ones—and then find other ways, other venues, to convey other suggestions. For example, ask the coach to work with teachers to support some of the other topics, or tuck mention of certain priorities into letters to the staff (away from any discussion of the classroom visits). From your visits, notice areas ripe for improvement, and lead group conversations around those topics. "Teachers, in my visits to classrooms, I've been thinking about word walls, and I am wondering what we believe about them." Or, "I am wondering how we make decisions about what goes up on word walls and how we can get our students to use them." Save the rest of your observations for later, or for yourself alone to ponder. Leading has a lot to do with knowing what to say—and also what not to say.

DVD

Principal to Principal

"Promoting Professional Development." Principals review practical aspects of supporting teachers in implementing a writing curriculum.

CHAPTER SIX

OCTOBER

Making and Meeting Expectations

I t is October, and reforms are underway. Teachers stop you in the hall-way to show you great pieces of writing, and when you are in the lunchroom, children talk with you about their stories. The paper order has doubled since last year. You have started to attend writing celebrations. You can almost hear your school humming with energy. At the next faculty conference, you plan to compliment teachers about the great work that they are doing. Although you know that actually only some of your teachers have come aboard this new initiative, the progress has still been dramatic. You plan to tell the staff as a whole that the school has taken a turn, that it has entered a new phase.

If something good is happening in at least many of the classrooms in your school, you should realize that your school, as a whole, is entering one of those teachable moments. The new momentum that you feel does not mean your job is *done*; it means that your job has *begun*. It means that your school is brimming with promise and that this is your opportunity to help writing work its magic. This chapter will help you know ways that you can take the glimmers of good work and fan them into flames.

To do so, this chapter will first put a spotlight on the challenge of creating close-knit, grade-specific teaching cohorts. Then Laurie and I will outline what you can hope to see in writing workshops at various grade levels by the middle of October. Finally, we will help you work to create consistency across a grade level, ratcheting all your classrooms up to the levels of your most effective rooms. This work will necessarily require that you defuse resistance; we will address this as well.

This Month

- Create close-knit grade-specific cohorts.

- Build effective cohorts with grade-level meetings.

- Use grade-level meetings to prepare for teaching.

- Visit classrooms to assess student writing, grade by grade.

- Deal directly with resistance in order to nurture good teaching.

CREATE CLOSE-KNIT GRADE-SPECIFIC COHORTS

Start with this premise. You cannot lift the level of your whole school if you work simply with one teacher at a time. If you try to do this, you will move one teacher forward and then look over your shoulder to see that the others have slipped backwards. Your time is limited and precious. The best way to leverage that time is for you to work with your teachers within cohorts, groups of teachers who have something in common. In most schools, the cohorts that make the most sense are those comprised of all the teachers across a grade level. For your work and the work of your literacy coach to be effective, your grade-level cohorts need to be close-knit, learning communities.

Strive for Consistency of Teaching Within Grade Levels

Howard Gardner, the Harvard educator who is best known for his work on multiple intelligences, has written a couple of books on leadership. A decade ago, when Howard spoke to our community of school principals, he told us that to lead, you need to give yourselves time to go into the mountains. You need to sometimes look down over everything and reflect. I think the image is an important one because those of us who can be consumed by the details of leading our very particular place do need to give ourselves opportunities to see the big picture of our work, to view what we are doing from a more distant perspective.

If you step back and think about the social fabric of your school, you will probably see that the teachers across some grade levels in your school operate as close-knit teams. Try this. Mentally, if not physically, walk in and out of all the classrooms at the grade level in which relationships seem especially cohesive. Do those rooms look and feel similar? Stop at a child's desk in each room—just pull close to a randomly selected child. Page through a collection of that youngster's work, looking at it in such a way that you see fingerprints of teaching. As you look at one child's work in one room and another child's work in another room, compare and contrast the teaching that underlies the work. Does the teaching in each room seem somewhat similar? My hunch is that in grade levels where teachers work with collegiality, you will see consistency of instruction, and more than this, you will see that the teachers' collaboration has already lifted the level of their teaching, creating a consistency of strong instruction that doesn't exist in more socially disjointed grade levels.

Take another grade—one where relationships are fractured. Do a similar walk-through at that grade level. You may find that the different classrooms feel vastly different, one from the next, and you may feel convinced that one or two of those teachers are doing a substantially better job than the others—perhaps these differences underlie every curriculum area or perhaps they are just in the area of focus for this book, the teaching of writing.

Either way, if you mentally or physically visit rooms and find vast differences in the quality of teaching between those rooms, ponder your response to this. I believe something is the matter if these differences don't fill you with a sense of disequilibrium. Your job is to make sure all children are given the opportunities they deserve. The thought that there are vast differences within a single grade level should ring in your brain with the urgency of a fire alarm. As you read this, you may protest—and yes, of course, you are right that there will always be some teachers who are especially strong and some who are the opposite. But your strong teachers need to function like tent poles, lifting up the level of instruction across the school or at least the grade level. This will only happen if it is someone's job—and that someone needs to be you—to be sure the strengths of particular teachers are "socialized" and the wealth distributed.

Encourage Classes in a Grade to Progress in Sync

So how does a principal make it more likely that the teachers across grade levels function as close-knit cohorts? More specifically, how can a principal make it likely that effective teachers lift the level of teaching across their grade levels?

First and foremost, if you want your teachers to work closely together (remember that we are writing as if the members of a cohort will be all the teachers across a grade level; you may imagine different cohorts in your school), Laurie and I strongly recommend you encourage members of each cohort to follow a shared sequence of units of study. The specific nature of that curriculum must be open enough that the teachers have input into it, but aligning the teaching in one classroom to the teaching in another is so fundamentally important that it must become one of your personal priorities.

Earlier in this book, we talked about the importance of teachers approaching their school year having already decided to proceed through a mutually agreed upon sequence of units of study. Although yes, it is important to approach the year with this plan in mind, those intentions and plans will be for naught unless you weigh in to make shared curriculum a reality. If your teachers are relying on the Heinemann *Units of Study*, this shared resource may lure them to travel the same general curricular path, but unless you urge teachers to progress in sync with each other, you'll quickly find that some teachers let weeks go by without finding time to teach writing, while others zoom ahead.

If your teachers are relying on the published *Units of Study*, you can anticipate two related problems. One is that without intervention from you, teachers across a grade level will probably not stay in sync enough with each other that grade-level grouping can work its magic. The other problem is that some teachers will proceed incredibly slowly through the units of study, inventing interim minilessons and spending several days persevering on one minilesson. I think it is essential that a unit of study take no more than five weeks of time, especially for teachers who are somewhat new to teaching writing and to teaching a specific unit. It was never the intention that before a teacher proceeded to another day and another minilesson, every child would master a concept taught in the preceding minilesson—the curriculum spirals for just that reason. Writers will not necessarily all grasp a technique that is taught on any one day—frankly, most writers spend a lifetime trying to actually grasp what it means to write with focus, detail, voice, drama, and the like. If your teachers tell you that they need to spend more than four or five weeks on a unit of study, ask them to try doing otherwise. For at least this one year, ask them to set publishing deadlines, so that all teachers at a grade level say something like this: "We will hold our first celebration by the first week in October, and the next one by Veterans Day."

> If you want teachers across a grade level to plan, assess, and replan together, it is vitally important that one classroom stay roughly in sync with another.

For now, then, let us say that if you want teachers across a grade level to plan, assess, and replan together, it is vitally important that one classroom stay roughly in sync with another. If all your third grade teachers, for example, are nudging kids to revise, then in a grade-level meeting, those teachers can write together in ways that allow them to create relevant demonstration texts for their minilessons. In those grade-level meetings, they can also help each other revise the upcoming published minilessons to make these are more accessible for their third graders. The next time this group meets, teachers can bring student work together and study the revisions kids are—and are not—making. If one teacher's kids are revising up a storm and other teachers feel their kids are locking knees in protest, then the context is perfect for the one teacher's "intelligence" to be socialized.

Because the easiest way for you to keep classrooms across a grade level roughly in sync is to insist that teachers finish a unit of study and publish every month (or every five weeks), be sure to ask for the publishing dates well ahead of time. You can tell teachers that you need the dates on your calendar and on the school's calendar because you want to be sure that you or another administrator can attend. Meanwhile, of course, the now public publishing date acts as a deadline not just for the children in that classroom but also for the teacher. Deadlines make any writer spring into action. The good news is that while you emphasize your commitment to celebration, you will also help to create and reinforce an infrastructure that is absolutely essential to your school's progress.

Support Model Cohorts to Lift the Level of Teaching

Of course, making sure that teachers across a grade level are teaching roughly in sync with each other is a necessary but insufficient step to take if your ultimate goal is for teachers across grade levels to support each other. Another way to begin spreading the spirit of collaboration among teachers is by finding a grade-level cohort that's already working collaboratively.

If you have a grade level in your school which you believe could become a strong model, you may want to consider talking directly to those teachers, saying, "I'm coming to think that you have forged a professional community among yourselves that is breathtaking and that could become even more important to the three of you. I would love for us to think of ways I could support you as a unit and ways your collegiality could lift the level of teaching across your grade level. My real goal is to create a model that I could then show the rest of the staff. What I am seeing among you three is giving me an image of what this school might become." Your teachers' energy would soar!

Ruth Swinney did exactly what I have just described when she was the principal of PS 165. One of her teachers, Amanda Hartman, wrote a grant and secured ten thousand dollars for herself and her second grade colleagues. They would receive lots of children's books so long as they planned and assessed teaching together. Ruth helped those teachers develop a system for working together, and then she identified other grade levels that she believed stood a chance of working in similar ways. She said to these teachers, "The four of you third grade teachers could become an amazing support group for each other if you had more time to meet and some shared resources. Could I free you up to listen in on the way the second grade teachers conduct their grade-level meetings, and could you think as you watch them, 'Are there ways we could work together that would be equally helpful for us?'" In such a fashion, Ruth helped one grade level after another in her school begin to fashion new images of possibility and to work with each other in dramatically new ways. I'll describe those ways in greater detail later in this chapter.

BUILD EFFECTIVE COHORTS WITH GRADE-LEVEL MEETINGS

One of the most effective ways to help teachers across a grade level work as a close-knit planning and support group is to establish grade-level meetings. Talk to your staff about other schools you've visited. Read about schools whose grade-level meetings are essential to those schools' lives. Perhaps over the past decade in your school, similar meetings lost their luster, becoming merely times for administrative busywork, and were thus eliminated. Your hope now is to revive them.

Relay to your staff the observation that too many of them are operating in isolation. That might have been okay years ago when pressures weren't so intense, when teachers were not asked to solve so many problems. But in today's world, the pressures on teachers are so great and the knowledge base about methods of teaching well is so extensive that it is no longer possible for a teacher to know enough on her own. If a school is going to become smarter, then one teacher on a grade level needs to develop expertise in understanding the ways that children's spelling reveals their level of development in phonics, for example, and another teacher needs to become the guru for children's literature. That way, our teaching can be like a potluck feast; each person can bring something different to the table, nourishing us all.

Make Time for Grade-Level Meetings

It is important that you provide enough time for teachers to meet in their grade-level meetings and that you do this in ways that do not impose on teachers' free time, creating resentment. If you go to enormous lengths to adjust schedules so that teachers have more school-sanctioned time to work with grade-level colleagues, you will find that more often than not, teachers end up finding these groups so supportive that they invest their own free time in these relationships. That's a great bonus, but it is not something you can count on. Your first job is to do the creative scheduling required so that you free up time for grade-level cohorts to meet. Those groups need more than one hour a week together, and this is especially true now when you are trying to channel those teachers to begin using these groups as support structures. Here are some ways other principals have carved out time for these meetings:

Ways Some Principals Have Carved Out Time for Grade-Level Meetings

✦ You might decide to cancel a few faculty meetings, for example, and in their place schedule grade-specific study groups. Those grade-level meetings might occur concurrently in the time slot that would normally be used for faculty meetings, but teachers may also be willing to agree on different times, making it possible for you and/or the literacy coach to attend the grade-level meetings.

✦ You might find a way to keep all the kids at a grade level occupied at either the start or the end of the day, one day each week (or two days each month), freeing their classroom teachers to convene as a group. For example, perhaps your music teacher can lead some whole-grade work for second graders in the auditorium at the end of Tuesday, and in turn you'll provide the necessary help for that teacher to release the kids directly from the auditorium. If you can find a way to establish a ritual such as that, then all your second grade teachers could convene for a grade-level meeting every Tuesday afternoon, forty-five minutes before the end of the day.

✦ You could, then, use per session pay to support teachers continuing to study after school for an added half hour or hour. All in all, these two structures together could mean that all your second grade teachers would work together for between seventy-five and ninety minutes every Tuesday (in addition to their regular grade-level meetings). Ideally, all the teachers at every other grade level would have similar meetings on other days.

✦ Some schools simply extend the morning recess by making use of parent volunteers. That is, while most children line up to go inside at 8:10 on Mondays, the first graders are told, "Remember, on Mondays you have extra play. We'll gather in half an hour." That half hour of extra recess time is not enough time for teachers to do substantial work, but if teachers agree to come half an hour early as well, receiving per session pay for that half hour at the start of the day, this would mean that these teachers could meet for an hour, once a week, at the start of the day.

Of course, these extra meetings are in addition to the prep times that you normally allocate (or that are within teachers' contracts).

✦ Finally, some principals that I know have extended every day's lunchtime by ten minutes, which means that one lunchtime a week is time that teachers "owe back." This then means that one lunch a week is earmarked as a grade-level meeting. Principals distribute those grade-level working lunches across the week so that an administrator or the coach is free to attend. That is, fifth grade teachers may always spend their extended lunch period on Monday in a grade-level working lunch. Meanwhile, fourth grade teachers may do this on Tuesdays, and so forth. Of course, it also makes sense for you to do everything you can to give teachers across a grade level common lunchtimes and common prep times because the unofficial meetings are as valuable as the official ones.

Establish Norms for Grade-Level Meetings

Once you have gone the extra mile to schedule time for these meetings, bear in mind that the start of the year (and the start of a new procedure) is the best time for setting standards of behavior.

Start and end meetings on time.

Be sure to begin your meetings on time every time. It is almost inconceivable that people will arrive on time if meetings do not start on time. Why *should* they if chances are good the meeting won't get underway for ten minutes? It can be difficult to start the meeting at the appointed moment if only half the group has arrived, but if the meeting doesn't start promptly, the outliers will arrive late, see that the meeting has not begun yet, and think to themselves, "Good, I'm not late." It is, therefore, incredibly important to start a meeting at the moment when it has been scheduled to start—this is true not only for grade-level meetings but for all meetings. You won't personally always be on the scene, so you'll need to work with whomever is the facilitator. Brainstorm strategies for handling late comers.

My own personal strategy is to close the door when it is time to start, using the closed door as an additional way to signal, "You are late." It is also important to me that I do not repeat everything that people have said to each of the stragglers. The whole point should be to signal to people, "These meetings are precious, and every minute is well used. If you come late, of course you will miss a lot."

Respecting people's time also means that meetings need to end on time. If a meeting is scheduled to last for half an hour after the end of the school day, after that half an hour, the facilitator needs to say, "Our time is up. Anyone who has other things planned, you should go. If a few of you want to stay and finish this up, that is up to you, but the meeting is officially over." It is not fair for people who plan to stay for half an hour to end up feeling that it is almost impossible to leave once that time is over, and if grade-level meetings are only for people with over-the-top levels of commitment, then they will not be a useful structure for supporting whole-school consistency.

Rely on a facilitator.
Each meeting will profit from the presence of a facilitator. Often this will be your coach. Many principals try to attend one meeting per month for each grade, attending more frequently only if a particular grade needs extra support. If your coach is unable to be present for any reason, ask a lead teacher to step in as facilitator for that meeting. I recommend this request be official—that is, that you send an email or otherwise explicitly state that so-and-so will take the place of the coach who can't be present. It is not easy for one colleague to elbow past others, saying to them, "I'm the facilitator."

Of course, the facilitator is not a boss but an enabler. In most meetings, the facilitator is the one to watch the clock and to say, "Should we get started?" Usually the facilitator then says, "Let's talk for a minute about our agenda," and he reviews the agenda that was in place prior to the meeting (perhaps this is a standing agenda). Then he asks, "Are there other things we should add to this agenda?" Once the agenda has been established, the facilitator is the one to herd the group along so that everything on the agenda is covered (or if not, so that this is decided together). This means that if the meeting will be forty minutes long and there are four items of roughly equal weight on the agenda, after about eight minutes the facilitator will say, "We should be moving on to our second item soon. What do we need to do before we move on? Any action plans?" If an action plan needs to be made, one person will probably need to volunteer to take responsibility for that action, and the person facilitating will be the one to ask who will agree to take this role.

If your school has not yet established norms for how meetings proceed, it is not enough to simply hope that those who have been asked to facilitate will do so in these ways (or in other preferred ways, if you arrive at those). Be explicit with your facilitators. If your coach and assistant principal are each leading grade-level meetings, you are leading faculty meetings, the director of special education is leading yet other meetings, then convene your various meeting facilitators to talk together about how you can all align yourselves so that meetings progress in one of two or three agreed-upon ways. The way I've just detailed will probably be one commonly used template, and there may be another template or two. For example, another template might involve a large group meeting dispersing into smaller groups. The essential thing is that facilitators recognize that together you are all working to establish a professional learning culture in the school and that one way to do this is to induct people into some shared expectations for how meetings will proceed.

Communicate expectations clearly.

It goes without saying that you will want to be transparent with teachers. At a faculty meeting or in a letter to the faculty, tell people that you have been giving careful thought to your own role as the teacher-for-the-school and that, just as many of them will sometimes realize that they need to pay more attention to the norms and structures within their *classrooms*, you have come to realize you need to pay more attention to the norms and structures within the *school*. Then lay out some of your tentative hopes for how meetings will proceed. Be sure you say, "I have asked the facilitators of meetings to keep groups progressing efficiently through the agenda the group agrees upon" so that when one colleague says to others, "I think we need to move off this topic," or, "Let's keep an eye on the clock," this person will be acting as your ambassador, deriving authority from you. It goes without saying that if the group challenges the facilitator for playing this role, you need to back the facilitator (while also investigating the problem and inventing new solutions).

> You will want to be transparent with teachers. At a faculty meeting or in a letter to the faculty, tell people that you have been giving careful thought to your own role as the teacher-for-the-school.

Keep working meetings small.

Some groups will be too large to work mostly as a whole. In these instances, the facilitator will need to plan some of the meeting time for the whole group and some of it for small groups or partnership conversations. If there are four or more teachers per grade, the meetings are more productive when the facilitator plans for people to talk in partnerships or triads, with these small groups then coming together for intervals in the midst of the meeting to share what they are figuring out. Partnerships among teachers will be best if they are long-term arrangements and if you help the partners spend time—even just a small amount—in each other's classrooms as well as talking in meetings. Some principals or facilitators choose to hold meetings in rotating classrooms. You will be amazed how much teachers can learn just by observing one another's physical environment!

Use Grade-Level Meetings to Prepare for Teaching

Of course, the logistics of the grade-level meeting alone won't make these meetings significant. The agenda will do that. You, the literacy coach, and teachers will want to think about the nature of these grade-level meetings. What will happen during them?

Teachers who are teaching in sync with each other will appreciate meetings that help them prepare for their teaching. Grade-level meetings are vitally important because they provide opportunities for the literacy coach and for colleagues across the grade to compile knowledge and experience so that each teacher feels prepared to lead minilessons and conferences during that week's writing workshops. If your teachers are leaning on the *Units of Study* books, this means that teachers reflect together on how to tweak the minilessons they offer and on how to write their own.

This can be a time for teachers to give those minilessons to themselves and each other, carrying out the writing that minilessons entail. This serves many purposes. For one thing, the opportunity to share writing can often meld people into a warm, cohesive group. It can also provide an opportunity for every teacher to preview the upcoming minilessons and to gain invaluable insight into those minilessons. A writing technique may sound very simple, but actually putting that technique into action is usually more complex, demanding, and interesting. If teachers experience the content they will be teaching, they'll understand it in a much richer way. They will learn about teaching writing from the inside. This, of course, will also allow teachers to test out the published minilessons and to have the grounds to sometimes say, "This needs to be different." Finally, by allowing themselves to function as students of their own teaching, teachers will develop the bits of writing they need to make published minilessons their own, as well as to be in a position to write their own minilessons.

If all the teachers across a grade level are working together to teach the same unit of study—say these are first grade teachers whose children are all writing how-to books—then the teachers, as a group, can develop the insights, resources, energy, and teaching plans they need to support that unit. In many schools, teachers across a grade level compile all they learn into units-of-study binders. That is, the second grade teachers in a school will gather all their shared ideas about the second grade writing curriculum into a whole set of binders, one of which will be titled "How-To Writing." This binder might include plans for how the second grade teachers will tailor the minilessons in the published book to suit second graders. The plans might include a list of teaching points and a calendar. Teachers who write their own minilessons might contribute those to the binders. Perhaps someone finds a chapter in a professional book related to the unit of study—it goes into the binder. Samples of student work go into the binder. As teachers name predictable problems their kids are encountering and invent ideas for small group work, these, too, go into that binder.

Later in this chapter I will talk about the importance of visiting all the classrooms at a certain grade level so that you familiarize yourself with that grade level's writing work and identify writing workshops that are functioning well. Once you have done this work and you or, more likely, the coach has helped those strong classrooms become even stronger, you can use them as resources for your grade-level study groups so that your best writing workshops lift the level of the others. This will lead to more consistency of strong instruction across each grade level. Later, I'll discuss methods for doing this well.

Help Grade-Level Cohorts Study Students' Writing

You will probably want to make it likely that teachers at every grade level spend some time looking at student work and using it to help them think about instruction. If you encourage teachers to look at student work in the company of each other, this can be a way to nudge them to deal with hard truths. A teacher who claims, "My kids can't," will find it harder to maintain this position if the other teachers across the grade level have lots of examples that their students can do the same work.

Just as it is important to establish norms related to attendance in meetings, it is also important to establish norms for sharing student work.

Be specific about the student writing every teacher will share.
Start by holding yourself accountable (and asking the coach to do the same) for structuring studies of student work well. For example, if you and the literacy coach decide to ask teachers to bring student work, let teachers

know well in advance what you'd like them to bring. Especially as you induct teachers into the rhythm of doing this, make a point to send a reminder or two so there won't be any reason for some teachers to come empty-handed to the meeting.

We recommend that you ask teachers to bring a very specific selection of student work. If teachers come to meetings carrying armloads of texts, the chance that those texts will be discussed is minimal. It won't be long before teachers cease bringing those armloads, feeling justified for that decision. So, for example, for the second grade level meeting in October, you might say to teachers, "Please make sure that you have cleared student folders out so that all the writing they did prior to the first publication is no longer in their daily writing folders. That should go into cumulative folders. Would you choose two students—one who struggles and one who is stronger—and bring just their writing folders." Teachers of older students can't bring only the writing that students have done since the first publication because much of the students' writing will be in writers' notebooks that cumulate across many months, but again, these students' folders (where they keep their rough drafts) will be cleared out after each publication. Upper grade teachers might be asked to bring notebooks for two students. These could again be students who represent the high and low ends of the spectrum of writing abilities, but, of course, it would be equally or even more interesting to suggest teachers bring the work of two students who are fairly representative of what most of the class is doing. Either way, be sure to establish clear parameters for the work that teachers will bring; make sure that they bring only a limited amount of student work and that all teachers select similar work.

The point is that you want teachers to grow theories off the work that they study, and this will be easier to do if each of the teachers has selected work using a similar criterion. If one teacher brings the work that her best student wrote that morning and another brings the collection of work her most struggling student has done all year, the two teachers will each be bringing something utterly different to the table—and won't be able to draw conclusions across the work.

Smooth over contrasts in student writing samples.
Once teachers have convened, student work in hand, you'll need to tread carefully. Writing researcher Mina Shaughnessy, author of *Errors and Expectations*, wrote, "Writing creeps across the page, exposing as it goes

all that we don't know. Writing puts us on the line and we don't want to be there." The truth is that, just as our own writing puts us on the page, exposing all that we do not know, so, too, does our students' writing put us as professionals on the page. If three teachers come to the meeting loaded with reams of pages that their two students have written, and a fourth teacher's students have each written just a paltry amount, nothing needs to be said. That fourth teacher will look to the right and to the left and chances are good that she will get the message. So be gentle!

> The truth is that, just as our own writing puts us on the page, exposing all that we do not know, so, too, does our students' writing put us as professionals on the page.

For now, you may deliberately want to say something that diffuses the contrast between the work accomplished in one class and in another. For example, you may say something such as, "One of the hard parts about teaching writing is that we teach one minilesson to a whole class full of diverse writers. Let's look at the upcoming minilessons in the *Units of Study* books and imagine the kids that are represented by this student work all sitting in those minilessons. Then let's think about ways in which that minilesson will and will not work for all these diverse kids." In that way, you'd let teachers off the hook for having students whose work doesn't measure up to that which others are doing. I recommend doing that. If you want to create professional learning communities that work, you need to make sure that everyone can gather around the table without feeling shame.

On the other hand, as I have said before, you, as the school principal, should feel deeply uncomfortable over inequities you see in the education that children are receiving across your school. It will be instantly clear to you from the writing work that teachers bring to grade-level meetings that the children in some classrooms are writing up a storm and children in other classrooms are not getting chances to write. And you do need to make sure that you visit the teachers who are not making time for writing and say to them, "It's clear to me you are having a hard time getting to the writing workshop. Can you and I sit down and think about your schedule and see if we can figure out ways to use time differently so that your kids do get to write every day?"

Once you feel as if you have made expectations clear to teachers, supported them, and given them concrete help, be prepared to hold teachers accountable for their teaching.

Study the volume of student writing.

If you've decided to use grade-level meetings as a forum in which you hold teachers accountable for teaching writing, then first and foremost, ask teachers to bring student work (as described earlier), and right there in the meeting say something like this: "I've been learning that there is a close connection between the amount of writing that kids actually do and their growth in writing over time. Let's look at the work we've brought—I know it is just the work of two kids, and it is just the work they've done since their first publication—but let's look at this and simply count how much each child has done." If you'd like, you could pass out a record sheet so the teacher can record what she finds. If the child is a K–2 writer, the teacher will want to count how many books the child has written, how many pages in most of the child's books, how many words/sentences/lines on most pages. If the child is an older child, the teachers can count the number of entries written either since the start of the year or since the last publication, and the average length of each entry.

Then, of course, you'll want to let this lead to a conversation about how the teachers can all find ways to make more time for writing and can encourage students to write with more volume during the time they do have.

Study teachers' responses to student writing.

Of course, each time teachers meet, each time they bring student work, the focus can be different. You may find it helpful one time early on to simply ask teachers to read over one entry—either an entry you bring to the table, or say, the most recent entry contained in the student work they've brought. Then ask the teachers, "Jot down whatever you notice in the child's work. Record some things you might teach this child."

So often, teachers will focus on conventions only and record only errors! Be alarmed when this happens. Be alarmed because your teachers are seeing first through the lens of "what is not working," but wince even more because very often your teachers' responses to children will echo your responses to teachers. Ask yourself, "Do I notice in what teachers say and do only what they are *not* doing, only what is missing?" Resolve to change your ways!

If you criticize your teachers for what they are seeing in student work, you'll only replicate the deficit model. Try demonstrating to teachers the journey you hope they take by taking onto yourself the very problems you see in them. That is, try telling them about a time when someone asked you to record what you noticed in student work, and then tell them that the person then said, "What you see in student work says more about you than it says about the student. We do not see with our eyes but with our beliefs." Tell the teachers that you were aghast, noticing that you'd only recorded all the things the kid was doing wrong. And tell teachers that, as a principal visiting classrooms and as a teacher like them, trying to help kids grow, you do know that it is terribly important to realize that we can choose the lens through which we look. You can look out the window onto the playground and watch kids playing, looking through the lens of noticing how kids do or do not play differently based on their gender. Alternatively, you can look out the window during play time and notice the colors that children wear. Or you could notice the posture of adults who work with children during recess time—some adults stand tall, supervising, others crouch to children's eye level. You can choose what you will see. Similarly, you as the principal can visit classrooms looking through the lens of noticing ways that students collaborate with each other. You can look at the use of space in the classroom, or at the role children's literature plays in different writing classrooms, or at any one of a zillion different things. And teachers, too, can choose to look at student work through a variety of lenses.

Vary the ways you study student writing.
You will, over time, want to help teachers look at student work through a variety of lenses. Here are a few that you might demonstrate:

- Teachers can reread student work looking for the presence of details.
- Teachers can look at student work looking for evidence that the child is spelling some high-frequency words with automaticity.
- Teachers can look at student work and notice how students tend to start off their narratives (or end their narratives).
- Teachers can look at student work and notice the time span that students' narratives tend to cover. Are these stories of a twenty-minute episode? Of an hour episode? Of a month? Are they more all-about texts than narratives that recount an event that took place over time?
- Teachers can look for evidence that children are valuing their writing—or are not valuing it. For example, if children are putting spelling or math work into their notebooks, or if they have scribbled on pages in their notebooks or torn pages from them, this does not suggest they are valuing those notebooks.

Visit Classrooms to Assess Student Writing, Grade by Grade

Earlier, I suggested that you respond to the buzz in your school over student writing by realizing that your work is not done, but has, instead, just begun. This is a teachable moment for your school. People are still new to the teaching of writing, so chances are good that many of your teachers are still in a learning posture regarding writing instruction. It will be much easier for you to intervene now, capitalizing on teachers' early successes to push them further, than it will be to intervene at a later point, once teachers feel as if they have arrived.

Establishing cohorts is a vital part of your work, but it is only half the job. The other half of your job is to get into classrooms again this month, watch teaching, and look at student work. You need to do this with some expectation of what you should ideally see so that you have a sense for what to support, what to ask for. It is not helpful if you turn somersaults over work that is nowhere close to what one should expect.

During this particular round of visits, I'll help you to focus on student work. If that will be the focus, ask teachers to be sure that each child's writing folder is out on the table that day (sometimes teachers will otherwise keep the folders in bins to make table space less congested). Ask teachers to leave the folders on the tables during the minilesson, too, so that while you listen with one ear to the minilesson, you can meanwhile browse through folders of children's work. You can't afford to lose any time. If your school is very large, you may divide these classroom visits with the assistant principal, or you may need to resort to simply looking at the students' work after writing time is over. You might decide to tell the teacher that you will be in another time of the day just to look at the writing. In this case, ask the teacher to gather the folders in one place so you can collect them as unobtrusively as possible. Alternatively, you might decide to look at writing during the late afternoon after everyone has left the building, when you can spend some quiet time.

> Establishing cohorts is a vital part of your work, but it is only half the job. The other half of your job is to get into classrooms again this month, watch teaching, and look at student work.

You only need to look at a sampling of work from each classroom. The sampling needs to be random, however. Teachers are human, so of course they will try to arrange it so that you see the work of their best children! If a teacher hands you a few folders, take those folders in hand and then do not look at those folders. Instead, go and help yourself to some other folders and look through those.

In the upcoming sections of this chapter, you will learn what you can hope to see in October of the school year—assuming a school begins after Labor Day and assuming this is your school's first year leading writing workshops. Afterwards, we will discuss ways this will be different in schools that have had established writing workshops in place for years. Then we will share ideas for what you can do when these expectations are not yet in place—which is, of course, a likely scenario.

October in Kindergarten: What to Expect

Start by visiting all your kindergarten classrooms, making these visits in one or two concurrent days. Tell the teachers the days you will visit their grade. "Kindergarten teachers, I will come to you on Monday and Tuesday during writing time."

Kindergarten, of course, has its own special challenges. First, everything we said earlier about your focus on the written products won't really work for kindergartners. At this grade level, you need to, in fact, watch the children at work on their writing. Then, too, oftentimes kindergarten teachers will have assumed that writing workshops couldn't possibly be developmentally appropriate for their kids. "After all," these teachers will say, "my kids don't even know their letters and sounds."

Do not be surprised, then, if you visit classroom after classroom and find that in fact, very few of your kindergarten teachers have actually even launched writing workshops! This is not an unusual state of affairs, but by all means you must jump into action immediately. There is almost nothing that a kindergarten teacher could teach that would be more developmentally appropriate than a writing workshop, and writing workshops are more spectacular at this grade level than at any other. Trust me. My colleagues and I have worked with thousands and thousands of kindergarten classrooms, including classrooms in the poorest sections of New York City, and there has never been an instance when kindergarten children were not ready for writing workshop at the very start of the school year.

The secret, of course, is that teachers need to tailor writing workshops so they match kids—and this is challenging work.

Do not let your kindergarten teachers convince you that their kids are not ready for the writing workshop. Be sure they launch writing workshops tomorrow, if they haven't done so already, and that they devote at least forty-five minutes or an hour a day to those writing workshops every day for the next month. Encourage the teachers to follow the unit of study laid out in the published series—it is perfect for kindergartners (less so for second graders). If, after a month, the teachers still insist their kids aren't ready for the writing workshop, that will be another story (they won't, though, so we do not even need to discuss how you'll respond if they do!).

You may well discover that although you are visiting classrooms in October, many kindergarten teachers didn't start teaching writing on day one of the year (next year they will!) and, therefore, may not yet be in their second unit of study. Let's assume, therefore, that the teachers are somewhere towards the middle of unit one, *Launching the Writing Workshop.* What should you expect?

First, instead of looking at the written work, watch the kids. You want to see that they all feel as if they can do this thing called writing and that they are all able to function with a lot of independence. If children can carry on as writers without needing a teacher at their side every minute to support each and every next step, then this means that teachers are, in fact, free to actually teach. So watch and see.

Kindergarten children, by the middle of their first unit of study, should be able to select paper for themselves (there may not yet be any variety of paper choice, but they can at least reach for the paper themselves, not needing to be on dole). The paper will probably have a space for the child to write his or her name as best the child can, and otherwise will probably not have any lines. The kindergarten child—let's imagine this is a boy—should be able to think of what he will put onto the paper without needing help choosing a topic. He should be able to get started putting what he imagines onto the page—through a picture that at least gestures towards being representative. If you ask, "What is your story about?" (call it a story although it will look more like a drawing), the child should be able to say something like, "I am writing about the park" or, "That's me on the swings" or, "When I went to the park." The content will probably come from the child's life, but it may not be a narrative—that is, the child may not be telling about one time when he did something (and that is fine). Ideally, the child will add details to the picture.

> Watch the kids. You want to see that they all feel as if they can do this thing called writing and that they are all able to function with a lot of independence.

You should see that some children are gesturing towards writing in one of two ways. Either they will label the picture or they will write on the side or underneath the picture. The writing will probably not be anything you (or the child) can read. The child may possibly have used knowledge of sound-letter correspondence to record a couple of initial sounds (as in writing an *m* for *me* beside the child's self portrait). Alternatively, he may have used a rudimentary knowledge of the fact that each sound in a word translates into a mark on the page to write the word *sun* as three marks (and these could be letters or letterlike marks). When the child finishes the drawing, you should see that he has a way to get started on the next piece of writing without needing intervention from the teacher.

If what you see matches what I have described and you wonder why this is a worthwhile use of children's time, consider the changes you will observe over the next two weeks. First, in short order, children will write stories that span several pages and that are sequentially organized and hold together as coherent narratives. These stories will tend to be mostly oral, but children will be able to say aloud the story almost as if they were dictating their writing: "I went to the park. I went high on the swings. I almost touched the leaves. Then I got off." Then, too, you should see that within two weeks, every child is labeling lots of items on his or her pictures and using letters to represent initial sounds, if not initial and final sounds. The letters will not always be correct, but still children will be beginning to grasp the concept of saying words slowly enough to hear sounds, and then the concept that a spoken sound is represented by a letter. Children will use whatever sound-letter correspondence they have learned to record sounds.

There is a rule of thumb you will want to keep in mind. Before kindergartners can begin to read conventionally (before it is reasonable to put them into leveled books and to support them through guided reading groups), you and they both must be able to read at least stretches of their writing. Generally, schools aim to move children into conventional reading by January of kindergarten. This means that by the end of December, a child who is ready for this will write, "I rode my bike" somewhat like this: "I rod mi bik." Even if children do not know sound-letter correspondences, they should be stretching out words and recording sounds as best they are able by mid-October (this assumes your kindergartners got a late start; if not, the timeframe would be earlier). In late October, I have written principals in schools that are linked to the Teachers College Reading and writing Project and said, "Please make time to look through the writing that your kinder-gartners are doing. Do you see evidence that every child is writing a whole lot—probably this means they are writing four to five booklets a week—and that every child is labeling several items on each page? This is vitally important!"

This write-up has no doubt put undo emphasis on spelling. Forgive me. It is, of course, also crucial that children see themselves as writers, that they approach writing with confidence and energy, that they believe their stories are interesting and important, and so forth. Your coach can help you know other things to look for at this crucially important grade level.

October in First Grade: What to Expect

I'll assume your first graders got started in writing workshop at the start of the year, which means that when you visit classrooms in mid-October, you should first of all see that each child has already published a piece of writing. In most classrooms, these finished pieces will be hung on a bulletin board that has been divided into a grid, with one square for each child. Expect teachers to hang next month's published pieces on top of this month's, so that you can track growth over time. Expect, too, that the published pieces will be in children's own spelling, perhaps with translations written in tiny letters in some marginal place.

Look through one child's folder and notice first the dates of the pieces. If pieces are not dated, be sure to give the class date stamps tomorrow and to insist that every piece always be dated. Children quickly learn to date-stamp every day's work. As you look over the dates of the student work, check that September's writing is no longer in this folder. Once a class has published the written work for that month, it gets taken from the work-in-progress folder and either sent home or saved in cumulative folders. This may sound very pedestrian, but teachers will need help managing all these papers, and frankly, consistent management structures will make your job as supervisor easier. For example, once earlier work has been emptied, you can contrast the volume of writing that one class and another does just by weighing the folders! It is much more complex to contrast the volume of writing in one room with another if there are no consistent ways of managing the paper chase.

If you notice that teachers in many rooms have not yet cleared out the writing from the start of the year, don't be surprised, but do make a note to follow up not just with this grade level but with others. These grade-level write-ups will not all address this concern—but this doesn't mean, of course, that we don't expect you to comb through the folders and others across all the grades. You needn't wait until you visit those rooms, either, before clarifying expectations.

Children will be writing in booklets by now, on a variety of paper. Some children will be writing in booklets that do not contain any lines for writing. These children will be labeling their pictures, and, we hope, will be beginning to use several sounds to represent a word. Once you can somewhat make out what the child is trying to write, that child needs to graduate into writing sentences under the picture and into using paper with a line or two underneath the space for a drawing. Other children will have paper that contains space for a picture and space for a sentence or two. Yet other children may have multiple lines. Be very careful that teachers are not limiting children's level of performance by giving them paper that does not stretch their abilities. In a first grade classroom in which most of the children attended kindergarten, you should expect that at least a third of the class will use paper on which there are three to five lines for writing, and these children will write more than one sentence on each page.

> Be very careful that teachers are not limiting children's level of performance by giving them paper that does not stretch their abilities.

Once you have determined when the class published, you can also figure out how many school days there have been since publication and how much writing each child in the room tends to produce each day. At this point in first grade, you can expect that most children write approximately a booklet (a story) a day. This will be equally true whether the class is filled with high-need kids or with kids who have had all sorts of advantages. The differences based on prior schooling and home life may well affect the maturity of kids' spelling and the length and complexity of their sentences, but either way, expect that first graders produce something like a book a day at this point in the year. Only your very strongest first graders will regularly work across two or three days on a story, and those stories will tend to contain many sentences on each page. That is, the stronger the writer, the fewer pieces of writing they produce—but the more complex and mature that writing will be.

If you are able to sit with a child, ask that child to read her writing. If the child is a beginning reader, expect her to read with her finger under the words and to read with one-to-one matching. Ideally, as such a child reads, she will notice instances when she left out a word (which happens) and will make insertions.

Expect to see children use invented spelling. This means that children are drawing on all they know and on the resources in the room to spell as well as they can. Invented spelling is not "free spelling." The fact that children use invented spelling simply means that the children themselves are doing this work, and it means their work reflects what they know and can do.

It is incredibly revealing to study children's spellings, and many phonics programs suggest that this is the single best way to assess a child's knowledge of phonics. In general, you will want to see that a child represents every sound that he hears in a word with a letter. That is, you'd hope that a child spells *phone* with at least three letters, one representing the sound made by *ph*, one representing the sound made by the long o, and one representing the sound made by the final consonant *n*: *fon*. The concept that each sound must be represented by at least one letter is one of the building blocks of written language. The hope is that your children master that concept in the fall of kindergarten.

You should also see that first graders have a growing command of high-frequency words. These will be words that teachers explicitly teach, and the classrooms should probably have word walls on which these words are displayed. Expect first graders to spell *you, it, we, like, home, Mom*, and so forth with automaticity.

You can expect to see that first graders are writing what we refer to as "small moment stories." These will tend to be chronologically organized narratives in which the author recounts something he has done. Ideally, these narratives will contain a few details and will tell not only what the child did but also his thoughts, responses, or feelings. A fairly modest first grade small moment story might read like this: "I went on the monkey bars. I went from bar to bar. Oh no! My hands slipped. I fell. I was sad." Some children will write stories that are richer and sound perhaps like this: "My mom, my brother, and me went to get some ice cream. I got a double chocolate cone with sprinkles. I was happy. My mom got a baby cone, but she is not a baby. Then my dog jumped up and ate my ice cream. I got a new one."

Children's focused stories will tend to encompass twenty minutes or an hour of time, not a whole vacation. When children write with focus, this often leads them to write with details—as in the detail in the above example about the child's mother getting the baby cone despite the fact that she's not a baby. Details add tremendously to a story. If you notice that children are not writing a small moment, glance at the teacher's demonstration piece on the white board often located at the front of the room by the meeting area.

Often the teacher's demonstration piece is not the best example and could very well be the reason the children are not writing small moment pieces.

You may also see that writers are including their responses to events (their feelings). This is a good sign. Elaboration, in general, is something to support. Then, too, you may see evidence of writers beginning to use story language. (Note the start of stories, for example. Do they begin *One day* or, better yet, *One sunny day*, or do they in other ways gesture towards using story language?) Endings, too, are a great place to look for evidence that children are using story language.

If you do have a chance to watch youngsters working during writing time, watch for their independence. If you enter the room at the end of the minilesson, watch to see how they access their materials and transition to writing. If you enter during writing time, glance over at the writing center. Ready-made booklets should be available, as well as one or two kinds of paper that they can add on to their booklets. The paper should be different from the paper used at the start of writing workshop. If you are not sure whether children are getting materials on their own, sidle up to a couple of kids and ask them to explain the routine for getting started writing. This short interruption will teach you a lot.

October in Second Grade: What to Expect

Your second graders need to write longer stories than those written by younger children. Second graders generally write in little booklets that are five or more pages long, with each page containing almost a paragraph of writing—say, seven sentences or so. Second graders will probably write two or three of these little books each week. These youngsters may still sketch in order to plan the content that will go on each page of a booklet, but the space allotted for these sketches will be significantly diminished.

Check that children are choosing their own topics. That's easy to see— look across the work done by several children and make sure they are not all writing on the same subject, even if it is an open-ended one, such as one episode from my summer vacation. Assigned topics, even open-ended ones, indicate that children are all writing in sync with each other—and that teachers are, therefore, not following the workshop method. If teachers are leading a true writing workshop, you'll see children who are writing about different topics (of their choosing) at different rates, drawing on a variety of writing strategies.

Check, too, that if the teacher is teaching children to write narratives, the story ideas that children are selecting are appropriate for this genre study. This means the texts tell about a character (the writer, probably) doing one thing, then the next thing, then the next. A plotline is essential to a story.

Look more closely at the narratives children are writing to see if they are focused in time. Eventually youngsters will learn a variety of ways to focus a narrative, and they may be able to write focused narratives that span more than one stretch of time, but for now, the easiest way for teachers to move children towards writing well-organized, detailed, and vivid stories is to encourage them to zoom in on limited stretches of time. For example, a child can tell the story of a friend who has moved by zooming in on the afternoon when the moving truck arrived, and the child watched her friend's house being emptied into the truck, and then watched as the truck and the friend drove away. Notice that in this example, the story may span an hour or two of time. The story could, alternatively, span just the last twenty minutes of that episode. Either of these would qualify as small moment stories. Be sure that teachers are not misinterpreting the injunction to focus and aren't channeling their children to write stories that can literally fit inside a single moment!

> It is challenging for second graders to write stories that are true, focused, and also significant.

It is challenging for second graders to write stories that are true, focused, and also significant. Some children have no trouble writing focused stories about tiny events—but those stories may be inconsequential to them. There are two ways to respond to this. One is to talk to children about choosing moments that fill the writer with big feelings—a sad time, a scary time, a hopeful time. Usually, for second graders, moments that are laden with feelings are also moments that brim with significance, although children will not understand the concept yet of these moments being meaningful or significant.

The other way to guide children whose vignettes center on seemingly insignificant moments is to help writers realize that big feelings lurk in those everyday moments. A haircut, for example, can be told as just a sequence of actions—but actually, haircuts are big deals. Haircuts matter. A good writer asks himself or herself, "What is the really important thing about this haircut?"

Take note of not only the topics that children are addressing (and their investment in those topics) but also the qualities of writing they are incorporating into their narratives. Notice, for example, the leads to their stories; second graders likely will have progressed from beginning stories with captionlike sentences ("This is me going to the store") to beginning with a character (themselves) on stage who acts ("I got on my bike and started pedaling to the store"). Some second graders will begin their stories by depicting the setting ("One snowy morning . . ."). Applaud this effort. You will also notice that second graders make an effort to conclude a story. They may do this by having the character make a closing action. Perhaps the character turns off the lights, for example, or closes the door. Some second graders will end the story by telling the reader the lesson learned: "I will never go to that store again."

In addition to crafting their beginnings and endings, second grade writers pay attention to developing their characters in several ways. They use dialogue as one way to help readers get to know characters. They may also include some of their characters' thinking. For example, a writer might say, "I walked into the kitchen. I wondered if my mom was going to get mad." You'll want to celebrate instances when children tell not only their characters' actions but also their reactions.

You will also see second graders take more control of conventions of language. Their sentence structure will be more complex; you'll notice this especially because their stories will include more varied (if not more correct) punctuation. Children's spelling will be easier to read, with more words spelled conventionally. Any spelling approximations will at least be decipherable. Children will spell well over a hundred sight words conventionally.

October in Third, Fourth, and Fifth Grades: What to Expect

When you visit the upper grade classrooms, you'll want to check, as you did in the first and second grade classrooms, whether children have already published. Expect that they have done so and that they are well into their second unit of study.

Look at the published work. There will not be gigantic differences between the pieces that third and fifth graders do. In fifth grade writing, the font will be smaller, the texts longer, but across these grades children will all retell true-life episodes. In many classrooms and especially in the younger grades, children may write their narratives across a few pages, with each page telling the story of one step in the sequence of events. Page one might tell about a child ascending towards the top of a mountain during a mountain hike. Page two might tell about the child reaching the mountain top and looking down from it. Page three might tell about lunch on the mountain top, and page four might tell about the start of the descent. Frankly, this example may be more focused, still, than the work you see, but you should see evidence of temporal focus. Ideally, this focus will help writers write with details and write narratives as stories rather than as summaries. Become accustomed to noticing the difference between summaries and stories. In a *summary* of the mountain climb, the piece might go like this: "I remember when we climbed a mountain. It was a lot of fun. The climb was tiring. My legs felt like they were going to fall off. Finally, we got to the top . . ." In a *story*, the same piece might sound like this: "'When will we reach the top?' I called out. I sat on a rock to rest my legs. Then I thought, 'It can't be much longer' and started to climb again . . ."

Chances are good that the published work of some children will not be focused or detailed, nor will it sound especially like a story. That is normal. More important is that children are attempting this. As you look through children's notebooks from the start of the year towards the present, you should definitely see lots of evidence of instruction and of progress towards writing chronological, detailed, storylike narratives.

> As you look through children's notebooks from the start of the year towards the present, you should definitely see lots of evidence of instruction and of progress towards writing chronological, detailed, storylike narratives.

Look also for evidence that children's volume of writing has increased dramatically. A child whose first entry at the start of the year was half a page long produced that amount in a single day of writing at that point. Now look at the entry the child wrote most recently, and contrast it with that original piece. You should see that the writing is becoming dramatically longer.

In general, most third graders can produce approximately a page of writing during one day's writing workshop. Of course, some writers, strugglers in particular, write in miniscule letters so while their pieces fill only a half or two-thirds of a page, they aren't short. I worry about the self-concept reflected in some of that writing and would encourage those children to let their writing use a bit more air space.

By fifth grade, children should produce more than a page of writing in one day's writing workshop, and of course the font will decrease in size (hopefully without seeming to say, "Excuse me for existing.").

Like primary students, children in grades 3–5 should put the date on every day's work. Most principals and teachers also ask upper grade children to record whether the work was written in school or at home, and of course this helps you. Make sure there is time for both. Most upper grade teachers assign at-home writing several days a week. The challenge is to make sure children are writing in school. Look at the entry lengths for at-school and at-home writing, expecting them to be comparable to each other. Become accustomed to leafing through the notebooks, saying to yourself, "I see Monday's in-school writing and Monday's at-home writing, I see Tuesday's in-school writing, I see Wednesday's in-school writing. Where is Thursday's writing? Friday's?"

In general, the flow of a month for writers in grades 3–5 will look like this: For just under half of most months, children will write in their writers' notebooks and you will expect approximately a page of writing in school and a page of writing at home each day. Then for a good portion of each month, children will write outside their notebooks, working on rough drafts. These will be stored in their folders. At this point in the year, most children will write one- or two-page drafts (unless children are writing in the booklets I described earlier), and they will revise the drafts by adding flaps to them in which they insert more elaboration. To do this, children may scissor open the original draft to insert extensions, perhaps writing several leads or several endings (these may be written with flaps on the actual draft paper or on other paper, perhaps in the notebook).

Next, children will edit their well-revised drafts, and then finally they will recopy these into final drafts. Final drafts will not be perfect unless the teacher actually writes them—which is a waste of teacher time and not helpful to kids. Revel in your children's pieces and hang them proudly. This is children's best work, for now, but the children themselves are works in progress.

Do your best not to feel insecure about posting work that contains errors. You could have a case for work that is posted in the hall, but not for work that is posted in the classroom. Perhaps teachers can title these displays of finished work in politically astute ways, hanging an announcement over the entire display that says, "See Our Works in Progress."

Cull the information you gather and look for patterns. Make notes of students you are concerned about, as well as any teaching that might raise concern. If you notice a problem consistently across a grade, make that grade an emergency. This might sound like a drastic and grandiose assumption to be making early on in the year, but viewing work in this way is often a litmus test, and the results will continue to haunt the well-being of this initiative and the school if there isn't an early intervention. Students can't afford a huge gap in their progress, and you can't afford it either. All grades should be in sync with the school at large.

DEAL DIRECTLY WITH RESISTANCE
IN ORDER TO NURTURE GOOD TEACHING

About five summers ago, Laurie's front lawn was turning yellow and discolored. The plush carpetlike grass now felt like scratchy straw. First, Laurie blamed it on the hot summer sun and began watering the garden daily, sometimes even twice. Then she blamed it on the chemicals and changed the chemical applications. Then, she got a different gardening service. One morning, as she was walking down the driveway, Laurie stooped down on the lawn, hoping that a stroke of magic would hit each blade of grass, rejuvenating it back to the way it had been before. A patch of grass seamlessly came out. Laurie turned the patch of grass over. Clusters of bugs were pulling at the roots. Laurie lifted out another patch, turned it over, and saw the same. She wanted to pretend that she never saw those bugs and walk down the driveway to the car as on any other normal day. But Laurie knew herein lay her problem, and herein lay her success.

I tell you this story not because Laurie has not solved all her gardening problems, but because as school leaders, you need to turn over "patches" in your school and not run away from what you see (and don't see). Be happy to find problems, and know that these will later turn into your successes. In his book *Good to Great*, Jim Collins rallies leaders of the corporate world to face head-on the hard truths. He says, "There is a sense of exhilaration facing these brutal facts and saying, 'We will never give up. It may take a long time, but we will prevail'" (2001, 68).

As you walk your building, you will, in general, be pleased with what you see. You will look at student writing and believe it is similar to the writing on the DVDs. You'll notice that a few teachers who have only had writing workshops for two short months will be teaching as though it had been encoded in their DNA. Classrooms will look impressive, and you'll begin to feel like a proud parent, marveling at the growth spurts all around you. While you won't see (or expect to see) model classrooms just yet, there will be evidence in most classrooms that this is the priority for this year.

However, if your school is like most others, there will be a few exceptions. You may have heard some rumblings and gathered some clues that things are not going precisely as you had hoped in all classrooms. A couple of your teachers are not receptive to having the coach in their classroom. They come to professional development sessions without paper, and they come to grade-level meetings without the materials they are asked to bring. They don't want to teach in ways that are different. They have heard that these are "best practices," but they would prefer to use best practices from a different time. You learn that your visits to some teachers' classrooms do not make them feel supported, and moreover, they believe what they were doing before was fine. They are resistant.

Each summer at the Teachers College Reading and Writing Project's institutes, we always offer sections for principals. At those sections, the most common question that principals ask is this: "How can we work with resistant teachers?"

Resistance comes in a lot of different forms. Sometimes it will be disregard for your requests. Perhaps you have requested that all your teachers display student pieces on the hallway bulletin boards, and, instead, three teachers chose to uphold their past tradition of hanging store-bought holiday decorations. Perhaps you have urged teachers to arrive at lab sites and study group meetings on time, and you've already made a great point of being sure that these teachers' replacements reach their rooms on time, yet still the teachers straggle into the meetings, coffee cup in hand. Sometimes, the resistance will come from teachers announcing to you that their kids aren't ready to write and can't produce the expected volume. Often the resistance will be unspoken and invisible until you get into the classroom, look at the students' writing folders, and see that these teachers simply haven't made time for the teaching of writing. The following are some thoughts to help you deal with resistance.

Form a consistent approach.

My first suggestion is that you and your ambassadors—the coach, the assistant principal—act consistently in response to resistance. All of you need to uphold the same message so that your school has a consistent approach. In *Good to Great*, Jim Collins points out that in order to lead an effective organization, your school has to not only have discipline (and this means for teachers as well as for children), but also a culture of discipline. This is not easily achieved, but it is essential. In his book *Change Forces*, Michael Fullan discusses some of Collins' findings. Fullan writes, "All companies have a culture, some companies have discipline, but few companies have a culture of discipline. When you have disciplined people, you don't need hierarchy. When you have disciplined thought, you don't need bureaucracy. When you have disciplined action, you don't need excessive controls. When you combine a culture of discipline with an ethic of entrepreneurship, you get magical alchemy of great performance" (1999, 9).

Address the resistance; others are watching.
If the resistance is public, others will watch your response. You have no choice but to respond. If you have requested that all your teachers display student pieces on the hallway bulletin boards, and three teachers chose, instead, to hang store-bought holiday decorations, teachers across the school will look at those bulletin boards as an indication that your injunctions can be disregarded. Be sure to address the behaviors of teachers who defy your requests without talking to you about their concerns. Do so not only for those people to learn that disregarding your requests is unacceptable, but more importantly, because the whole community will be watching. The norms you establish in your community matter very much, and all of us establish those norms in large part by the ways we do or do not choose to work with boundaries. Your words, alone, do not establish norms. Your words and your actions, in combination, do this.

This does not mean that you need to publicly scold those teachers, but it does mean you need to do something to address the resistance. If the bulletin board has store-bought decorations on it, you may want to start with a warm, jesting comment. Humor or a light injunction is probably the most appropriate response for the time being, but use it right away, before the problem grows. Humor can also dissipate tension. "Mary Lou, it is so *creative* of you to use holiday decorations as the back drop for student writing! When will the writing go up on top of those pumpkins?" Of course, if the resistant teacher doesn't rectify the matter, you may need to take a more direct approach—perhaps even a public one. Be sure that your response is not a public humiliation, but a gracious nudge.

Realize that where there is smoke, there is usually fire.
Resistance is complex because people are complex. Generally, when teachers arrive late to meetings, when they do not remember to bring the requested student work, when they sit in a grade-level meeting and, instead of participating, grade their students' spelling tests, when they plop a gigantic bag onto the table obscuring their view of the coach, these behaviors are all indicators of trouble. If you've heard that a couple of your teachers are not receptive to the coach, chances are good that the tensions are greater than you've heard. And if some teachers regularly come to professional

development sessions without paper, chances are good that this is no accident. These teachers are probably unhappy about your efforts to reform the teaching of writing, or they are unhappy with the coach or the staff developer. They are resistant—and you need to think long and hard about how to handle the difficulties.

Before you do anything else, make sure your evidence is correct. Is it resistance or something else? Perhaps you visited the kindergarten and saw that no child has written anything for a week. It could be, however, that the date on the date stamp hadn't been changed regularly and for that reason it only appeared that the kindergarten children had not been writing daily. Perhaps teachers haven't launched writing because they are still waiting for the shipment of supplies that you'd promised. Make sure that the problem really does exist before you take it on.

Decide to study the problem: Listen.

What's really going on? Schedule an appointment to talk one-on-one, away from the public eye, with the dissenter, and in that meeting try to create some open (but limited) conversation. "It's been clear to me that you aren't crazy about this new writing initiative. I need to understand your reservations. Can you take five minutes to explain to me the big concerns you have about this, and then can we talk together in order to find a way to go forward that feels okay to both of us?" You could say it differently. "Let's take ten minutes to clear the air, to put gripes on the table, and then we'll try to see a way out of this morass."

Then listen. As you listen, resist the assumption that the problem is the other guy, that the dissenter is wrong. Frankly, chances are pretty good that you inadvertently offended this person, that you stepped on toes in ways you didn't intend, and even if the person with whom you are talking doesn't realize this, chances are that the dissent is a response to actions you took.

There is another option. The person could be dissenting out of firm beliefs. If you have tried to rally your whole school to use the *Units of Study*, this teacher could be angry because she believes you are trying to push a scripted curriculum onto the school or because she believes the *Units of Study* do not showcase fiction as much as they should. So listen. Listen, because this is a democracy and dissent is part of the American tradition. Listen, because your fondest hope is that your teachers will be critical thinkers and questioners. Listen, because your teachers will never teach well if they can't draw on their own beliefs.

Look for common ground and areas for acceptable compromise.

If a dissenter is resisting the writing initiative because he holding tight to goals that you believe could serve the school well, then you can say to that teacher, "I believe your goals need to be our goals, as a school. I do not think we feel differently about the goals. I think our differences are only about the path to those goals, and I'm asking the school to take on the writing reform as a school, for now. But I am 100 percent convinced that once we are, as a school, working together to learn this approach to teaching writing, then we will need to outgrow this approach, to do yet more. And I'd love it if you could be ready to help us go past this starting point. But could I ask you to try, for now, to help me bring the whole school together around this writing reform? Could I ask you to take a leadership role just for now, for the next four months, and then I promise that you and I can talk again and can think about how you could also lead us to go beyond this work? Because I have no doubt that we will need to do that."

Your dissenter's goals may not be your goals, and you may not respond in that way. But, in any case, listen well to what this teacher has to say, and respect his right to say it. Listening should not just be a courtesy. Listen to learn about points of agreement you and the dissenter share. Listen to learn ways in which you can allow the dissenter to tweak aspects of the writing workshop. If he does not think partnerships can be started in the first month of school and would prefer to wait until the second month—go for it. If the dissenter wants to abbreviate minilessons for now because his children don't seem able to listen—great, the rest of us can learn from how this goes. That is, you need to convey that some aspects of the writing workshop are negotiable—while others are not. If the dissenter wants to assign topics and to be sure every child is writing on the same topic—no, it is really important to a writing workshop that children have chances to write about topics of their own choice, so that needs to be a schoolwide policy.

> Listening should not just be a courtesy. Listen to learn about points of agreement you and the dissenter share. Listen to learn ways in which you can allow the dissenter to tweak aspects of the writing workshop.

I have sometimes found that my strongest dissenters end up as my strongest team members. Dissenters are often people with convictions, with backbone, with the tenacity to hold to their convictions—and those are exact qualities you especially want in your efforts to reform the teaching of writing.

Recognize that resistance can come from being overwhelmed.

Sometimes resistors are just teachers who need help. They may have camouflaged their lack of understanding as resistance. Or they may simply have encountered enormous difficulties when they tried to teach writing. Of course they resist the writing workshop—it isn't working for them! These teachers need a huge infusion of help right away. If the problems include classroom management problems (which is apt to be the case,) these teachers need first to receive one-to-one help, presumably from the literacy coach or from the assistant principal if she is a good teacher. Usually it will help if this teacher and the coach visit other classrooms with an eye only on how those teachers are managing their rooms. (Often this means visiting classrooms of teachers whose teaching may not be radiant but whose systems are well-oiled, and these teachers are often not the superstars who regularly receive visitors, so you'll be helping the host as well as the visitor.) Then the teacher and the coach will need lots and lots of time (perhaps a full day) to rethink rituals, systems, rules, expectations so as to be able to restart the year on a better footing. I usually think it helps if a few people help the teacher put an entirely new face on the classroom, too, rearranging the desks, perhaps adding a new rug, some new flowers.

When children come into the room, the classroom teacher will need to say to them, "I've rearranged the room because we are going to turn a page in the story of this room. We're starting a whole new chapter. And things will be different from now on. So today, the coach and I will be showing you how we'll act in this new chapter. First, let's talk about how we convene for meetings. Every day, we will often gather in the meeting area, and right now I'm going to show you how we go about doing that. Then we'll practice a few times so we get this really perfect."

The coach will need lots of time in that classroom for a few days, just to help the teacher install new rituals and procedures and expectations. That teacher will need tons of compliments from you, as will the children in that room. The new approach, like a fragile seedling, needs the sunshine of your approval.

Recognize that resistance can stem from the fear of losing control.

Sometimes, teachers who worry about losing control over their classroom become fearful, and that fear translates into resistance. They prefer to have their rooms in rows rather than clusters; they worry about conferring with one child instead of controlling the whole class; they worry about students going "off task." They have not yet built the trust that children will be able to talk productively. Writing workshop makes these teaches feel insecure. They worry about having kids sit next to each other.

Many times, these teachers already have challenges around classroom management, and the lack of what they see as control will only make it worse. Teachers in this category would benefit most from interacting with the coach in a one-on-one situation. Classroom work should always include very clear and direct demonstrations of management techniques.

These teachers would also benefit from visiting other teachers whose instruction is rigorous and whose children are independent. Ideally, they should visit classrooms of students similar to their own. If a teacher struggling with management issues has a lot of English language learners, for example, try to find a similar class. It would be a wise use of the coach's time to gather together the teachers that fall into this category and work with them as a group and point out all the structures that support the independence of children they (the teachers) might not yet be using. Be prepared for these teachers to tell you that their students are different, that they can't do these things. In your visits to these classrooms, make sure that your compliments are focused around management and independence. Compliment teachers if they are now letting children get their own paper. Compliment teachers if they have rearranged their seating. Compliment teachers if partnerships are up and running. Ask your coach to make a cheat sheet of techniques that you can look for.

Recognize that resistance can come from feeling undervalued.
Resistors may be experienced teachers whose preeminence as superstars has been challenged by the new reforms. These teachers were the ones that administrators before you relied on because of their expertise. Now, finding their knowledge is no longer highlighted in the same way, they feel undermined.

You know how to help people in this position regain their footing! Find ways for these teachers to know that you value their skills, their experience, their wisdom. Ask for their advice. Find ways their teaching is exemplary, and send others into their rooms to learn from those pockets of excellence.

One of those teachers may have expertise in math, and you may have sidelined math as well as that teacher through your focus on writing. Call her into the office and tell her that before long, the school will be thinking about math and you'd love it if you and she could be thinking about the new directions the school might take at that point. Another teacher has tremendous experience helping with parent communication. Recruit these teachers to lead others in their areas of expertise. Meanwhile, separately, compliment any progress you see in their teaching of writing. On the other hand, you needn't pretend that the teacher is doing good work if he is not. Do not allow much time to go by before saying, "I can't live with your kids not getting a real chance to learn to write. What can I do to make it more likely that you'll start teaching writing with the same intensity you bring to teaching math?" Don't let much time pass before rallying these teachers to be invested in the writing reforms. These are your leaders, and disgruntled leaders can do your school a lot of harm.

Work with each resistant teacher individually.
Struggle happens for different reasons. One person's struggle is not another person's struggle. If one of your teachers treated all struggling readers the same, you would want to help her try to look at each child separately and find the reason for the struggle and possible ways to help. You need to do the same with your resistant teachers.

Know that the best way to deal with resistance is to nurture a culture of kindness and respect in your school.
Congratulate acts of kindness and generosity among the staff. Send notes of appreciation when you see one teacher going out of her way for another. Pay attention to the small ways in which people contribute to the community, and let them know their efforts are appreciated. "It was so kind of you to bring donuts to that meeting," you can say. "How incredibly nice of you to go to the trouble of copying this poem for all of us!" "I noticed you staying late after the meeting to restore Jenny's room to order. That was so kind of you, so like you. These little acts of generosity that you do mean the world."

The biggest suggestion I have for you is that you cannot be an ostrich, putting your head in the sand and ignoring your resistant teachers. You need to ferret out indicators of resistance, you need to know clearly which teachers are resisting you, and you need to understand that although resistance comes in a lot of different forms and exists for a lot of different reasons, the fact remains that some teachers have not taken up the new writing initiative, and this will only be a schoolwide initiative if you are willing to work past the hard parts so that in the end, yours is a school where teachers teach writing and where kids are given opportunities to flourish as writers.

You need to be willing to talk firmly and clearly about the code of behavior you expect in your school. A teacher can disagree with a colleague and can say so. But acts of rudeness and incivility are not acceptable.

Whether you like what the coach is saying or not has nothing to do with the fact that you cannot sit in a grade-level meeting and correct math homework or talk on your cell phone. That's simply rude and, therefore, unacceptable. You can let people know that complaints (verbal or nonverbal ones) are masked requests. Instead of folding one's arms and rolling one's eyes, it would be preferable to voice your suggestions and your requests using words.

So deal with resistance. No one else can. Your coach can't be the person who says to these teachers, "You must." Your outside staff developer can't be the one who conveys this message. This needs to be your job. You need to have a list of teachers who are resisting, and you need to make a plan to visit their classrooms more regularly and to develop action plans with those teachers that include positive steps forward that the teacher agrees to take. You need to invest your own time and resources in enabling that teacher to have success teaching writing (and in other ways), and you need to be especially alert for any indications of progress and to support those with heart and soul.

The real goal is that your school is one where teachers are invested in the common good and are willing to set aside individual gain for the common good. The single most important suggestion I can make for those of you wanting to do more to nurture that sensibility is that you must hurry to the bookstore and get yourself a copy of the book *A School Leader's Guide to Excellence: Collaborating Our Way to Better Schools*, written by two of the leaders I respect more than any others in the world—Carmen Fariña and Laura Kotch. Their book will help in zillions of ways, but it will especially help you create a culture of collegiality, and that will be the strongest antidote to resistance.

"Lab Sites and Study Groups" and "Planning the Curriculum." In these two sections, principals discuss specific strategies for promoting collaborative learning and planning among teachers.

CHAPTER SEVEN

NOVEMBER

Engaging with Parents

I n the fairy story of Rapunzel, a child is born at long last to the king and queen. To celebrate, they invite the entire village to a banquet on the day of their infant's christening. Seven good fairies come, and each bestows the infant with a gift; one gives the gift of wisdom, another, the gift of generosity.

In my ideal version of that fairy tale, the good fairies would give their gifts not to the newborn infant, but to the parents on the child's behalf. The good fairies would sprinkle their magic dust on parents, giving them wisdom, generosity, tenacity, imagination. Parents would hold these gifts in custody and, in time, would pass them on to their child. Because parents were generous, children, too, would become generous. But in real life, there is no magic wand that helps people become the parents that they long to be.

This Month

- **Create a forum for teaching parents.**

- **Talk to parents about the school's approach to writing.**

No job requires more, yet most parents do not take classes or attend conferences or receive on-the-job supervision in this, the most important job of their lives.

Each teacher in your school has his or her own job; each has responsibility for a different portion of the school's population. You, too, have a contingent that is squarely in your hands. The students' parents are yours. They look to you as den leader, super parent, coach. Others will contribute, too, but ultimately, the job of organizing your parents' learning lives will be yours.

You may be sputtering in protest. You may feel as if I have just thrown a hot potato at you that you do not want, and you may be dying to heave that potato in someone else's direction. And there may be people on your staff who will catch that potato, who will support you in your role. But I believe that in every superbly functioning school, the principal has embraced the role of teacher-of-the-parents.

I'm convinced that working with parents can be a source of great pleasure if you are proactive, finding as many opportunities as possible to communicate with parents so they become partners with you. And I am equally convinced that working with parents can be a source of terrible angst if you are reactive, waiting for one parent after another to question, to attack, to arouse opposition.

The author Avi was wise when he said that if you are going to teach a child to write, first you need to love that child. If you are going to teach a parent, too, first you need to empathize with that parent. You can be a source of information, helping parents have the fortitude to turn off the television, to unplug the computer, the Nintendo, the iPod. You can be a source of inspiration, rallying parents to fall head over heels in love with the best of children's books and to move heaven and earth to be sure their children share that love. You can be a source of clarity, helping parents decipher all the conflicting information they get from media and neighbors about hot-button topics such as phonics, spelling, standards, and state tests. You can be a source of companionship, too, by creating a space in your school where parents forge support communities for themselves.

> If you are going to teach a parent, first you need to empathize with that parent.

Among all the other things you do with parents, you'll want to tell your parents about the new work your school is doing in writing. It is almost inevitable that your decision to spotlight the teaching of writing will be met with widespread support, and it will also be the case that long before parent-teacher conferences in November, many parents will have seen changes in their children. Most will be intrigued with and pleased by those changes. Kindergartners will have come home and searched for paper, announcing "I gotta write a story." A flyer lying on the floor will have been folded into a story booklet. At restaurants, children of all ages will have used napkins and placemats as stationery. Children will have told parents about the emphasis on writing about small moments, and they'll have looked up from family events and said, "I can write about this." Parents, then, will be eager to understand the new buzz. We urge you to proactively teach them about the teaching of writing—and to see writing as just one case in point.

CREATE A FORUM FOR TEACHING PARENTS

Before you can think about what you will say to parents about the teaching of writing, you need to think about how to reach those parents in the first place. You will, no doubt, have an established forum already in place for talking to parents. But it could be that only a small contingent of parents actually attends your PTA meetings, and if this is the case, you will want to think about the reasons for this. Just as kids are not all the same, parents, too, are not all the same. As Carmen Fariña and Laura Kotch emphasize in *A School Leader's Guide to Excellence*, it will very likely be the case that only a contingent of your parents will be front-row participants in your PTA meetings. Sometimes this same contingent of parents will also be the people who step forward to organize your schoolwide fund-raisers. When Carmen became principal of PS 6, she found that this small cohort of parents wielded great influence in the school and that too often this influence benefited a select few. "This small but prominent group of parents was speaking for all parents, when most other parents never attended meetings or joined committees," she realized (2008, 152). When Laurie was an assistant principal in a school of 1,400 children, many families worked two jobs, and attendance at the once-a-month evening PTA meetings averaged only fifty people. But if people's sons and daughters were performing and if parents could bring younger brothers and sisters to those performances, everything changed. Hundreds of family members thronged to Laurie's school, PS 148, for evening Author Celebration extravaganzas. Those evening events, then, became Laurie's opportunities to teach parents about the school's curriculum. Of course, those events were only the beginning. Your job as teacher-of-the-parents begins with your recognition that you will need to provide a variety of ways to reach out to the parents of your children.

These are a few ways that principals we've worked with have reached parents. Some of these ideas might work for your school, and others won't. You'll need to think carefully about the diversity of your parents and organize outreach methods to reach them all. Here are some suggestions:

Ways to Reach Out to Parents

✦ Ask parents to write letters introducing their children. Ask teachers to write each parent a letter or email before the school year begins, inviting those parents to write, letting the teacher know more about the child. A sample letter may look like this:

> Dear Parents,
>
> I'm writing to ask you to help me become a partner with you in your child's education. I will only have your child for a short time in this trip through life—just one fleeting school year—and I want to make a contribution that lasts a lifetime.
>
> I know my teaching must begin with making your child feel at home in my classroom, and with helping all the children come together in a

learning community made up of particular, unique individuals, who have
their own learning styles and interests and history and hopes. Would you
help me teach well by taking a quiet moment to write me about your
child? What is your youngster like? What are some of the things you know
that would be important for me to know? What are your child's interests? I
want to know how you know how your child thinks and plays and how
you see your child as a learner and a person.

Sincerely,

Miss Marotta

✦ Make a year-opening speech. Give a state-of-the-school address within
the first few weeks of each new school year, and in that speech talk
about the teaching of writing (among other topics). Just as you need to
be the inspirational leader for teachers, you need to be this for parents,
too. The good news is that you can and probably should say similar
things to all your different constituents so you won't need to plan vastly
different beginning-of-the-year presentations.

✦ Offer grade-specific curriculum nights. Together with the teachers on a
grade level and the literacy coach, you can teach parents about the curriculum for that grade. Do this early in the year. It usually works to teach
parents as you would teach children. Lean on the *Units of Study* books.
You'll find that those lessons are truly multilevel.

✦ Also offer whole-school curriculum nights. Devote one of these to informing parents about the teaching of writing. This could be for K–5
parents, with everyone staying together for the whole evening, or it
could involve you (or you and the literacy coach) talking for a little while
about aspects of the teaching of writing that pertain across the grades,
followed by grade-specific meetings led by teachers. Those teachers
could talk about the teaching of writing, or they could involve parents in
a simulation of a writing workshop, or they could use children to
demonstrate aspects of the teaching of writing. Another option would
be for parents to attend author celebrations (which will be described in
more detail elsewhere), celebrating children's published work.

✦ Write to your parents directly. Perhaps you'll do this in a monthly
newsletter, or perhaps you'll simply send home a letter describing your
approach to the teaching of writing. Many schools also include a de-

scription of their approach to writing in the parent handbook. A sample letter might look like this:

> Dear Third Grade Families,
>
> Welcome to the exciting world of third grade! This will be a year of many new experiences and growth. One of the biggest changes this year will occur in writers' workshop. Every child will have a writer's notebook—a special place to record stories, ideas, and observations. Inspiration can happen at any moment, so we know that children will want to bring home their writer's notebook. Please work with your child to decorate the cover so it reflects your child's life: pictures of family members or friends, sports, musical instruments, favorite foods, and so on. It is important that your child bring his or her writer's notebook to school each day.
>
> Sincerely,
>
> Miss Marotta

✦ Provide parents with a glossary of educational terms teachers will use with children. Children will come home talking about "stretching out a word" or "writing how-to books," and parents will want to understand what the child means. Of course, parents know what the words mean in real life, but they will seem to have taken on special meanings for the child. Sending home a glossary of terms can help parents feel like insiders.

✦ Use parent-teacher conferences as a time for parent education. Teachers across the grade level can plan how they will use parent-teacher conferences as a forum for teaching parents about the writing workshop. Certainly every teacher will have student work at each conference: the child's first piece of writing, a few pieces along the way, and a recent piece of writing. The teacher can show parents how to look at growth in writing through a variety of lenses. "We can look, for example, at Bobby's progress spelling high-frequency words such as because, said, when, and so forth." The teacher could, in a similar way, help a parent shift and view writing through the lens of a child's command of narrative craft, a child's increasing ability to use what the teacher has taught, and so forth.

✦ Offer Open School Day (or Open School Week or Open School Fridays). On these days, you can invite parents, grandparents, and other caregivers to join the child in school for a regularly scheduled time. Some schools are open all day every day for a week in November in honor of National Parent Month. Other schools earmark an hour at the start of the first Friday of every month. Others set a date in which classrooms will be open a week after parent-teacher conferences. During this time, ask teachers to lead writing workshops. If they are uncomfortable leading minilessons before this audience, they can instead use the time for independent writing, showing parents how the parent, too, can confer with young writers. Teachers could function a bit like staff developers or literacy coaches, saying "Can the parents come over here for a minute so I can talk with all of you?" and then taking a few minutes to summarize the architecture of a writing conference, perhaps demonstrating one, before sending parents off to try their hand at conferring.

✦ Create a Newcomers Welcoming Committee so that parents who are knowledgeable about the school help bring new parents aboard. Be sure that you have provided this committee with materials that inform the newcomers about the school, including the school's approach to teaching writing.

✦ Create a Parent Advisory Committee, making sure that the full diversity of parents is represented on this committee. Urge this committee to poll parents and to bring their ideas to the table. Be sure to refer to what you learn from this group when you describe initiatives at this school. "I heard from many of you that you wanted the school to provide a more rigorous approach to teaching writing, and so we've tried to do this. Let me explain . . ."

✦ Invite specific parents to join specific think tanks or task forces. For example, there may be a task force on student publications. Parents who are at the table in that task force will be more willing to step forward to fund-raise or to organize parent volunteers. Similarly, you could invite parents into a task force to support the school library or classroom libraries. There is never a time when you will not want more fund-raising for books, and the work of organizing books is always more than any one person can handle.

✦ Organize courses for parents on topics of special interest. These topics might be designed to support parents' work with their children, with titles such as "Help Your Child Write Essays" or "Help Your Child Spell and Punctuate." Alternatively, the workshops might be designed to inform parents about the school's approach, with titles such as "How Are Schools Today Teaching Children to Write Essays?" and "Spelling Matters: What Does Research Suggest About Teaching Kids to Spell?" If you worry whether your school has the needed expertise to teach these courses, then set the date well in advance and give a teacher or your coach responsibility now to be ready for that important job. Be sure to encourage that person to include student work from the school, to rely on video snippets on the resources CD-ROMs in the *Units of Study* packages if he needs support, and to organize little archives for the parents. Be sure, too, that you are part of the program—talk briefly and then be a front-row participant. Remember that if you invite a teacher to teach one of these courses, you are giving that individual a chance to outgrow himself or herself. The request itself will lift the level of teaching in your school.

✦ Plan an orientation night for the upcoming year at the end of each school year. Use this as an occasion to emphasize the importance of kids' engaging in summer reading and writing and to provide parents with ideas for how they can support their child's reading and writing. It is impossible to overemphasize the importance of summer reading and writing.

✦ Consolidate all these invitations and dates into a centralized calendar of events for parents. Develop systems for communicating—through regular newsletters, a school website, or other media. You won't use every forum I've discussed to reach parents, but you *will* use many of them. The best way to communicate these forums to parents is to distribute a yearlong calendar at the start of the year that contains dates of all upcoming occasions, and to be sure that communication about these calendars actually reaches home, have parents sign a form indicating they've seen it. You will still send more information home during the year, including reminders, and it will be best if every child in the school brings home parent information on the same day. That is, perhaps in your school you and your teachers can say, "Every Monday, your child will bring home a red folder. The red folder will contain any information you need to read, plus the child's homework for the week." Such a system will be a tremendous boon to parents.

Tucking letters to parents in with a child's report card makes it likely that parents will see those letters. It also helps if a portion of the bulletin board at the main door of the school is set aside as a vehicle for communicating with parents. Obviously this (and all communications) needs to be in more than one language for parents who are not native speakers of English.

Talk to Parents About the School's Approach to Writing

Parents are dying to know that you recognize the importance of writing. They have always regarded writing as one of the basics. For generations, those basics have always been reading, writing, and 'rithmetic. Of all of those basics, writing is the one in which parents can actually see a child's work right before their eyes. Writing puts a kid on the line, and parents often don't like what they see. These days parents are especially keen for kids to finally have good writing instruction because they know that kids need extraordinary writing skills in order to excel in middle and high school and in order to meet the exacting demands of those all-important college admission tests: the SAT, ACT, AP tests, and the like. So parents will be with you if you gather them together, in one forum or another, and say, "We've decided that ours will be a school in which writing is taught in a systematic, organized, whole-school fashion, with the work of one grade building on the work of the preceding grade, and with children receiving explicit instruction in the skills and strategies they need in order to write narratives and expository writing really well."

Spotlight Children's Writing

Make sure that the talk you give about the teaching of writing is both child-centered and professional. The easiest way to be child-centered is to put kids at the center by sharing student work. Early in your talk to parents, say, "I want to open by telling you a story." Then tell about a child who slipped a note under your office door, or one who shyly stuck a story in your hand, or another who was found writing a poem on the sly. Read aloud the work. The literacy coach can help you find pieces, looking especially for those that will appeal to parents. Some pieces will need to be enlarged through an overhead projector so that parents can enjoy the child's drawing and spelling, although at the start of the year, don't expect parents to join you in appreciating approximated spelling in children beyond first grade—those pieces are best read aloud. Choose pieces that you think will touch parents.

I once began a meeting with kindergarten parents by saying, "I feel like I know each one of you in a very intimate way. Your kids have been writing up a storm this year. They are told, 'Write about something that matters to you.' They can all choose their topics, but the funny thing is they are almost universally writing about *you*! Take this piece, written by one of our kindergartners:

> The sun is like a mommy
> With a tremendous warmth
> Its rays so hot and nice
> When it shines down upon the town
> Its warmth you can't believe."

I went on to say, "I've learned about your acts of heroism—how one of you scooped up your daughter when a rat was approaching her on a subway platform, and I've learned about your kids' attentiveness to you—how one child lies in bed waiting for the garage door to open, waiting for the footsteps that mean Dad is home."

Sharing children's work warms up the room in ways that are important, and you may decide to make this into a ritual. You may decide to begin every PTA meeting as well as every other parent event throughout the year with a shared piece of writing. Bringing the voices of children into the room will delight parents and will remind them that ultimately, all that we do is for the sake of our children.

Explain the Writing Curriculum

After sharing just a bit of children's charming, idiosyncratic, funny writing, you'll want to be sure that your language shifts so that you also talk about the teaching of writing in ways that help parents know that you not only love their kids, but that you will also educate them in rigorous ways. The good news is that you can accurately talk about the teaching of writing in your school while using terms such as these:

explicit, direct instruction
systematic, organized curriculum
assessment-based
expository writing
teaching the skills and strategies kids need
rigor
standards
expectations

tracking kids' progress

an emphasis on revision and editing

providing students with time on task, with time to practice

developing stamina

the conventions of written language

In addition, there are some big ideas you may want to convey:

We need to *teach*, not just *assign*, writing.

You could give parents a broad overview of the field of writing. You could tell them, for example, that when they were in school, most teachers assigned writing and corrected writing, filling margins of children's work with red-inked *awk*s and *run-on*s, (you'll hear boos and hisses from the sidelines), but that no one really taught writing. Some kids wrote well and they were regarded as "gifted" in writing, and many kids did not write well. Since then researchers have realized that when writing is not just assigned and corrected but is also explicitly taught, then all kids can learn to write well. And researchers have shown that to teach writing explicitly, we can't just hold up finished writing and say, "Write like this" and expect a child to write a polished piece any more than we can teach baking by holding up a finished cake and saying, "Bake a cake like this" and expect the child's cake to be edible. Instead, we need to teach writing like we teach baking, by showing kids the step-by-step process, the recipe, and by teaching them the specific methods that experts use. That is, teaching someone to cook means showing them that if they need to whip the egg whites, there are tried-and-true ways for doing this; in the same way, writers benefit from learning tried-and-true ways for writing strong leads, for developing a thesis statement, for deciding when to paragraph.

> Researchers have realized that when writing is not just assigned and corrected but is also explicitly taught, then all kids can learn to write well.

Writing practice is crucial to writing development.

You will probably tell parents that there is widespread agreement across the nation about methods of teaching writing and that increasingly elementary schools are using methods for teaching writing that are also used in colleges and among professional writers. The most important aspect of any writing program is the acknowledgment that writing is a skill and, like any skill (swimming, playing piano, baseball), people get more proficient with practice. Therefore, the most important part of any approach to teaching writing is the expectation that writers will write, and they will write a lot.

Writers not only write, they also write like professional writers.
This is no different from what already occurs in your school's science program. In science, there is widespread agreement that all scientists use the scientific method—hypothesizing, collecting data and the like, and so when children study science, they do so in ways that allow them to use these same processes. Similarly, in writing, there is widespread agreement that writers use the writing process. Writers rehearse (they plan for their writing), they draft (they write quickly, in rough draft form), they revise (they reread their writing and make substantive changes in content, organization, and language), and finally, writers edit (they check that their words are precise, they condense, refine, and correct). You will want to tuck into this the recognition that children will not do one-shot writing. They will not be assigned to write a perfect story on an assigned topic and to bring that writing in, completed and corrected, the next day. Is that how real writers write? Of course not!

Drafts are meant to be rough.
Real writers take some time to plan their writing, trying out one idea and another for how the writing will go. Real writers write a very quick first draft, just trying to get the broad outlines of the text into place, not worrying that every word is perfect. You may say, "For real writers, drafting is more like playing in clay than inscribing in marble," and you might even show on an overhead the rough draft you scrawled when you first began thinking of your remarks on teaching writing. Some parents could mistakenly think that the concept that a child writes a rough draft as well as a final draft represents lax standards, so you want to emphasize the rigor behind this process. Because children, like you and like every published writer the world over, write rough drafts before writing final drafts, this means that writers have time to reread, examining the structure and clarity of the first effort, thinking, "How can I make my best work better?"

To help parents feel at home with revision, explain that all of us revise most of the time. When we want to hang a picture on the wall, we don't just bang in a nail and presto, we are done. Instead, we rope someone into holding the picture up in a tentative spot, and then we back up and eye the scene, calling, "Move it a little to the right. Now a little bit down." That's revision. Or we go to make a clay rabbit, and we shape the clay into ears, and then we pause and hold the clay figure at arm's length, eyeing the ears. Then we pull back to adjust them, bending one ear over, making the other just a bit bigger. That's revision. And writers know that revision is crucial to the writing process.

Spelling is important.

There is no question you will need to give special attention to spelling. Spelling matters so much that I often tell teachers, "In your first letter home to parents at the start of the school year, be sure to tell parents that you will be teaching spelling and that you will give kids a spelling test every Friday." I go on to point out to teachers that while there is lots of evidence that a school needs to adopt a thoughtful approach to spelling, there is no research suggesting that there is something essential about spelling tests or, especially, about spelling tests on Fridays. But I am convinced that many parents care more about the teaching of spelling than about almost any other topic, and if parents receive a letter at the start of the year that says, "We'll have spelling tests every Friday," that one sentence will win over parental support more than anything else the teacher could possibly say. For some parents, there is something enormously reassuring about spelling tests on Fridays, and meanwhile those tests take all of five minutes to give, so why would a teacher hesitate?

> Let parents know that part of teaching writing is teaching kids to become more proficient at editing.

Of course, the fact that a teacher calls out five words, asks kids to jot them onto paper and then to exchange papers and correct those quizzes has almost nothing to do with whether that teacher in fact teaches spelling well, nor with whether that teacher has helped kids to write more and more conventionally. You will also need to be sure that your teachers do have a responsible approach to teaching spelling (more on that later). For now, the important thing is to let parents know that part of teaching writing is teaching kids to become more proficient at editing.

Editing is important.

Tell parents that starting in kindergarten, every writer will be asked to reread and edit her writing, doing this as best she can. A kindergartner may only be able to look back to check that she has included the author's name and page numbers—five-year-olds can't independently assess to be sure their spelling is perfect! And the important thing will be that children learn to reread and edit as best they can and to improve their skills in using written conventions and editing over time.

You can also let parents know that in your school, teachers emphasize that the skills children do first during editing transfer over to become skills they use with automaticity in their first drafts. If, at the end of September, children revise their personal narratives by focusing on the skill of paragraphing, then a week or two later, when those same children write new rough draft entries, teachers will want to check that children remember to write their drafts in paragraphs. This is important for teachers to emphasize to children and for you to emphasize to parents. The broader principle is that what children do first through editing needs to move forward in the writing process, becoming part of what kids do with automaticity. Of course, this is a goal, and teachers and children will need to work to achieve that goal—but the important thing is that you convey to parents that a concern for mechanics is absolutely part of your approach to writing.

Children will learn how to write all the kinds of writing that exist in the world.

Children learn that they can find writing they admire and think, "What did this author do that I can try?" Then they can try their hand at writing in ways that resemble whatever it is they admire. You may want to emphasize that children will refer to published work as mentor texts or touchstone texts, and over time they will come to learn that there are a hundred lessons that can be learned from even just one single mentor text.

If you'd like to show parents an example, Mo Willems' picture book *Knuffle Bunny* is loaded with lessons on narrative craft. You could invite parents to pore over the book, thinking, "What has this author done that our kids, too, could benefit from doing in their stories?"

Answer Parents' Questions

Over the years, we've found that there are a handful of predictable topics that parents will want to discuss:

Questions about editing: No matter if your presentation on writing includes a full discourse on editing, parents will likely still have more questions on that topic. Some parents will ask about whether you "accept errors" in children's work. In response, you'll want to talk about the importance of a child's growth—growth over time. Tell parents that if you insist every child's writing be perfectly spelled at all times, then you'd be insisting on teachers and parents doing kids' spelling for them. Let parents know that researchers suggest our goal be for children to spell with 90 percent correctness in their first draft writing by the time they are in fifth grade and to also develop skills by that time that are necessary for the children to research spellings they do not know. Emphasize that fifty percent of the words children write the same thirty-six words—high-frequency words—and you are working hard to be sure all children learn to spell those words (and others like them) "in a snap."

Questions about spelling: Some parents may persist with more questions about phonics and spelling, in which case you can remind them that spelling and phonics are taught outside the writing workshop as well as within it. Perhaps your school has studied an approach towards phonics such as Donald Bear's *Words Their Way* or Gay Su Pinnell and Irene Fountas' *Phonics Lessons: Letters, Words, and How They Work*. If so, mention this approach.

Questions about reports and other sorts of content area writing: Some parents may push you to clarify whether children are given opportunities to write nonfiction texts. They may ask, "Is all the writing *creative*?" I've come to believe that those who word a question in that way are usually disdainful of creative writing, as if it's all whipped cream and rainbows. I try to resist the temptation to rise to the challenge and instead validate the very reasonable interest in children developing into well-rounded writers who can work with a diverse range of genre. I emphasize the expository *Units of Study*: the K–2 unit, *Nonfiction Writing: Procedures and Reports*, in which children write all-about books and the two units at grades 3–5 that focus on writing thesis-driven essays. I also emphasize the importance of writing across the curriculum.

Questions about homework: Be prepared to address questions about homework. I recommend that teachers ask older children to carry their writer's notebooks between home and school and to write often as part of homework. In the *Units of Study* books for grades 3–5, I've included a ton of homework assignment sheets, each one giving children detailed ideas for work they can do at home, and each one designed in such a way that a teacher can personalize the assignment. (Make sure teachers are drawing upon this resource! When parents see well-crafted, thoughtful homework assignments, this helps them to feel more comfortable about the work that children are being asked to do—the homework assignments serve as an important form of parent education.)

You can find examples of these homework assignments on the CD-ROMS in *Units of Study*, in case you want to have them handy to show to concerned parents. Be sure to tell parents that children in kindergarten through second grade will tend to not come home with homework assignments from writing workshop. Even though there are no written assignments, parents should expect that their children will be bubbling over with stories. Encourage them to ask their kids, "What did you write about today in writing workshop?" Let them know that young children don't always remember the events of a day; in these instances, parents can say to them, "Well maybe tomorrow you can try to remember, and we can talk about it when you come home."

> You, as the teacher-of-parents, need to remember that there are very few resources for parents, and you need to remember what an enormously difficult job it is to raise children.

Parents can help children realize all the little things that happen in a day that make for great stories. Loosing a first tooth, trying out a new pair of sneakers that the child always wanted, helping mom make cupcakes all are wonderful possibilities for stories for writing workshop. "Are you going to write about that tomorrow in writing workshop?" a parent might ask. Or at bedtime, a parent might say, "Wow, look at all the stories that you have just from today! Let's say all of them on our fingers so you can choose what you want to write about tomorrow."

You can also tell parents to anticipate that their children will collect papers they find around the house to use as writing paper—and that this is worth encouraging. Children might use the reverse side of old flyers, or borrow printer paper lying by the computer and fold sheets together to make booklets. Encourage parents to have writing tools—perhaps crayons or pencils— in a predictable place at home. Let parents know that perhaps the best job they can have is to be their child's cheerleader. "I love that story. Can we read it together?" Or, "Grandma is going to love this card. Let's go put it in an envelope and mail it to her now." Your teachers will want to elaborate on all these options, but for now it is important to give all parents a few quick ideas.

I think that you, as the teacher-of-parents, need to remember that there are very few resources for parents, and you need to remember what an enormously difficult job it is to raise children. Parents of elementary school children can be thorns in the side. They can be demanding and difficult. But, as a Jewish philosopher once said, "The decision to have a child is the decision to forever have one's heart walking around outside your body." The questions and demands and worries that parents have all come from caring and from a need for support.

"Involving Parents." Principals describe ways of informing and involving parents.

CHAPTER EIGHT

DECEMBER
ENGAGING WITH CHILDREN

Schools have become frenetic places. Everyone is rushing to teach, to cover curriculum, to get to topics. Eve Merriam, the great poet, has written a poem that has an important message for those of us in schools:

> There go the grownups
> To the office,
> To the store,
> Subway rush,
> Traffic crush;
> Hurry, scurry,
> Worry, flurry.
>
> No wonder
> grownups
> Don't grow up
> Any more.
>
> It takes a lot
> Of slow
> To grow.

THIS MONTH

- **Value the voices of children.**

- **Don't wait before bringing specialists into writing reform.**

- **Check in on children's writing progress.**

Writing gives many gifts to a school community. Among the contributions writing can make is this: Writing helps us slow down so that we hear the voices of people that we do not always take the time to hear. When we teach children to write, we give voice to people who have sometimes been silenced.

As David Booth, coauthor of *Stories in the Classroom* has said, "The stories which our children make and tell about themselves should be honored in our classrooms, for it is through their stories that they build their self-esteem and sense of belonging in the world" (1990, 128). He has said, "Our children story about us all the time. They story about our new shirt (was it a birthday present?) and our new suntan (where did she go on vacation?), but sometimes, teachers do not 'story' about their children." Stories, on the other hand, are at the heart of the writing workshop. A teacher does not need aquariums and geraniums and elaborate learning centers to teach writing well, but teachers do need to listen to kids in order to teach writing well. Classrooms need to brim with kids' stories. Teachers do not need to be super-teachers to teach writing well, but they do need to love and respect kids and to listen with open hearts to their stories, helping them to listen to each other with equal respect, and eventually, to themselves.

VALUE THE VOICES OF CHILDREN

In your role as principal, it is important that you demonstrate a willingness to crouch low so as to be on eye level with children. It's important that you listen to children's voices and their writing with open-hearted responsiveness. If a child tells you he had a hard weekend because her teddy bear fell in the mud, your instinct might be to brush the child's concerns away with a laugh. We as adults know better than to worry about a stuffed animal's feelings. When you feel yourself about to chuckle at a wee person's heartbreak, listen harder. This youngster is holding the concerns of his life in his hands and bringing them to you. You are being entrusted with this child's life. This is a gift and an honor. Listen through the words, through the details, to the child. What a sweetheart this little guy must be if his weekend was destroyed because his teddy bear fell in the mud! Sympathize. Question. Is that yellow bear a particularly special companion? What did this youngster do to solve the problem? Is the bear okay now?

I won't forget the day a nine-year-old girl told her classmates about bringing a friend home from school and proudly taking her friend up the stairs to her bedroom. The girls were going to organize a giant wedding for dolls. When the child opened her bedroom door she found, to her horror, that all her dolls and teddy bears were hanging from nooses. (Her brother had thought this trick would be funny.)

What I remember about that little girl's story is the horrified gasp that I heard from the teacher and then, in turn, from all the kids in that classroom. That teacher mentored the class in gasping, in listening with such an open heart that she was right there in the doorway, looking at all those dolls dangling from nooses. That gasp told me so much. Children will write for teachers who gasp and wince at the hard places, who laugh aloud at the funny places, who rejoice at the small childlike triumphs—like a teddy bear whose fur is back to normal now.

The best way to create a school full of people who listen is for you, as the principal, to be someone who listens. You'll find that sometimes teachers bring you work that they want to dismiss, and it will seem to you that the teacher is brushing aside not only the writing but the writer. When this happens, prepare yourself. Say to yourself even before you bring your eyes to the page, "I will be blown away by this child's work." A great teacher of writing once described her teaching by saying, "There is never a time when I pull my chair alongside a child and a miracle doesn't happen." Read that child's work, ready to find miracles.

I remember visiting a crowded school in the Bronx and being rushed in and out of classrooms. Every teacher, it seemed, wanted me to stop by to bless the class. I was late leaving the school and didn't want to make these drive-by visits to one classroom after another. But then I noticed that after stopping in every room along the hall, the principal actually steered me past one doorway. "What about that room?" I asked, suspicious. "We don't need to go there," the principal assured me.

My suspicion grew. I turned around in my tracks and went to the bypassed room. I opened the door. What I saw were twelve children in a converted lavatory. The rooms still had the tiles and mirrors from when the room had held toilets, not desks. I looked up at the principal, and he read the question in my eyes. As I suspected, these were kids with IEPs.

Although I was very late already, I could not go without supporting those children. So I said to them, "I came because your principal was telling me you guys are authors—and I am an author, too! May I read your writing?"

> The best way to create a school full of people who listen is for you, as the principal, to be someone who listens.

Within minutes, the children had all handed me their stories, and I began reading them aloud. I held the first story in my hands. It said: "I got pizza. Then I ate pizza. I like pizza. Yum, yum."

Try this. Go back to that little story and reread it. This time, read it with reverence, as if every word is precious. Picture that pizza as you read it— with the melted cheese, oozing over the edge, the smells wafting. Read the words with all this in mind, even including a bit of drama.

You'll realize that you can read *anything* as if it is beautiful literature. Simply reading student work aloud incredibly well is a gift. That day, I read one story and then looked the writer in the eye, clasping my hand to my chest. I read the next story, letting a long silence fall after the ending, while I regrouped myself in order to carry on. All I did was to read aloud, but I read the pieces in a way that said, "I hear you." You can do the same.

Listen, too, to the words. Really listen. Take this little piece, for example. It was written by a first grader and came with a drawing of a cat and a dog, standing under a rainbow, surrounded by hearts, all in the requisite pink and blue colors. The story goes: "The dog and the cat are in love. They got married. The end."

You and I can both shrug over that little story and set it aside. But listen again. The DOG and the CAT are in love! This is what I said to the child: "Wow. This is such an important story, isn't it?" The child looked a bit startled, but I pressed on. "Most people think that dogs don't love cats, they only love dogs. But your dog is a brave dog and your cat is a brave cat. They don't worry about people who say, 'Dogs can only love dogs, and cats can only love cats!' They love whom they love. And the world you create in this story is a really important one, because you are saying we do not need only to stay with people who are just like us, we can be brave like your dog and your cat."

As you listen to children and help teachers listen to children, too, you'll want to make sure that certain children in your school have not been marginalized as writers. The teaching of writing is a *schoolwide priority*; it is your job to make sure that eventually all your teachers, including teachers of special needs kids, are included in your school's writing initiative. Teachers who are marginalized will resent the writing initiative, as well they should. Meanwhile, when teachers are marginalized, children, too, are marginalized. Hopefully, you've made a point to be sure everyone is at the table all along.

Don't Wait Before Bringing Specialists into Writing Reform

It may well be that at the start of this reform, your first goal was to make sure your "regular" classroom teachers received as much professional development as possible. That's okay—as long as you do not wait another minute before bringing anyone who has been marginalized into this initiative.

Begin by thinking about the support you have provided to teachers who work with specialized populations of children. Have you and the literacy coach and the outside staff developer reached out to your teachers of English language learners, to the teachers of children who have IEPs, to teachers of talented and gifted children, to teachers of prekindergartners, to librarians?

The next suggestion I have is this: Apologize. Tell people you were sitting at home over the weekend, thinking about the school, and you realized that you'd made an awful mistake to not bring everyone in on the writing initiative from the start. Then let them know you really need their ideas, their input, so that together you and they can figure out how to tailor the writing workshop so that it works for every child. If you tell teachers you value their input, you make it much more likely that they will listen to you and to your ambassadors. Show these teachers how the writing workshop looks, and help them get it started in their places of work, with the plan that eventually you and they can talk about ways to tweak the writing workshop so that it is tailored to their kids.

> If you tell teachers you value their input, you make it much more likely that they will listen to you and to your ambassadors.

As you do this work, you'll be aiming for your school to be a place where the motto can be "No excuses." Every child merits an education in writing. In fact, writing workshops have been especially successful for children who are, for one reason or another, sometimes marginalized. Writing gives each and every person a voice, allowing individuals to bring their ideas and passions and life story and perspective to the community. For people who have at times been silenced, writing has special power.

To best support your children with special needs, you will want to recruit specialists to participate in professional development. Before you can do this, of course, you will need to plan how that professional development will proceed and to think, also, about ways in which you and others will tailor your messages to those you will now be teaching.

First, it goes without saying that you cannot lump all the teachers of children with special needs together anymore than you can lump the children themselves together. There are gigantic differences in the sort of help you will ideally provide to teachers of English language learners and to teachers of children with IEPs. But the formats for the help you provide each subgroup may be similar.

Ways to Support Your Specialized Teacher

✦ Ask your coach or your outside staff developer to provide a series of workshops for the separate groups of specialized teachers. If your experts (the coach, the classroom teacher) do not feel as if they have specialized expertise on how to tailor the writing workshop for a particular population, encourage that person to say to teachers, "I am going to teach you about the writing workshop *in general*, and then, later we can work together to get this started with the kids you serve and to invent ways to tailor this to the needs of your specific kids." Pool people's various talents to meet every child's needs.

✦ Encourage your coach, staff developer, or lead teachers to provide specialists with the same sort of professional development that other teachers have received. This means selecting a classroom for the lab site room, bringing a group of professionals together with a group of children. The teachers will probably want to select the classroom—as long as the room does not rotate, the choice of one room or another is not an especially significant one.

✦ Ask a specialist or a group of specialists and the coach to work together in a classroom or in several classrooms (say, of teachers of English language learners). It may be that the coach and the specialist work as twosomes (or triads if there is more than one specialist), moving in and out of several writing workshops while the coach points things out quietly to the specialist.

In any case, think of this work as an entrance ramp onto the ongoing highway of professional development. Once you have given the specialist some specific help, she should join an existing cohort of teachers, receiving professional development alongside everyone else.

Keep in Mind General Principles for Supporting Struggling Writers

As you and others work to include your specialists in writing professional development, keep in mind a few guiding principles for supporting struggling writers. First, strugglers are not all the same. When learners are successful, that means to some degree they "have it all together." Successful learners, then, sometimes tend to resemble each other. Struggling learners, however, do not have it all together. Strugglers do not all struggle in the same way or for the same reasons. This means that it is really important for teachers to assess their strugglers so they understand what strugglers can do and what they cannot do. It goes without saying that because all strugglers are not the same, all strugglers cannot be taught in the same ways. So it is important for teachers to develop plans tailored to particular children.

Also, everyone needs opportunities to engage in work in which they feel successful. This means teachers need to find ways to be sure that every writer has an opportunity to succeed at writing. One way to do this is to discover what a child knows, and then to attach writing to that knowledge. If a child knows rap music, then among other things, that child should write rap songs! If a child knows fish, then that child can write the guidebook to caring for the school's fish tank.

Common Ways Writers Struggle and Ways to Support Them

✦ Some writers' developmental levels match those of younger children. Although we tend to describe the teaching of writing by talking about how teachers might work with children at a *specific* grade level, in fact, what we mean is at a particular time in their development as writers. If they happen to be at a point in their development as writers where younger children tend to be, then they can benefit from the sorts of instruction others at that level receive, regardless of grade level. If a fifth grade child is a beginning writer, whatever the reason for that might be, that child will benefit from using methods that are appropriate for her level of writing proficiency. This means that some fifth graders should be writing in the booklets that one generally expects to see in a second grade.

It also means that fifth graders who are beginning writers can still write up a storm, as second grade writers are apt to do, producing volumes of stories! Sometimes, teachers don't raise an eyebrow when a struggling fifth grader (who writes more like a second grader) produces almost nothing during writing time. "He's just a beginning writer," the teacher may say, by way of an explanation. That teacher needs to visit a second grade classroom and to realize that beginning writers don't become better by sitting over the blank page day after day. They become better by writing a lot and doing so in ways that match their skill level.

✦ Some writers struggle to come up with a topic. These strugglers benefit from idea-generating strategies. They might say, "I don't know what to write about." Teachers can spot these struggling writers because they often sit with a blank page in their writer's notebook and get little accomplished. The teacher who observes this and identifies such a child would want to confer with the child at the start of writing workshop. He could draw on a teaching chart, "Strategies to Generate Entries" from

Units of Study and guide the child through one of the strategies from that chart. If, for example, the child spends a lot of time with his grandmother, the teacher can situate the strategy of "Think about a person who matters to you, then list clear small moments you remember with him or her" with that knowledge. The teacher might say, "I know that you spend a lot of time with your grandma. Let's think of different times with your grandma." Teachers need to give children the feeling that they are brimming with topics. We need to show them that they don't just have one topic, but in fact three and maybe even four or five.

✦ Other writers struggle because they need extra support understanding the minilessons. Often these children require additional time and practice with the teaching point and the strategy in it. The teacher might start by gathering a small group of students who fit in this category and coaching them through using the strategy. On other days, these struggling writers will benefit from being paired with partners that are at a somewhat higher ability. In these instances, the children checks in with each other, retelling the lesson to each other in "kid language."

✦ Other writers struggle because of limited knowledge of the conventions of writing. Especially in the upper grades, when students become aware that they are "weak" writers they are less willing to write for fear of embarrassment. A teacher can gather these students together and provide additional instruction in one area of conventions or another—capital letters or end marks, for example. Teachers should reassure these writers that writing is never perfect and encourage them to write the best they can. Partners can help each other with mechanics as well.

✦ Writers might struggle if they haven't developed the stamina to write for long-ish blocks of time. This kind of writer benefits from having several kinds of quick check-ins. Ask the child to set a volume-of-writing goal. Make sure the goal is one the child can attain within a reasonable amount of time. Compliment the child when he is successful, and then move forward to the next step—aiming for a bit more writing in a bit more time.

For more support in this area, you and your coach and teachers could refer to Colleen Cruz's book in the Workshop Help Desk series entitled *A Quick Guide to Reaching Struggling Writers.*

Support English Language Learners (ELLs)

When teachers ask, "How can instruction be tailored to support ELLs?" you need not rattle off a hundred answers. Instead, ask the teacher to join you researching that question. As part of this, you and the teacher will want to think about ways to give ELLs access in the context of minilessons. Teachers may need to modify minilessons for their ELL students. For example, teachers might imbed gestures within their minilessons. A teacher might say, "You want to choose a seed idea that is small," squeezing her two fingers together, "not a big large watermelon topic," lifting her arms and making a big circle. Or she may show children what zooming in is by closing her fingers around her eyes, imitating binoculars.

When you visit classrooms, then, be sure to not only look at these children's folders and notebooks, though this is very important, but to also make sure that instruction is tailored to student needs. As you coach teachers who work with ELLs, be sure that they are differentiating their instruction in many different ways based on the different needs of children who do not speak English. Some children are literate in their first language, others are not. If a teacher knows that a child is literate in his first language, the teacher will want to encourage the child to write in his first language as well as in English. You may protest. Perhaps neither you nor the teacher can speak or read the child's first language. This is irrelevant. If those of you who are native speakers of English and I were to live in a nation where people did not speak English, even if we needed to spend six hours a day in a place which did not allow English and even if no one could read what we wrote in English, we would still want to read and write in our first language—and so, too, should children.

Support Children with Special Needs

In classrooms with two teachers, one a licensed general education teacher and one a licensed special education teacher, both teachers should be part of the same staff development.

In self-contained special education classes, that is to say, classrooms in which every child has an IEP, often the pace of the curriculum is altered. The amount of writing time that children are able to sustain is often less than that of students in general education classes. If your teachers are using the *Units of Study* books, each session can be tailored into three sessions spread out over the course of three days. Any teaching points within the sessions that are supplemental can be edited out for clarity's sake. That teaching can be saved for another minilesson.

It is helpful for teachers of students with special needs, especially those in the upper grades, to have the K–2 *Units of Study* books in addition to the grades 3–5 set of books. Upper grade teachers will often need to adapt many of the suggestions from the primary books to suit the needs of their students. That is, some of their students might do best not working in a writer's notebook, but instead having the same paper choice options that children in primary classrooms have. It can help them to focus first on their drawing before they write their story.

Often in classrooms that have two teachers (one a general education teacher and one a special education teacher), one teacher leads the minilesson while the other teacher positions herself where students might need the most support and coaches those students. The two teachers most often rotate this role. Alternatively, if both teachers teach the minilesson, they can each model different strategies appropriate for different writers. If, for example, the minilesson is about ways to add dialogue to writing, the teachers can model different ways to do that with varying levels of sophistication—adding speech bubbles, using quotation marks, using paragraph indents, and so on.

When only one teacher is teaching the minilesson, the other teacher can research individual children to figure out what they are learning from the minilesson and how to support them learning even more.

CHECK IN ON CHILDREN'S WRITING PROGRESS

As you have been doing all along, you will need to continue your classroom visits. Here are some general patterns and stages to look for with children at each grade level.

December in Kindergarten: What to Expect

The Heinemann *Units of Study for Primary Writing* are geared towards grades K–2, which is a big range. There will be times when teachers tell you, "The units seem too hard for my kids," and there will be times when they tell you, "The units seem too easy for my kids." If your kindergarten teachers tell you that November seems too hard for their kids, they may be right. Certainly this will be the case if most of the children didn't enter kindergarten already knowing quite a few alphabet letters and their corresponding sounds. The third unit in the Heinemann series is designed to help children make sure that they and others can read their writing. This is a perfect unit for children who are ready to write a bit more conventionally, but many kindergartners will not be ready for this unit for another month or two. This means that in November and/or December, kindergarten teachers will be called on to design their own units of study.

Many teachers will take to this effort with enthusiasm. It is, after all, a lot of fun to design curriculum. But other teachers will use this as an excuse to let writing workshops grind to a halt in those classrooms. You won't want to let this happen.

If nothing else, encourage kindergarten teachers to reteach the October unit of study on small moment stories, only this time they should try to make sure that as many kids as possible have graduated from simply labeling items in their pictures to writing sentences underneath these pictures, a bit like the first grade children will have done in the preceding month. Teachers could even name this unit, "Writing Stories Like First Graders," and the title alone will make this a surefire hit. Your kindergarten teachers can visit first grades to get a sense for how the unit unfurled at that level. In fact, kindergarten children, too, could visit the first grades! Imagine teachers saying to the kindergartners, "Do you guys think you are ready to write stories like these children did?" The answer will be a resounding yes whether or not the little ones truly *are* ready.

> Help your people to be resourceful and tenaciously committed to continuing to teach writing even when the going gets tough.

This solution—suggesting kindergarten teachers reteach the October unit, this time trying to ratchet kids' writing up a level so it more closely resembles the work of first graders—is just one possible solution to the problem kindergarten teachers will face. I hope that you infer larger principles from this example. That is, when teachers run into a closed door, remind them that there's got to be a window! When you feel as if teachers don't have the knowledge needed to move forward, try to imagine who on your staff could be called on to help. Help your people to be resourceful and tenaciously committed to continuing to teach writing even when the going gets tough.

In general, this will be a month for great growth for kindergartners. Their stories should be increasingly sequential, detailed, sensible, and readable. Youngsters should be able to read their own stories, pointing under the words. Most of the words for many of the children should be readable—not correct, but readable.

There will be some children, however, who are not close to writing in ways that they and you can read. These children need one-to-one attention *now*, not later. If a knowledgeable person intervenes now, these children will not fall behind, but if these children do not receive intensive help now, they will very likely end up struggling as readers. Marie Clay, the great New Zealander who founded Reading Recovery, the intervention program for first graders, has done extensive research to suggest that one of the greatest indicators of future success or struggle in reading is a child's early abilities in writing.

December in First Grade: What to Expect

If your first graders are involved in the unit of study *Writing for Readers*, this means they're continuing to write lots and lots of small moment stories, only their focus now is to make their stories more readable. That is, they are using more high-frequency words from the word wall, they are taking time to stretch words out and record as many sounds as they hear, they are using white space between words, and they are drawing on a knowledge of lower and upper case letters and of punctuation.

When you are in these classrooms, be sure to try your hand at reading children's stories. Young writers will watch, hoping you will actually read their writing. Don't hesitate to let children see you struggle when in fact you do struggle, but if a child has written in a way that is readable (though not yet correct), don't overexaggerate your struggles.

> When you are in these classrooms, be sure to try your hand at reading children's stories. Young writers will watch, hoping you will actually read their writing.

Earlier in the year, if you couldn't read a child's story, you might have either looked for an adult translation, perhaps scrawled in cursive in an inconspicuous spot, or you might have pretended that you could read the story and said, "What a story! Will you read it to me?" If the child clearly was inventing rather than reading the story, earlier in the year you will have gone along with the role-play, the approximation. But this unit is all about letting the cat out of the bag. It's about letting kids in on the fact that sometimes a reader just can't make out what the writer is saying, try as the reader may. The point is not to dispirit the child, but instead to nudge the child to supply enough information so that readers can, in fact, read the text.

So struggle away, doing everything you can to read the story, and if you can't read it, show the child how upset you are. You would so love to know the content of this text! Maybe next time the writer will listen extra carefully to the sounds in words and put a lot of sounds down on the page.

The other thing to remember if you visit during this month is that sometimes children's fixation on writing in ways that people can read their writing will lead production to ebb. Children should still be writing approximately one story a day; if you see children spending days and days on one measly page of a story, up the ante.

December in Second Grade: What to Expect

Look at the stories that your first graders are writing, and look at the stories your third graders are writing. Then make sure that the narratives your second grade writers are producing feel halfway in between. Your second grade teachers will presumably be relying on *Units of Study for Primary Writing*, K–2, which were really written with kindergarten and first grade children in mind. They are appropriate for second graders who haven't yet had an introduction to writing, but in general your second grade teachers will need to ratchet up the expectations just a bit. In the book for coaches, I have included lots of help for teachers of second grade writers. As part of that help, I suggest that second grade teachers may want to alter their curricular calendars somewhat, and I suggest ways for doing so.

> In general your second grade teachers will need to ratchet up the expectations just a bit.

All of this means it is challenging for me to predict the writing work that will be taking place in your second grades. But in general, my sense is that children will be writing either personal narratives or fiction. Either way, children will write in a sequence of five to eight pages, each containing space for at least four or five sentences. You should expect that most of your second graders have a repertoire of perhaps seventy-five to one hundred high-frequency words that they spell correctly—words such as *said* and *then*. Expect that they write in lower case letters unless there is a reason to capitalize (they will not always have this right, but second graders should be well past the stage of writing Bs and Ds as capitals in order to distinguish one from the next.

At this point you should be able to read your second graders' stories with ease. These stories will contain many multisyllabic words. While there will still be words that are spelled in children's best approximations, many of the vowel patterns that children are using will be ones that they have learned. These attempts mean that children will come close to conventional spellings in many cases. In addition, your second graders should write with fluency. As a result, their stories may ramble a bit, but this is better than the alternative—stilted and underdeveloped pieces.

Second graders' knowledge of punctuation is also expanding. Expect that children will use periods effortlessly, as well as question and explanation marks. Some children might even attempt commas, although their choices will often be a best "guesstimate." When children are gesturing towards doing this, celebrate their awareness. It matters less that a child at this stage is using the punctuation correctly and more that he has made a deliberate attempt to do so.

Second graders are now more inclined to think of their audience. They have attended several author celebrations and received enough feedback to be able to anticipate their readers' responses *prior* to a celebration. This means that during writing, students ask themselves questions with the reader in mind, "Will my reader understand this part? Will my reader laugh here? Will my reader see that I was sad here?"

December in Third, Fourth, and Fifth Grade: What to Expect

The third unit in Heinemann's upper grade *Units of Study* series is on writing essays. This is a challenging unit and an important one. Your literacy coach could share with you the chapter I wrote helping people coach into the unit. In this small section of this chapter, I will give you just the broadest overview of this unit.

Although children will be writing essays, you may not at first identify the writing as such because it will likely be centered on personal topics. One child, for example, may write an essay around this thesis: "It is hard being an only child because parents put too much pressure on you, you have no one with whom you can share things, and because you are always the first child and therefore the guinea pig." Another might write, "Soccer teaches me sportsmanship. It teaches me to win gracefully, to lose cheerfully, and to care for my team." The rationale for essays centered on personal topics is this: It is easier for children to learn the structure and voice of an essay if they are not also juggling demands of an unfamiliar topic. The structure of the essays they write, however, will not be very different from the essays they are expected to write on the SAT exam. My son, for example, wrote, "The Louisiana Purchase was an important decision for economic, political, and social reasons."

This unit, like any unit, will have its own ebb and flow. I imagine that children will spend the first week learning to grow provocative ideas in their writers' notebooks. I hope the entries they write during that week are not boxed up in little essay formats. I'd look at them to help teachers and students value insight, precise language, new thinking, elaboration and, as always, volume. It is not easy to write long when one needs to carry a cargo of ideas in one's writing, and so typically at the start of this unit you will see that students' entries are shorter than they were earlier in the year. Therefore, we hope, students will write several in a day. Certainly the overall volume of writing should not be going down, even though the length of any one entry will decrease.

After approximately four or five days of gathering entries in writers' notebooks, children will spend a day working on what we describe as "boxes and bullets." This is a very fundamental idea—and it is challenging even to many educators. When outlining for an essay, it is important to think structurally. A writer takes a topic—for now, say, teaching writing is challenging. Then the writer needs to think of categories to elaborate on that don't overlap. The categories should also be comprehensive—covering the whole of the topic.

I would not explain this concept to children in this way. You can watch and see how the teachers teach children to think structurally. But you meanwhile may want to think about ways you can take the concept of "boxes and bullets" into schoolwide work. For example, if you need to write a letter to parents, you could try using boxes and bullets. You might write, "Dear Families. December is a month for celebrations. We have been celebrating literacy, math, and the arts." Then you could elaborate about first one, then the next, and then the third category.

Once children have written their thesis statements using boxes and bullets, they'll start writing out of notebooks. Just as many of us use index cards for recording research so that we can categorize and sequence those cards, so, too, will children gather evidence for each of their subordinate claims using separate sheets of paper which they'll file in folders. One folder might be titled: "Soccer teaches me sportsmanship because it teaches me how to win," and another might be titled, "Soccer teaches me sportsmanship because it teaches me how to lose." On any given day, a student might write an angled anecdote to illustrate two or three claims (that is, two or three topic sentences). This, again, is a time when children's level of writing productivity can slip—one tiny anecdote illustrating a time when the child learned sportsmanship by learning to lose won't be work enough for the entire day's writing workshop!

> Children will spend a day working on what we describe as "boxes and bullets." This is a very fundamental idea— and it is challenging even to many educators.

Children collect material in their folders for a few days and then tape bits of paper together to construct a first draft. The process is overly elaborate, and there are ways teachers may decide to streamline it. I am still convinced, however, that the manipulative nature of this helps youngsters come to understand the structural thinking that is essential in expository writing.

If teachers find this unit of study difficult, don't be surprised. Cheer them on. It is important. The upcoming unit on fiction will be enthralling for kids, so remind them that we all have that to look forward to.

DVD

Principal to
Principal

"Gathering Data and Assessing." Principals focus on student learning and progress.

CHAPTER NINE

JANUARY/ FEBRUARY
ENGAGING WITH TEACHERS

E ven as a child, I always loved the end of one year and the start of another. I loved cleaning out my old folders of schoolwork, beginning with clean new folders. I loved organizing my desk, sharpening my pencils, purchasing new school supplies. Above all, I loved the chance to look backwards and to look forwards.

As a principal, you'll want to embrace any occasion you can find to help your school look backwards and look forwards. January, then, will give you a chance to reconvene your people and to once again step up to the job of being the inspirational leader for your community. Perhaps you'll write a New Year's letter to your teachers, or you'll host a back-to-school party at the end of the first day, or you'll open your first faculty meeting of the new year by talking about your resolutions for the school.

For some of you, the temptation could be great to use this occasion to embrace new topics, new innovations, new directions for the school. I strongly urge you, instead, to remember that teaching writing well is an infinitely complex undertaking and, moreover, that if writing is going to help your school become a learning community, you need to help your teachers reach towards deeper levels of learning. All too often in our schools, people learn a tiny bit about a topic—say, the teaching of writing— and then declare themselves to be finished. "I do the program," teachers tell me. "I know how to teach writing," they explain. "I took the course. I've been inserviced." I am reminded of the Pulitzer Prize winning writer, Don Murray, who once said that if you know how to teach writing, watch out. If you know how to confer with young writers, watch out. If you understand the qualities of good writing, watch out. If you find it easy to make reading-writing

THESE MONTHS

- Invite teachers to put problems on the table for discussion.

- Support teachers in overcoming predictable problems.

- Help teachers develop and share personal expertise.

connections, watch out. Watch out lest you suffer hardening of the ideologies. Watch out lest you lose the pioneer spirit that has made this field a great one.

Murray's counsel is especially important for teachers, because in our schools, the most at-risk learners are teachers themselves. Teachers are apt to take their first versions, their earliest efforts, and enshrine those early efforts, saying, "I'm done." Don't we all do this in one way or another? How crucial it is, then, that you, the school principal, not support these tendencies by pronouncing your teachers to be experts on the teaching of writing! To the contrary, you will want to do everything possible to help your teachers see themselves as beginners on a very long journey. Help them look ahead with excitement to all the incredible learning that lies in store around the next bend. For, as Michael Fullan has often pointed out, the reason schools rarely change is not that there are no innovations in school, nor is the reason even that teachers are resistant to innovation. Fullan writes, "It is, instead, the presence of too many innovations, so people never have a chance to go from mandates towards personal beliefs" (Teachers College, 1/24/07).

In the months ahead, you'll want to be sure that you support your teachers' learning curves in the teaching of writing. You'll need to do so in ways that enable teachers to take more personal ownership for the innovations in writing and to become more invested in the teaching of writing. You need to do this work, realizing that you will be asking your teachers to do what teachers rarely do—to go beyond the first rush of implementation reforms and to become invested in deepening, refining, and revising their own teaching. Borrowing the words of Jim Collins, you will be asking your teachers to go from *Good to Great*. For the next few months (and really for the next few decades), your work will be to encourage teachers to name and overcome challenges. You will cultivate leadership amongst your teachers, and support them in overcoming predictable problems they encounter.

INVITE TEACHERS TO PUT PROBLEMS ON THE TABLE FOR DISCUSSION

On the final day of our July and our August writing institutes, I always give the closing speech. I think of these closings as benedictions, and I work hard to make the last words I say be as helpful as possible. Every year, my closing is different, but no matter how I organize my talk, I always include one message: "You are going to go back to your home schools. You'll reread your notes, you'll recall everything you have learned, and then you'll get started.

You'll launch a writing workshop. You'll send the kids off to write, and then you'll head out to see what kids have done. I can promise you one thing. It is this: Your methods won't work. And that is the truth. It is inevitable that there will be problems. Kids will tell you they have revised, but you'll look more closely and see that draft one, draft two, and draft three are practically the same, save for some added punctuation in one draft, some corrected spellings in another. You'll pull close to one child, intending to hold a lovely, intimate conference, and you'll look up to find that nine other kids have lined up beside you for help. You'll no sooner send kids off to work than it will be like popcorn, as child after child springs out of her seat, saying, 'I'm done.'"

> We all set out intending to climb every mountain, ford every stream, follow every rainbow, until we find our dreams . . . . [W]hat happens next is this: We encounter problems.

In those final closing speeches, I always tell teachers (and these are people who have just devoted their summer to perfecting methods of teaching writing), "Not only can I promise you that when you teach writing, you will encounter problems, I can also promise you that the success or failure of your teaching will depend on how you respond to those problems." This is not only true in teaching writing; it is also true in life. In life, all of us have motivations; all of us have big plans, tall dreams. And we all set out intending to climb every mountain, ford every stream, follow every rainbow, until we find our dreams. Then in life, as in any story, what happens next is this: We encounter problems.

In stories, when the character encounters difficulty, the character doesn't say, "Ah, heck, I don't want that goal anyhow." The story doesn't come to the part where it goes, "But then, one day . . ." and then, lo and behold, the character bales out, and the story is over. No way! When the character encounters difficulty, this is the time for rising action. This is when the story really begins, the tension mounts. This is when the character reaches inside himself and finds resources he didn't even know were there. This is when the little train, trying to take a load of toys over the mountain, starts huffing and puffing, saying "I think I can, I think I can . . ." This is the time when a little girl who has found a wondrous world at the back of a wardrobe continues to seek it out even though her sister and brothers don't believe it exists.

In writing workshops, too, your teachers will start off with the best of intentions. Your teachers will have big dreams. They'll gather kids for minilessons, and they'll send them off to write. And as your teachers move from desk to desk, child to child, the one thing I can promise you is this: There will be problems.

Some kids won't write with punctuation. Some will ramble on for pages and pages and pages. Some will resist writing. Some kids' writing will get worse and worse. If you and your teachers say, "I knew it. This approach to teaching writing doesn't work," and regard problems as evidence that the school should forgo this approach, then I wonder if any approach to teaching will ever really work in your environment. Teaching (like writing) must involve a cycle of doing one's best work, and then pulling back to ask, "What's good here that I can build on?" and "What's not so good here that I can tweak or refine?" The really crucial thing is that you and your teachers come to a place where you regard problems as invitations to invent, to problem solve, to find resources in yourselves and in each other that you never knew were there. Problems can galvanize your entire community to outgrow itself through resolute, resourceful, tenacious work.

> Problems can galvanize your entire community to outgrow itself through resolute, resourceful, tenacious work.

Before teachers across the school can feel as if they own this approach to teaching writing, you and the literacy coach need to invite teachers to identify specific problems they've encountered. Teachers will only own this approach if they can draw on their own lifetimes of knowledge in order to invent responses to the problems they identify. First, though, you need to decide whether the time for this work is, in fact, January. That is, you will probably feel that you can only say to teachers, "Let's talk about issues we have with this method of teaching writing" when your school is at a point where teachers have found enough that is good in the writing workshop approach that they won't take your words as an invitation to throw the baby out with the bathwater.

You may feel that in your school, or in some grade levels within your school, you need to keep a lid on the Pandora's box of discontent—or that discontent could get out of hand. If the writing workshop approach to teaching writing hasn't yet won over enough supporters and achieved enough success for you and the coach to risk saying to teachers, "Let's talk about some of the little ways in which these methods of teaching writing may be running into trouble. Let's also think about adaptations we can make for our specific kids," then your instincts might be right. But chances are good that by this time, teachers in your school will have seen dramatic improvements in student writing, and they'll have found that the writing workshop is a viable (though imperfect) method of teaching. If your teachers are feeling this, then by all means, make January into a time for putting problems out on the table, for addressing them in the public square. Over and over in my life, I have found that it is far more healthy to take the whispered innuendos, the unspoken worries, and bring these to the light of day.

After spending a few months trying to adopt an approach to teaching writing, some of your teachers will be chafing in the harness. Some of them will feel as if certain aspects of the writing workshop are not entirely working for them. And they will probably be right. You'd be wise to let teachers voice these questions.

Granted, some teachers will question things that I regard as holy, as essential, and this is probably true for you as well. I always worry when I say, "What would you change in our approach to teaching writing?" because it is inevitable that someone will want to return to a regimen of linking all the writing that kids do to responses to literature, or to the standardized test, or to something else that would make me cringe. Usually, however, if a couple of teachers suggest revising the approach to writing in a way that you believe is counterproductive, the good news is that others probably will share your belief, and in the discussion that ensues, your whole community will listen to that concern and respond in ways that don't compromise the teaching.

You may want to say something like, "Can we take some time to list the aspects of the writing workshop that seem to be working really well, and then can we also list aspects of the workshop that aren't working as well?" When teachers voice concerns, you listen, you respect them. The concerns that teachers articulate do not need to lead instantly to revisions in curriculum. Instead, they can lead to inquiry. So listen, and find concerns that seem to you to be generative enough that you can say things like the following:

- That strikes me as a really important question, not just for you but for many of us. Do you all agree?
- Have other people found this to be a problem?
- Should we research this further as a staff and see what we can invent in response?
- Would you be willing to be part of a study group on this?
- What do you suspect is the underlying issue here?

In responding in these ways, you will not only bring problems to the light of day, you will also help teachers see that problems are not reasons to abandon a direction, but are, instead, invitations to become students of our own teaching. Problems can lead us to dig deeper, to reach farther, to adapt, invent, and tweak. They can lead us to link arms together, relying on each other. They can lead us to become thinkers, inventers, teacher-researchers, intellectuals. This is the stance towards teaching that can provide a school with a learning life that is unstoppable, and the first step is for problems to be seen as invitations to learn.

Support Teachers in Overcoming Predictable Problems

Because I'm fortunate enough to work alongside a lot of communities of teacher-researchers, I can pass along to you some of the problems other teachers have encountered at this time of the year and some of the solutions they are exploring. However, please resist the temptation to function as the sage from on high, naming these problems and delivering these solutions. That does not empower your teachers. It will only discourage them! Instead, trail the teacher as he moves among kids, and jot down notes or engage in conversations as you proceed. Notice challenges that are derailing kids, including some I may describe to you (but notice them as they occur embedded in your teachers' classrooms). Then recruit teachers to work together to fashion responses to those problems. Join in this work. Try saying, "I wonder if . . ." and suggesting some of the solutions others are trying. Or you could say, "In Calkins' book, she said others were having this same problem. She shared a few tentative responses, but she isn't sure herself how to proceed. I'll convey some of her ideas, but then let's see if we can come up with others . . ."

Address General Midwinter Problems

It is not hard to imagine predictable problems that teachers are apt to identify, and it may help you to have thought about possible ways to begin responding to those problems, turning what can feel like gripes into invitations to study more deeply and to become more self-reliant. These are some of the issues teachers are apt to identify and some of my thoughts about them:

"I'm not getting around to every child."
Some teachers will feel they are not getting around quickly enough to children, and they'll worry that many kids, therefore, aren't getting the help they need as writers. This will definitely be the case, so it's a good sign that teachers recognize the issue. You and the literacy coach could do some research, identifying which teachers *do* seem to travel more quickly through their classroom (without compromising the quality of their interactions), and you could suggest that other teachers observe this group, making an inquiry to

figure out what these teachers are doing. You could also suggest that teachers spend more time leading small groups; that they do briefer, more informal small-group work; and that they get to this work more often. Then, too, conferences and small groups, both, will be more efficient if teachers spend a bit of time looking over student work outside of the classroom. They might jot down names of four to five children who need one kind of instruction and four to five children who need another kind of instruction, and then use these notes to help them cut to the chase sometimes in their interactions with kids.

"I need a couple of months for each unit."
Some teachers will tell you that everything takes a huge amount of time and that they can't begin to move kids through a unit of study in a mere month. They'll say each unit of study really requires two months. I resist this and would love to help you do so as well, while also helping you to be responsive to your teachers' concerns.

If teachers voice this worry, tell them that you and the coach need a bit of time to gather some data. Then visit classrooms and look through collections of student work, trying to piece together how often teachers have actually had writing time. That is, are they actually teaching writing at least four days a week? Then gather data about how much time for writing there tends to be in a classroom during one day's writing workshop. To do this, watch a child writing—actually moving his pen down the paper—and note how much the child writes in ten minutes. If the child has written half a page of lined notebook paper in ten minutes, and he tends to produce just about that much each day of the writing workshop, then you have the data you need: that child is actually writing only ten minutes a day. Collect similar data on another randomly chosen child or two.

My sense is that when you do this work, you will see that the units are taking teachers a very long time because children are not actually getting time to write and are, therefore, not producing a volume of writing. Tackle that topic first, by helping teachers and kids join together in a schoolwide research project through which kids across the entire school (or grade, or classroom) chart the number of pages written, the genre of writing, and so forth. As you do this, expect that other issues will come up. One might be the length of time that is required for a minilesson, a midworkshop share, and a teaching share. That is, whole-group work may be devouring writing time. If that is the case, encourage teachers to streamline and to develop ways to make their transitions briefer and their pace quicker.

"The published minilessons eat up time for writing."

Some third to fifth grade teachers will tell you that they are relying on the minilessons in the *Units of Study* books, and they find that each minilesson consumes 12–15 minutes. Celebrate the fact that your teachers feel this is a concern and help them see how easy it is to adapt a minilesson. Sometimes in the *Units of Study* minilessons, I include a long prelude before the teaching point; a teacher can decide whether the prelude will work with this particular class of children. Often I include two examples; one will suffice for this year, the other saved for the next year. Usually I add tips that make the minilesson multilevel; only some of these will be pertinent. Streamlining a minilesson will not mean dividing it in half but rather weeding out the unnecessary bits.

The other thing to watch is whether teachers develop tight transitions, teach with a lively pace, avoid prolonged question-answer periods, keep turn-and-talks brief, and write on charts before or after the minilesson—all techniques that keep minilessons focused and rigorous.

"My kindergartners' writing isn't readable."

Some teachers will notice that certain children, especially kindergartners, lag behind in their knowledge of sound-letter correspondences and, therefore, are still not writing with enough proficiency that their writing is readable. That is, teachers will use student writing as a window onto their children's knowledge of phonics and will find some kids are not progressing as hoped. (This is a critically important issue; if teachers do not say this problem exists, you may want to look for it yourself.) You and your teachers can do some groundwork if you simply ask teachers to collect every child's writing on a given day, at which point you can together sort through the writing, dividing it into piles: Kids Whose Writing Is Readable and Kids Whose Writing Is Not Close to Being Readable. Kindergartners and especially first graders in the latter category will need more small-group and one-to-one help with writing, and you'll want to be sure that you rally people to provide that help within the classroom as well as perhaps outside the classroom.

These children also need a responsible education in phonics. Investigate that aspect of their education. Meanwhile, you may want to take these concerns as an opportunity to remind teachers that the K–2 *Units of Study* books address a wide span of learners. This is a good time of year to invite some of your kindergarten teachers (perhaps some from your school and some from other schools in the area) to form a task force so that together, this group develops a unit of study or two that could be taught in the autumn of the upcoming year. One or both of those units could be designed to help kindergartners progress as emergent writers. As part of this task force, teachers can also watch conference 10 on the DVD *Big Lessons from Small Writers*, in which Amanda teaches Bejida a strategy for putting stories on paper, and conference 13, in which Lucy teaches Jacob a revision strategy. It will also be helpful for teachers to watch strategy lesson 15, in which Kersandra teaches a small group of students. This will help teachers think carefully about the methods of teaching they are using in small groups and one-to-one conferences.

"I feel like my second graders have outgrown the primary
Units of Study."
Some of your second grade teachers may feel that the K–2 *Units of Study* are not rigorous enough for their kids. This is an astute observation on their part. The difference between kindergarten and second grade is just about as big as the difference between second grade and graduate school, so there is no question that teachers will need to ratchet up the K–2 units so they give second graders a run for their money. In the books we've written for coaches, *Professional Development in the Teaching of Writing*, we've provided lots of support so coaches can rally teachers to invent curriculum that is patterned after the curriculum in the *Units of Study* books but that takes second graders farther.

"My writers aren't improving."
Some upper grade teachers will worry that their strugglers are not progressing as they had hoped. I've written in Chapter 8 about struggling writers, so you are likely to be ready for these concerns already!

Address Problems That Arise During the Fiction Unit (Grades 3–5)

Before looking for problems, recognize that *Writing Fiction: Big Dreams, Tall Ambitions* presents amazing potential for moving your writing program forward. If you visit classrooms during this unit, you should notice right away that the kids are tremendously excited to finally have the chance to write fiction, and their energy is apt to be contagious. This is often teachers' favorite unit of study. If the unit is working so well, how can teachers share what they are learning? In many schools, the upper grade teachers have taught second grade teachers about this unit, and second grade teachers then try a variation of it with their kids. Similarly, upper elementary teachers can share their experiences with the unit with middle school teachers, who in turn find their kids learn in leaps and bounds from the experience of writing fiction as well. Then, too, because this unit works really well, it is a natural to suggest that teachers may want to write a second unit that stands on the shoulders of this one. Might they consider a later unit on writing historical fiction or fantasy short stories or short mysteries? Could that future unit perhaps be aligned to a parallel unit on reading within that genre?

But I'm ahead of myself. All this potential comes with its own set of challenges. If you join the teacher in working with one individual student and then another, you and the teacher are apt to find that the kids' are encountering problems, and then you can help the teacher invent responses to those problems.

"Writers create drafts too quickly."

The first big problem will arise because the kids are so excited to write fiction that as soon as the starting gun goes off, they'll have written three pages. The teacher will pull a chair alongside the first writer, and she will be on page four of a very long (and probably very awkward) story. Maybe, just maybe, the teacher will be able to convince this one individual to revise her lead, but the youngster will have written so much that the conference will be longer than most, and the chances are small that the teacher will get to very many other youngsters that day. So, one predictable problem will be that the kids will write a lot and conferences will be slower than usual. Meanwhile, writing fiction well is not something most of us can do without a fair amount of rehearsal and revision, so consequently the stories will be pretty bad.

Teachers that I know have found a couple of ways to respond to the fact that kids' drafts of fiction stories tend to be long and their conferences are, therefore, slower than usual. First, it helps to be sure kids progress through a sequence of rehearsals even before they get started writing a single draft. Many teachers emphasize the importance of rehearsal and help kids realize that during rehearsal, they need to progress through many different plans for a story. Some teachers do this by having kids make a sequence of story mountains, using those story mountains as scaffolds for oral stories. (Story mountains are rather like timelines, outlining the sequence of a narrative.) This leads to another problem, which I'll discuss in a bit.

Teachers also find that they need to strongly support revision. That is, if children will only revise after a teacher spends ten minutes in a one-to-one conference, it is no big surprise that few kids end up revising. The fact that kids' have a lot of energy for this unit means that teachers can get away with teaching kids that after a writer gets started writing a fiction story, the writer pulls in the reins on himself, saying, "Whoa!" Then the writer rereads, rethinks, rehearses again, and starts a second version of the same story. Notice that the revision in this instance is not the sort that a writer pokes between lines or paragraphs. This revision, rather, requires an entirely new draft. And notice, too, that it is done after a writer has gotten a good start on a draft, written perhaps a page or two or three. Writers don't, however, tend to write the entire story, start to finish, before revising.

"The story mountain is challenging."
Your teachers and students might struggle with the concept of a story mountain as a planning tool for writing fiction. If that is the case, you may want to encourage teachers to ask, "What's the essential part of the concept of using a story mountain to write fiction, and what is not so essential?"

Earlier I mentioned that teachers will probably want children to progress through a sequence of story versions even before they write a single draft, and teachers may encourage children to draft several story mountains. You and your teachers may find that the whole idea of a story mountain is a bit complicated for kids. The youngsters can grasp that the story cannot be just a single event: A boy wins an award. The youngsters can grasp that they need to decide if "A boy wins an award" will be the *start* of the story—as it would be, for example, in a story that begins with the boy winning an award and then goes on to show how the boy's sister struggles with feeling lost in the shadow of her brother. Alternatively, the boy winning the award could be the cumulating event at the *end* of the story. Writers can grasp that a story needs to involve a small series of micro-events, perhaps taking place within two 15–20 minute scenes, and they can grasp that a writer needs to consider various story plans, but for many students it is tricky to figure out what goes where on a story mountain. What, for example, goes on the peak of the mountain?

> You may want to encourage teachers to ask, "What's the essential part of the concept of using a story mountain to write fiction, and what is not so essential?"

In the end, your teachers may decide that the essential thing to teach is simply that writers plan stories that each contain a beginning, middle, and end to a story. Or your teachers may decide to borrow a strategy many K–2 teachers use and suggest kids fold a piece of paper into a little booklet, and then very quickly sketch what happens first in the story (this goes on page 1,) what happens next (page 2), and so forth. Lots of upper grade classrooms have found that if children sketch rather than write the plans for their stories, and then touch each page and say aloud the exact words they might write on that page, this sort of rehearsal is more flexible and more appealing for kids than the process of creating a whole array of different story mountain drafts.

Address Problems That Arise During the Nonfiction Unit (Grades K–2)

In midwinter, while your upper grade classes are studying fiction, your primary classrooms will be using the *Nonfiction Writing* unit (or this will be on their horizon). Your teachers will no doubt encounter challenges that are unique to them, but chances are good that they'll also struggle with issues that have been challenges for hosts of other K–2 classes as well.

"My second graders are writing the same all-about books they wrote in kindergarten."

Your teachers may be unclear how they can differentiate expectations and their teaching. How will the work that kindergartners do be different from the work that second graders do in the same unit of study?

You'll want to applaud teachers who ask for help differentiating instruction and developing a spiral curriculum, one that supports students working in progressively more complex ways over time. One of your most important jobs as principal is to make sure that every member of your school maintains a steep learning curve, so you'll want to vigilantly watch for the questions teachers pose that could support substantive inquiry. This is one such question. You may, then, want to convene a study group to work together on the question "How will the K–2 *Nonfiction Writing* unit be taught differently for kindergarten, first, and second graders?"

When that study group begins considering that question, encourage them to think about development as occurring along a number of lines of growth. For example, one line of growth might be directed toward time and with time the nature of a child's writing process. Will all children ages five to seven engage in prolonged work on one significant report during this unit of study? In general, kindergartners cycle more quickly through the process of writing, often rehearsing, drafting, and revising within two days. Second graders, on the other hand, might invest a week on a single narrative. Perhaps your teachers will decide (as I'd recommend) that kindergartners write reams of little all-about books and second graders make a commitment to one area of expertise, writing just one or perhaps two books on that one topic.

Other lines of growth might include research or paper choice. Kindergartners might each write about a topic of personal expertise; second graders, in addition to relying on personal expertise, might conduct research in your school or classroom library. Then, too, the paper on which kids write can represent different levels of competency. Kindergartners might use paper that devotes large spaces to drawings; second graders might rely mostly on words, using paper that is not unlike the notebook paper on which third graders write. You'll want to encourage your teachers to look at children's writing across these grades and identify the lines of growth they want to develop.

"The children's nonfiction writing lacks voice."

This is often symptomatic of classrooms where there is an overemphasis on using texts to generate the content of children's own books. Often, children in these classes are encouraged to read and write facts simultaneously, which frequently results in children copying the information on their paper rather than composing information in a thoughtful manner. Teachers can encourage these children to rely less on the facts from the books and, instead, to think, "How can I teach others about what I know?" The goal is for children to be able to storytell their information just as they did when they told their small moment stories.

Teachers who try to jump right into all-about books on a content area topic from within the social studies or science curriculum are more likely to encounter this problem if children haven't first had the opportunity to write all-about books on a topic of their own choice. Show teachers that having students write on topics of their choice gives them a deeper understanding of the various structures of nonfiction writing, which is an important scaffold for them to have prior to moving into content area writing.

"Children are confusing nonfiction text features."

Young children are enthralled by diagrams, photographs, captions, and other text features, but if this is the first time that children are learning about these, they will not understand the terms and might confuse the purposes of each feature. Encourage teachers to incorporate these text features as they read aloud nonfiction books. "Look at this diagram of the snake," they can say, or "Isn't this an amazing photo of a baby?" A useful classroom chart that shows these text features will have each of these features delineated with an example that children can use as a reference. Mentor texts in the classroom library that contain these features can be an additional resource. If teachers draw on these resources to help children understand nonfiction text features, it won't be long before teachers hear their students say while reading, "I see a caption, " or "Look at the diagram."

Help Teachers Understand that Teaching, Like Writing, Involves Rough Drafts and Revision

You and your teachers have a choice. You can regard problems as problems, or you can regard them as opportunities. How crucial it is that the school leader encourages people to lift up the rug and find the loose ends, knots, and tangles that have been hidden there! How crucial it is that you help your entire community recognize that problems are inevitable and that our job is not to avoid them but to address them! Teaching, like writing, needs to involve time to step back and ask, "What's working that I can build upon? What's not working that I can address?"

Help teachers realize that one of the most important things they can do is to see problems, to name them, and then to gather with their colleagues to invent responses to those problems. Ideally, teachers will meet at least once or twice a week in grade-level study groups, and those group sessions can provide a time for teachers to bring problems to the table and to invent solutions. But there should be other ways for teachers to seek out help. Is there a structure in your school for teachers to ask for someone to cover their class for a few minutes so they can observe in the classroom of a colleague? When teachers encounter problems in their teaching, is there a structure that makes it likely that they'll pass this information along to someone who will then help organize an optional breakfast group on the problem? If your school is going to be a learning organization, it is incredibly important that people embrace problems and work shoulder-to-shoulder to invent responses to them.

In each of the instances cited above, the problem becomes an opportunity for investigation, for finding and learning from experts, and for teachers to lean on each other. Whatever the problems are that your teachers identify, you and the coach will want to respond with a spirit of receptivity and with a willingness to inquire. As you help your teachers tackle the problems they identify, you'll also find that you have created opportunities for teachers to play leadership roles, for every problem merits an inquiry, and those inquiries each need to be led.

Help Teachers Develop and Share
Personal Expertise

A number of years ago, I decided that it was time to research the effects of all the professional development that my colleagues and I had provided. A doctoral student interviewed teachers who had attended summer institutes, daylong conferences at the College, and classroom-based professional development, asking, "Of all the experiences you have had learning about teaching writing, which particular experience especially pushed forward your learning?" I couldn't wait to hear which of the Project's many offerings each teacher selected.

To my surprise, teacher after teacher responded by saying that they had learned the most not from one of the wonderful opportunities they'd been given to study, but instead from a time when they had taught other teachers. I remember one person, in particular, saying that the turning point in her life as a teacher was one afternoon when she led a workshop for teachers from another school. I recalled the event. A group of teachers had been scheduled to visit the school on a day when the principal wasn't on site, and a week before the visitors arrived, the principal had recruited the teacher to take the visitors (there were about six of them) on a tour of the school's writing workshops and then to meet with the group afterwards to answer questions. From my point of view, the event was no big deal, and yet that one experience propelled that teacher's learning forward more than all the carefully designed professional development opportunities our Project had ever provided for her. To think that all my colleagues' smartest, best efforts to teach that teacher amounted to a hill of beans when contrasted with the time this teacher shared what she knew about teaching writing with a handful of novices! At first, I was stunned by this. But then I remembered my own early years as a teacher and recalled the time a school in western Connecticut hired me to lead an after-school workshop on teaching writing. They probably paid me all of seventy-five dollars, and for that giant sum I needed to take a day off from teaching and to drive hours and hours over hill and dale to reach their school. Yet that one afternoon workshop transformed my sense of myself. My chest puffs at the memory of how thrilled I was to actually be called upon as an expert. It was just after I led that one after-school workshop that I bought myself a door and two file cabinets, creating a makeshift desk for myself, and began writing articles about my teaching. As they say, the rest is history.

One of my favorite quotations in the world comes from Erik Erikson, who once wrote—and I paraphrase here—human beings are constituted so as to need to teach because ideas are kept alive by being shared, truths by being professed (2004, 204). If you want to light a fire under your teachers, ensuring that they are deeply and passionately committed to teaching writing well, then you need to think about how you can create opportunities for teachers to feel that they have been called upon to play a leadership role in writing instruction in your school. There are a couple of ways you can go about creating leadership roles for teachers:

- Find and compliment teachers' areas of expertise.
- Distribute leadership among teachers.
- Support professional growth in teachers, inside and outside your school.

Find and Compliment Teachers' Areas of Expertise

Pause, right now, as you read this book. In the margin of this page, list initials representing your teachers. Beside each name, jot a word or two that represents what that teacher knows and can do especially well (make this something pertinent to the teaching of writing, if you can, for now). That is, ask yourself, "What is the area of expertise for this first person on my list? If this person were to mentor other teachers or teach an inservice course, what would be the topic?" Ask yourself, " If I were to release other teachers to watch this teacher, what would I want the others to note?" Readers, if you are drawing a blank for one teacher, try doing this for the second name on your list. If you find that you are either stumped once again or that you are writing the same vague generalizations for one teacher after another, then regard this as a wake-up call. You probably need to work harder to notice and to talk eloquently about each of your teacher's unique strengths.

If I've just made you feel as if I am scolding you, forgive me. Really, I write this section for myself, not for you. I seem to have a unique gift for being able to identify a person's weaknesses. I'm constitutionally designed in such a way that I can quickly hone in on the specific problem that underlies any teacher's teaching. And frankly, my first instinct is to do just that. But after years and years of work, I have learned that I must at least *try* to discipline myself so that I also notice and identify strengths.

Now, let me be clear. I think it is helpful that I can hone in on the next steps a person needs to take, and I think many people's tunnel vision is the opposite of mine. Many people see only strengths and cannot really imagine how a classroom could go from what it is to what it could be. But for now, I am talking to those of you who had trouble listing topics of expertise alongside your teachers' initials. I strongly recommend you try walking from one classroom to another, watching the classroom for a few minutes, and then after you leave the room, writing a note to the teacher in which you simply articulate what you believe that person's unique, special, rare gifts are as a teacher. As you do this, reach for specific, precise terms, and try to use a lot of words, not just one adjective, to capture what it is you admire. Try reaching for several ways to convey this one thing that you want to say, including using very specific examples. Think about how other teachers try to do similar things and try to name the qualities that separates this particular teacher's way of working from the norm. You might, for example, write a note like this:

> David, when I watched you working with Jerod, it struck me that you have a real gift for working with individual students. I think I've figured out the secret. Respect. You talk to your kids as if each and every one is a colleague. You seem genuinely interested in the thoughts these nine-year-olds have on their own writing processes, on what has worked and what has not worked. You ask the same research questions that others ask—"How is your writing going?" and the like. But I wonder if you realize that your kids respond to those questions utterly differently than they do for others. And I think it comes down to that one word, respect. They feel that you are learning from them, as if they are the expert on their own writing processes and you are enthralled by what they have to say. Congratulations. I'm going to listen differently because of you.

Or a note like this:

> Mary. Wow. I am exhausted from watching you teach. You are so high-energy, so keen to use every minute and every interaction to its fullest. At one point, I started counting how many teaching interactions you were engaged in, how many tips you were conveying to kids. In a five-minute period, I saw you engage in four teaching interactions! I think you accomplish far more than the average person accomplishes. Your rigor, your sense of wanting to make the best use of every minute, and your ambitiousness for your kids are astonishing. Congrats.

You need not actually visit the classrooms in order to write notes such as these. You could simply sit at your computer, take out a list of your staff, and grab a name, any name. Start an email to that person. Write, "Sandra" (or whatever the name might be). Then write, "It is Friday evening, and I've been thinking about you and want to jot a quick note thanking you for the way you . . ." You needn't have anything in mind when you begin that note and, specifically, for that last sentence. Just start writing, "I want to jot a note thanking you for the way you . . . ," and your fingers will come up with the words to finish that sentence. You'll find something to say even if you weren't at first feeling all that appreciative of Sandra. Once you have recalled a specific moment that merits thanks, ask yourself, "What does that particular instance represent about this person?" And write that. Simply continue the note, writing, "I realized, as I thought about the way you did that, that this one episode shows a lot about you. I love the way you so often . . ."

> Giving compliments to a teacher is not the same as putting that teacher in the role of expert, and you will want to go the extra step and do that.

I promise that if you (and if I) get into a habit of writing five emails like this each week—perhaps every Sunday evening—the tone of our workplaces will change. Our profession is full of people who give, give, give and who very rarely receive anything (other than a snowman coffee cup from a kid at Christmas). Those emails will become turning points in your teachers' careers.

Of course, giving compliments to a teacher is not the same as putting that teacher in the role of expert, and you will want to go the extra step and do that. Here is one low-key way to proceed. Take an issue that you think is worth highlighting for your school—say, perhaps, peer conferring. Maybe you decide that the partnership conversations (another way of saying peer conferring) in a lot of the writing workshops feel robotic and perfunctory. Ask your literacy coach, "Which classrooms do you think have strong, vital partnerships?" and then go to those rooms. Alternatively, you can identify an area of need, partnership conversations for example, and go on your own talent search. Carmen Fariña, the former Deputy Chancellor of New York City schools, called those investigations Glory Walks (in contrast to walk-throughs) because this time, you visit classrooms looking for bits of teaching to glorify. Find one classroom where you think something good is going on (in this instance, pertaining to partnership conversations). At the next faculty or grade-level meeting, or in an upcoming letter to your staff, let teachers know that you were taken by the partnership conversations you saw in that particular room. Offer to free teachers up so they can visit that classroom.

You may not want to oversell what you saw, setting people up to cut down the newest tall poppy. Instead, you might just say, "It seemed to me that something is happening in those partnership conversations that might be worth studying. I'm posting the writing schedule for that classroom, and specifically the times when those kids will be in partnership conversations. Will you try to stop by at one of those times to see what you think? Jot some notes about any ideas this sparks in you, and note, too, anything *you've* done with partnership conversations that could help our inquiry. We'll use what we observe and try to grow some new thinking on this important topic."

The important thing is that after you do this once with one topic, setting one teacher up as an expert, you must quickly identify another expert on another topic. Do this soon afterwards so you dissipate the negative reaction you are apt to get from singling out one person. Then, too, as you no doubt realize, the choice of the teachers that you will spotlight matters. I wouldn't advise that you make a fuss over the one teacher whom everyone already believes is favored, the one who is already resented by her peers. Nor would I advise putting this sort of spotlight on a novice teacher. You might, in fact, find a teacher who is especially respected by his peers, who has felt undervalued because this new initiative dimmed his halo. It could be that you are very clear about the teacher you'd like to spotlight, but you can't find anything to make a fuss over in that teacher's room. One option is for the coach (or another expert, such as the English language learners specialist) to work a bit with the teacher on a topic, with the expert setting the teacher up to be successful. Then that expert could pull back the training wheels, allowing the teacher to emerge with the expertise you applaud.

Distribute Leadership Among Teachers

There are lots of other ways to go about giving teachers leadership roles in your school. You could, for example, consider whether any of the jobs that you and other leaders are now doing could be given away in a manner that empowers others.

Leadership Jobs to Give to Others

✦ You may want to invite a few teachers to each lead a course for first-year teachers, student teachers, or paraprofessionals. Ideally, this course would be structured so that it meets regularly for at least four weeks. These adults all deserve mentoring, and this can be done in a casual fashion, or it can be done in this rigorous and planned way. If you decide to give this leadership opportunity to a teacher or two, talk up the value of such a course, so that everyone understands the importance of the work. Say, "I thought you'd be especially qualified to lead this particular course because you have such a knack for . . ." The course could involve work in classrooms as well as in a lunchtime or after-school study group. There could be several smaller courses, each on a specific topic, such as "The Art of Conferring with Young Writers," "Helping Kids Write Faster and More," or "When Writers Struggle with Spelling: What To Do, What Not To Do."

✦ You might ask a teacher to mentor a junior person, rather than to teach a course. If this is the choice, I suggest you pay the mentor to spend a whole day or two with the apprentice at the start of the mentoring work, and ask that the apprentice synchronize her teaching so that it is aligned with the teaching the mentor is doing. Be sure to praise the mentor to the apprentice and to institute a specific structure for the mentoring relationship. The mentor can't just press herself on the more novice teacher—that breaks the mores of our schools.

✦ If you currently use parent volunteers or would like to do so, a teacher could step into the important role of teaching those parents ways in which they can support writing workshops. Again, be sure to let the teacher know that this is a crucially important role and that you believe the teacher could institute a program that would be gigantically important across the entire school. What a difference it could make if parents helped teachers reach more kids and helped also by manning a school-wide publication center.

✦ Could you ask a teacher to help gather and organize materials, school-wide, for an upcoming unit of study? Perhaps you'd give that person control of some of the budget so she could figure out what teachers already have, what they need, and what materials she would recommend purchasing. That teacher would need to spend time behind the scenes with the literacy coach and with you; giving the person access to the budget could make up for the more onerous parts of the job.

✦ You could ask a different teacher to step into a lead role for each unit, so that, for example, one teacher is the lead teacher on poetry, one on a unit on revision. This person will take the role more seriously if you send him out for staff development on that topic or give him the green light to order some professional books on that topic. It could be that a person is the expert not on a unit of study, but on a concern—on spelling and punctuation across the school, on finding new mentor texts for every unit of study, on conferring record sheets across the grades.

✦ Could a teacher in the school function as the liaison to the outside staff developer, talking to the staff developer prior to that person's day in the school, working with that person to establish a schedule? This may seem like nothing, but for most of us, it is a thrill to rub shoulders with an expert.

✦ If your school hosts a lot of visitors, could you ask a teacher to be in charge of taking visitors on tour and meeting with those visitors afterwards to answer their questions? In one school I know well, the principal always asked that visitors come as a grade-level cohort and visit all the host classrooms at their grade level. At the end of the day, the principal of the host school asked the visitors, "Was there one teacher you'd especially like to learn from?" After the visitors identified one person, the principal said, "Would it help if that teacher came to your school for a day and led writing workshops with your kids, just to show you how he'd do it?" If the visitors wanted such support, the principal released that teacher (if the teacher was willing) to be an unpaid staff developer for a day or two. When I asked the principal why she was willing to finance this, she said she'd found that her teachers learned and grew in dramatic ways when they were put into positions to teach others, and she was happy to finance that sort of learning.

✦ If you write letters to parents describing the school's approach to writing, spelling, homework, and so forth, could you ask teachers to play the role of a visiting columnist, writing portions of those letters? Perhaps one teacher could be a regular columnist.

When you turn a responsibility over to someone, there are some rules that one needs to follow (rules that I neglect at my peril). They are obvious— but like so many leadership principles, they are easier to say than to do.

Guidelines for Delegating Leadership Roles
✦ The person stepping into the new role needs to talk with the person who has previously done the job or with the person who is creating the job if it is new. The person in the new role must fashion clear objectives and learn any tried-and-true ways to accomplish the job. Otherwise, this

person who is inheriting the job will invent new procedures and will be told only afterwards that there were preexisting ways to proceed. The person needs to be given any enabling tools and information.

✦ The person stepping into the role needs to be invited to plan, dream, and improvise so that he can bring his imprint to the job. But the person needs to bring those ideas past whoever will oversee the work. Therefore, it helps to say early on, "Why don't you think about how this could be done, and let's talk about your ideas on such-and-such a date so that we can fashion a plan?"

✦ It is crucial to be extremely clear from the start about any financial rewards this may or may not entail. Do not leave this open-ended nor avoid discussing the matter. If there will be no money exchanged, be sure to say so. Can you reward in other ways? Be explicit and straightforward. Don't leave anything unclear.

✦ Establish a clear timetable, one that allows the person to accomplish the job well before the final product must actually be finished. This allows time for the person to get feedback and to revise or refine the initial draft. One should expect that someone who is new to an assignment will not do everything perfectly. Be ready to help that person and to do so without taking away the job.

✦ If anything comes up pertaining to this topic, bring the person you asked to take a lead role in this area into those conversations. That is, we can't give someone a job and then cut her out of it.

✦ When a person does a job, give that person public acknowledgement. Post it on a bulletin board, write about it in a newsletter, let others know to go to that person for questions related to that work. Thank that person publicly.

Continue Supporting Professional Growth in Teachers, Inside and Outside Your School

As a principal, you need to learn about and channel teachers towards opportunities that exist for teachers to study more and contribute more to the profession or to your school. Do so in ways that convey your awareness of a teacher's particular strengths.

How important it is for school leaders to do everything possible to make sure that teachers outgrow themselves in leaps and bounds! At the end of a day, a principal needs to ask his teachers not only, "What did you teach today?" but also, "What did you learn today?" If schools are places where teachers' abilities are called upon, extended, and challenged, then teachers will not only learn more, they will also stay longer in that school. This is not a small thing. As every principal knows, the retention rate for teachers is far too low, and the consequences of that are enormous. In urban classrooms, almost fifty percent of new teachers flee the profession during their first five years of teaching. Even in suburban schools, principals know that holding onto teachers is no easy task.

I'm convinced that one of the best ways that a principal can retain good teachers is by making an all-out effort to be sure those teachers feel that their strengths are recognized and extended. Yet a school can be such a small world that it is not always easy for a principal to showcase teachers. Putting any one teacher's practices in the limelight can make other teachers feel unseen or less accomplished. What's the principal to do?

> How important it is for school leaders to do everything possible to make sure that teachers outgrow themselves in leaps and bounds!

I strongly suggest that school leaders look for ways outside the confines of the school to help teachers grow. For example, every state has a state chapter of the International Reading Association and the National Council of Teachers of English (and of similar professional organizations for social studies, math, science educators, and the like). Encourage specific teachers to become active members of those state chapters, attending the local conferences, helping to organize the events those groups sponsor, and applying to present at the state conferences.

These professional organizations have been intellectual lifelines for me and for many others. For three decades now, I have never missed attending the national conference for the National Council of Teachers of English. When I was still a classroom teacher, I remember attending the conference and listening to the sessions, thinking, "I could do this." I put in an application to speak at one of the national conferences, was accepted, and found myself in the big leagues. What a great joy it has been to attend sessions across all these years, coming to know the authors of books that mean so much to me and coming to understand that my own local challenges are not unique to me, nor must I invent solutions on my own.

Professional organizations can be an incredibly important venue for some of your teachers, but there are many other equally important ways for you to channel teachers towards professional opportunities. Have you thought, for example, what it might mean to a teacher if you slipped a professional magazine into the teacher's mailbox with a note on it saying, "When I read this issue, I couldn't help but think that you should be writing articles like these. Your ideas deserve to be shared. Think about it . . ."

Every year I get a form letter from an organization asking whether I want to nominate people for a particular award. It is easy to push that request to the side. My in-box is too full and I cannot possibly respond to every request. You probably do the same. You probably have seen, for example, that the National Council of Teachers of English gives out a Don Graves Award each year to a particularly strong teacher of writing. You may have shrugged that award off, thinking there are no doubt other teachers who are more deserving. But pause for a moment and realize that even if the teacher you nominate never does get the award, your nomination, alone, might be a big honor. There have been years, for example, when instead of bypassing letters asking me to nominate people, I have instead taken the time to advocate for a couple of people. I send those people copies of my efforts to advocate on their behalf. I write something like this: "In my in-box today there was an email asking whether I knew a principal who might deserve the honor of becoming one of this year's group of . . . I thought of you and wrote the attached letter telling them about your amazing work. I hope you receive this recognition, but even if you don't, know that I think you are the best!" I'm pretty sure this makes a difference.

You, too, can be on the lookout for ways to celebrate your teachers. Ask your secretary or your assistant principal to be on the lookout with you!

As you do this, remember that people benefit not only from gold stars and certificates of recognition. People also benefit from being given opportunities to outgrow themselves. Consider, for example, what it might mean to send one of your teachers to New York City to attend one of our summer institutes in the teaching of reading or of writing. Consider suggesting a teacher sign up at a local college for a course in fiction writing. Imagine whether one of your teachers might profit from encouragement to attend graduate school.

Be sure, though, that when you want to suggest a teacher write for publication, attend a conference, or sign up for a graduate course, you make your suggestion in a way that shows the teacher you have been thinking about that one particular person and his or her strengths. Even if the truth is that you just want one of your third grade teachers to attend the upcoming computer conference, you'd be wise to talk about this differently. "I've been thinking of the way you learn in leaps and bounds. You are such a powerful, fast-paced learner that I have my fingers crossed you might be willing to attend the upcoming computer conference as our school's ambassador. And I'd hope that afterwards, you could help the whole school become more tech-savvy."

Even just the fact that you believe a person has amazing potential and that you take the time to talk about how that person could reach for a new horizon can make all the difference in the world.

DVD

Principal to Principal

Review any section of *Principal to Principal* that addresses a topic of current concern.

CHAPTER TEN

INTO the FUTURE

BUILDING REFORM INTO YOUR SCHOOL'S INFRASTRUCTURE

When I finished writing *The Art of Teaching Reading*—a book that required almost a decade of work—I decided that to celebrate, I would get a life. I would begin to entertain. I'd fix lovely meals and I'd have company over to enjoy those meals, just like others do.

But, of course, first you need the proper kitchen. So I invited a kitchen consultant to help me make decisions. The kitchen consultant, however, began by asking very personal questions. "What is it you generally cook?" and "How many people tend to work together when you prepare a meal?" she asked.

I realized I'd never get an island or a second sink or anything if I told her that one of us usually stirs some macaroni into the boiling water, and then after ten minutes we drain the water, add the powdered cheese, and that's dinner! So, finally, I said to that kitchen consultant, "You don't understand. I don't want the kitchen for the person I am now. I want it for the person I'm soon going to be!"

> ### THIS MONTH
>
> - Make shared units of study part of your school's new infrastructure.
>
> - Make grade-level curricular planning part of your school's new infrastructure.
>
> - Write to support your school's new infrastructure.

I laugh at that story now, but I also think it carries truths that matter to me. I do think that in life, all of us try to outgrow ourselves and that we do so by role-playing. And I think that in order to step into new roles, it helps to do so in newly fashioned places, equipped with props that embody the new roles.

When I was little, I often pretended to be grown-up. I'd pretend to be a teacher working with a classroom full of young charges, a knight in shining armor, a fearless leader at the helm of a ship. When I role-played my way into leadership roles, I always did so by first creating places: a school in my basement, a castle on the stump at the edge of our school's playground, a ship docked alongside the creek in my backyard. I took on props, too—chalk, a staff, make-believe binoculars. I believe that all of us become who we want to become by building places and taking on tools that allow us to step into those roles.

When my sister, a single mother, phoned one September to ask whether I really thought it was necessary for her to spring for new school supplies every September (couldn't she just round up some old pens and pencils?), I encouraged her to make that annual trip to the store. "After all," I said to her, "you dress your kids up to assume the role of soccer player, of cheerleader. Don't we also need to give kids the props necessary so they step into the role of avid reader, of diligent student?" My sister got her kids pencil cases and assignment pads—and that matters.

> The time to take one-time reforms and make them into whole-school structures and rituals is now, as you end one year of innovation and head towards the upcoming year.

I say this, because this entire book has been about the actions you can take to support writing instruction across one unfolding year. But I want to end this book by suggesting that in the end, the curricular leadership you've demonstrated this year needs to become part of the bearing walls in your school. The actions you've taken, the events you've created, the occasions that you've shaped all need to become part of your school's infrastructure. The time to take one-time reforms and make them into whole-school structures and rituals is now, as you end one year of innovation and head towards the upcoming year.

I cannot tell you exactly how to do this, of course, any more than you can tell teachers exactly how to organize tables, rugs, and chairs in their classrooms. Some books end with DVDs attached to the back cover, and I wish this book could end with airline tickets attached to the back cover. Then I could bring all of you to visit one school after another where a visionary leader has made the writing workshop (and the reading workshop, too) into part of the school's infrastructure. If you were to visit one such school, another, and another, then you could see the variety and the consistency between those schools, and I suspect this would help you find your very own way to take all that you've done this year and make it part of the bearing walls of your place.

I cannot, however, provide you with the airline tickets or the magic carpet necessary for you to coast in and out of schools, seeing ways in which others have grown the writing workshop, and so I will do the only thing I know to do and use words to help you see what others have done. I trust you'll read the suggestions I share, realizing that of course I know that in the end, you and your people will invent your very own idiosyncratic ways to create a richly literate culture within your school.

MAKE SHARED UNITS OF STUDY
PART OF YOUR SCHOOL'S NEW INFRASTRUCTURE

I recommend that as you approach the end of one year, you consider ways in which you can be sure that your teachers never again teach writing in isolation. No one structure will ever create learning communities among your teachers, but the first and most essential structure you can put into place is the concept of shared units of study.

When Carmen Fariña was Deputy Chancellor of New York City's schools, she suggested that every principal across every one of New York City's schools set aside time for "June planning." Principals covered classes for all the teachers across a grade level, and those teachers spent half a day devising a curricular calendar detailing their units of study in writing for the upcoming year. (Actually, in many schools teachers plan their curricular calendars for other subjects as well as writing.)

Of course, June planning days are far more effective when there is advance planning for the meetings themselves. During the week or two before June planning, principals help teachers to plan. To do this, for example, they might do the following:

- Provide teachers with books, articles, interactions, field trips, or samples of writing that can help teachers at that grade level imagine a new frontier or two that the principal, coach, or staff developer thinks would help that grade level.
- Release teachers to observe in the classrooms of the preceding grade so they know what it is students can already do and alter their plans accordingly, making sure to provide not a repetitive but a spiraling curriculum.
- Perhaps ask different teachers to prepare for June planning in specific ways so that people do not come to this empty-handed.
- Make sure that stakeholders are present so that plans aren't made that later need to be jettisoned. This may mean ensuring that the school's staff developer is present and will almost certainly mean that the school's literacy coach needs to be present at every grade level's June planning.

If you want to be sure to institutionalize June planning, then you may want to ask teachers to send a letter to the incoming students at a grade level and to their parents, letting them know how the upcoming year will unfold. You may, on the other hand, want to ask teachers to send such letters home on one of the first days of the new year.

Alternatively, you can organize a time in which you will give all parents a state-of-the-school address, and in that address you can tell parents that across every grade level teachers plan and follow a shared curricular calendar. If you make these structures very transparent, you can be sure that when teachers do not adhere to what you describe, parents will no doubt come to you, complaining. This, of course, provides a system of checks and balances.

I recently brought fifty school leaders to visit the Oyster River School District on Long Island. The superintendent there, Phyllis Harrington, told the visiting principals that her philosophy includes the adage, "What you expect, you inspect." Because she expects teachers to teach shared units of study and to progress through those units with some expediency, she asks every teacher in the district to maintain a writing portfolio for each child, and she establishes due dates for those portfolios. At the start of winter holidays, the principal collects each child's writing portfolio, and Phyllis spends a day or two in the school office, looking through the portfolios. She knows what the units of study are that each grade decided to embrace and looks for three publications, representing three units of study, by December. She also looks for evidence of the writing that children do as they progress towards those publications. "I can't actually look at every child's portfolio," Phyllis explained to the principals. "But I dip in and out enough to get an idea of the way in which teachers are teaching shared units of study. I do this because I think it is important."

MAKE GRADE-LEVEL CURRICULAR PLANNING PART OF YOUR SCHOOL'S NEW INFRASTRUCTURE

Earlier in this book, I described some of the many ways in which school principals make time for all the teachers across a grade level to plan and reflect on teaching together. The specific ways in which you free teachers up to plan together will be up to you, but you cannot expect that grade-level cohorts will plan units of study together unless you provide regular, weekly time for these groups of teachers to meet together.

In addition, for these meeting to be effective and helpful enough to become permanent, you will want to provide leadership for those grade-level planning sessions. Usually, literacy coaches attend and help lead these sessions. If you do not have a coach, it will be especially crucial that you also support a teacher to function as the lead teacher for that grade. This is also a wise idea even if you do have a literacy coach.

In many of the urban schools I know best, one teacher from each grade officially assumes the role as lead teacher for writing at his grade level. Many of these schools contain half a dozen teachers at each grade level. In smaller schools, where there may be only one or two classes on a grade level, one person from the primary grades and one from the upper grades might assume such a role.

> Teachers will be vastly more likely to accept a lead teacher in writing if you also ask other teachers to play parallel roles in other areas.

I should caution you that any teacher who is asked to function as the lead teacher will probably run into trouble if she sees this as an invitation to take charge, to assign, to judge, or to order. Instead, I hope this teacher sees this as an invitation to serve. If the lead teacher makes a point of asking everyone what supplies they will need for the upcoming unit and then makes sure those supplies are ordered, then the lead teacher's colleagues will accept this sort of leadership. If the lead teacher plugs in the coffee pot before a grade-level meeting and stops to buy donut holes the morning of the meeting, then her colleagues will accept this sort of leadership. Especially at first, the lead teacher needs to see the role as one of enabling and supporting and facilitating. I recommend taking this a bit slowly.

Teachers will be vastly more likely to accept a lead teacher in writing if you also ask other teachers to play parallel roles in other areas. When Carmen Fariña was principal at PS 6, every teacher at every grade level was lead teacher in one subject or another! Of course, some of those subjects were closer to Carmen's heart and to the central work of the school than others, but distributing leadership positions in such a way can be helpful. The person whose role it is to be the math lead teacher will no doubt hope that her colleagues wouldn't give her a hard time when she steps up to lead in her subject area, so the implicit expectation is, "I'll follow your lead in writing if you, in turn, follow my lead in math."

Then, too, if there are ways in which you hope the lead teacher will step forward, you need to be explicit. If you would like the lead teacher to specify the nature of the student work that teachers will bring with them to grade-level meetings, then you need to say to your staff, "I have asked the lead teachers to specify what student work you will bring to meetings, but it is my decision that at every grade-level meeting, every one of us will bring three selected pieces of writing. These pieces of writing could represent the work that a variety of strugglers in our classes did the preceding day, or they could be published writing that shows the array of writing levels in a classroom—the lead teacher can specify. But I'm asking that we all bring three pieces of student writing to every grade-level meeting."

It is important that you give the lead teachers added access to professional development. These are the people that especially need to be released to attend conference days and to be sent to summer institutes. Their access to experts allows these teachers to step forward a bit, although I'd still suggest they do so saying, "Would it help if I run through some of the tips Don Graves has given about how to write short stories?" That is, at least when these leaders are just stepping into their roles, there are ways you can make it easier for colleagues to accept them. One way is for these lead teachers to portray themselves more as supporters and conduits of information than as gurus.

Some principals refer to the collection of lead teachers as their "articulation team" and give this group special responsibilities. For example, an articulation committee could make it more likely that teachers know what students will be taught in the preceding and following years, helping teachers be sure that each year builds on (instead of repeats) the preceding year.

These lead teachers can be instrumental in holding the grade-level groups together.

WRITE TO SUPPORT YOUR SCHOOL'S NEW INFRASTRUCTURE

In your classrooms, teachers will have used charts as a way to remind children of all they have already learned, making sure that youngsters continue to rely on preceding minilessons for their current work. In a similar way, you will want to think about ways you, your literacy coach, and your lead teachers can use written documents as a way to be sure that the work everyone has done to learn about teaching writing becomes part of the infrastructure of the school.

Many principals I know well use the school's handbook as one form of institutional memory. For example, you may want to write up the school's approach to teaching writing, or you may want to excerpt other documents within your handbook as a way to do this. Some principals include several sketches of classroom layouts within their handbooks or examples of editing checklists, classroom charts, and bibliographies of touchstone texts. Many principals include examples of letters that teachers have written to parents explaining their yearlong writing curriculum, inviting parents to author celebrations, or explaining policies related to conventions of written language.

If you decide to use your school's handbook as one form of institutional memory, be sure that you include several examples of whatever items you include. That is, include several alternate sketches of classroom design, several different versions of invitations to author celebrations, several different editing checklists. I recommend entitling these in ways that convey alternatives. A sketch of classroom layout might be entitled, "One Possible Way to Organize Your Classroom to Support Interaction and Engagement." An editing checklist might be entitled, "One Version of an Editing Checklist." Of course, it will be very important that the handbook, itself, become a living document, changing from one year to the next.

> The school's handbook might be one way for you to be sure that reforms in writing aren't blown away in the winds of time.

The school's handbook might be one way for you to be sure that reforms in writing aren't blown away in the winds of time, but you will want to provide other more informal records of the school's learning life. Above all, you'll want to be sure that teachers across a grade level begin to create binders or folders for each unit of study. That is, the third grade teachers will need to have a binder or a folder titled, "Fiction Writing: Third Grade." It could be that the first year came and went without people combining forces to create such a binder, and, in fact, teachers may end the first year feeling as if most of what they did during year one was to digest and use the information from *Units of Study* for grades 3–5. But certainly, as you end the year, looking back on all that has been accomplished and looking forward to the upcoming year, you will want to be sure teachers begin gathering materials into unit-specific binders.

One way to be sure this happens is to suggest that before sending student work home at the end of the year, teachers sort through the work and find samples of student writing that they can use in minilessons during upcoming years. Encourage teachers to also save work that can help any teachers who are new to a grade envision how a unit of study will actually unfold. Teachers will probably have conferring record sheets they could gather within a binder. They'd probably be eager to have someone take photographs of their most successful charts, saving these in a unit-specific binder.

Then, too, after teachers plan for the units of study they will teach in an upcoming year, you may suggest that each teacher take responsibility for researching one of those units, doing some extra professional reading on the selected unit and gathering recommended ideas and book titles.

Of course, teachers will also want to invent brand new units of study, and those, especially, will need binders full of support materials. There are some units that promise to be surefire successes. For example, it's always a success when kindergarten teachers design and teach a unit of study on list books or on songwriting. It is always a success when teachers in grades 3–5 bring the K–2 poetry book to higher grades, expanding on this book by leaning on work that Georgia Heard has done with poetry. It is always a success when first and second grade teachers invent a fiction unit of study. Of course, nothing is more successful than when teachers invent curriculum based on whatever it is they know and love. Be sure their hard work becomes part of the infrastructure of the school!

It is crucial, of course, that binders containing last year's charts, mini-lessons, conferring records, and teacher samples of writing are regarded as "improvable texts," not as the law of the land! That is, just as the school's handbook needs to contain a variety of examples of any one document, all bearing titles that are worded tentatively, "One Possible Way to . . . ," so, too, do these curricular binders need to contain lots of different versions of documents, unit plans, and the like. These materials, like the *Units of Study* books themselves, must all be resources that expand a teacher's imagination rather than scripts that turn teachers into robots!

Next year, then, be sure that you help teachers to lay out the contents of a binder and a *Units of Study* book, and to look over all these materials, thinking, "How can I take what is especially good from all this and improve on it, making the best that we know even better?"

After all, the reason to write is that teachers, all human beings, can learn from putting a text—our account of our lives and work—in the center of the conversation. At that point, we can work together to improve on it. Teaching writing, like writing itself, like living itself, is a continual process of drafting and revising, and then, writing, teaching, living again.

"Building a Literacy Program over Time." Two principals relate how literacy reform in their schools evolved across the years.

References

Allington, Richard. 2006. Address given at Principals as Curricular Leaders Conference, 6 December, Teachers College: New York.

Allington, Richard, and Peter H. Johnston. 2002. *Reading to Learn: Lessons from Exemplary Fourth-Grade Classrooms*. New York: The Guilford Press.

Anderson, Carl. 2008. *Strategic Writing Conferences: Smart Conversations That Move Young Writers Forward*. Portsmouth, NH: Heinemann.

Avery, Carol, and Donald Graves. 2002. *. . . And with a Light Touch: Learning about Reading, Writing, and Teaching with First Graders*, 2nd ed. Portsmouth, NH: Heinemann.

Baker, Russell et al. 1998. *Inventing the Truth: The Art and Craft of Memoir*. Edited with an introduction by William K. Zinsser. Boston: Houghton Mifflin.

Barth, Roland S. 2007. Address given at Principals as Curricular Leaders Conference, 7 November, Teachers College: New York.

Barth, Roland S. 1990. *Improving Schools from Within: Teachers, Parents, and Principals Can Make the Difference*. San Francisco: Jossey-Bass.

Barth, Roland S. 2001. *Learning by Heart*. San Francisco: Jossey-Bass.

Barton, Bob, and David Booth. 1990. *Stories in the Classroom: Storytelling, Reading Aloud, and Roleplaying with Children*. Portsmouth, NH: Heinemann.

Baylor, Byrd. 1995. *I'm in Charge of Celebration*. New York: Simon & Schuster.

Bear, Donald R. et al. 1996. *Words Their Way: Word Study for Phonics, Vocabulary, and Spelling*. Upper Saddle River, NJ: Merrill.

Bear, Donald R., Francine Johnston, and Marcia Invernizzi. 2006. *Words Their Way: Letter and Picture Sorts for Emergent Spellers*. Upper Saddle River, NJ: Pearson/Merrill/Prentice Hall.

Beers, Kylene. 2007. Address given at Principals as Curricular Leaders Conference, 30 January, Teachers College: New York.

Berdan, Kristina, et al. 2006. *Writing for a Change: Boosting Literacy and Learning Through Social Action*. San Francisco: Jossey-Bass.

Calkins, Lucy. 2001. *The Art of Teaching Reading*. New York: Longman.

Calkins, Lucy. 2005. *Big Lessons from Small Writers: Teaching Primary Writing (DVD)*. Portsmouth, NH: Heinemann.

Calkins, Lucy. 2006. *A Guide to the Writing Workshop* in *Units of Study for Teaching Writing, Grades 3–5*. Portsmouth, NH: Heinemann.

Calkins, Lucy. 2003. *Nuts and Bolts of Primary Writing* in *Units of Study for Primary Writing: A Yearlong Curriculum*. Portsmouth, NH: Heinemann.

Calkins, Lucy et al. 2007. *Seeing Possibilities DVD (3–5): An Inside View of Units of Study for Teaching Writing*. Portsmouth, NH: Heinemann.

Calkins, Lucy et al. 2003. *Units of Study for Primary Writing: A Yearlong Curriculum*. Portsmouth, NH: Heinemann.

Calkins, Lucy et al. 2006. *Units of Study for Teaching Writing, Grades 3–5*. Portsmouth, NH: Heinemann.

Calkins, Lucy, Amanda Hartman, and Zoe Ryder White. 2005. *One to One: The Art of Conferring with Young Writers*. Portsmouth, NH: Heinemann.

Collins, James C. 2001. *Good to Great: Why Some Companies Make the Leap . . . and Others Don't*. New York: HarperCollins.

Cooney, Barbara. 1985. *Miss Rumphius*. New York: Puffin Books.

Cruz, Colleen. 2008. *A Quick Guide to Reaching Struggling Writers*, in Workshop Help Desk Series. Portsmouth, NH: Heinemann.

Ehrenworth, Mary, and Vicki Vinton. 2005. *The Power of Grammar: Unconventional Approaches to the Conventions of Language*. Portsmouth, NH: Heinemann.

Erikson, Erik H. 2000. *The Erik Erikson Reader*, selected and edited by Robert Coles. New York: W. W. Norton.

Fariña, Carmen and Laura Kotch. 2008. *A School Leader's Guide to Excellence: Collaborating Our Way to Better Schools*. Portsmouth, NH: Heinemann.

Fletcher, Ralph. 1993. *What a Writer Needs*, with a foreword by Donald M. Murray. Portsmouth, NH: Heinemann.

Fletcher, Ralph, and JoAnn Portalupi. 2001. *Writing Workshop: The Essential Guide*. Portsmouth, NH: Heinemann.

Fullan, Michael. 2007. Address given at Principals as Curricular Leaders Conference, 24 January, Teachers College: New York.

Fullan, Michael. 1999. *Change Forces: The Sequel*. New York: Falmer.

Fullan, Michael. 2003a. *Change Forces with a Vengeance*. New York: Routledge-Falmer.

Fullan, Michael. 2001. *Leading in a Culture of Change*. San Francisco: Jossey-Bass.

Fullan, Michael. 2003b. *The Moral Imperative of School Leadership*. Thousand Oaks, CA: Corwin Press.

Gardner, Howard. 1995. *Leading Minds: An Anatomy of Leadership*. New York: Basic Books.

Goldberg, Natalie. 2006. *Writing Down the Bones: Freeing the Writer Within.* Boston: Shambhala.

Henkes, Kevin. 2007. *Chrysanthemum.* New York: Greenwillow.

Lamott, Anne. 1994. *Bird by Bird: Some Instructions on Writing and Life.* New York: Pantheon.

Lewis, Rose. 2000. *I Love You Like Crazy Cakes.* Boston: Little, Brown.

Mermelstein, Leah. 2007. *Don't Forget to Share: The Crucial Last Step in the Writing Workshop.* Portsmouth, NH: Heinemann.

Merriam, Eve. 1990. "A Lazy Thought," from *There Is No Rhyme for Silver* in *Jamboree: Rhymes for All Times.* New York: Dell Publishing Company.

Murray, Donald. 1989. *Expecting the Unexpected: Teaching Myself—and Others—to Read and Write.* Portsmouth, NH: Boynton/Cook Publishers.

Murray, Donald M. 2004. *A Writer Teaches Writing,* 2nd ed. Boston: Thomson/Heinle.

Parsons, Stephanie. 2007. *Second Grade Writers: Units of Study to Help Children Focus on Audience and Purpose.* Portsmouth, NH: Heinemann.

Peters, Thomas J., and Robert H. Waterman, Jr. 1982. *In Search of Excellence: Lessons from America's Best-Run Companies.* New York: Harper & Row Publishers.

Pinnell, Gay Su, and Irene Fountas. 2003. *Phonics Lessons: Letters, Words, and How They Work.* Portsmouth, NH: Heinemann.

Pressley, Michael. 2001. *Learning to Read: Lessons from Exemplary First-Grade Classrooms.* New York: The Guilford Press.

Ray, Katie Wood, with Lester Laminack. 2001. *The Writing Workshop: Working Through the Hard Parts (And They're All Hard Parts).* Urbana, IL: National Council of Teachers of English.

Ray, Katie Wood, with Lisa B. Cleaveland. 2004. *About the Authors: Writing Workshop with Our Youngest Writers.* Portsmouth, NH: Heinemann.

Reeves, Douglas. 2006a. Address given at Principals as Curricular Leaders Conference, 6 November, Teachers College: New York.

Reeves, Douglas. 2006b. *The Learning Leader: How to Focus School Improvement for Better Results.* Alexandria, VA: ASCD.

Reynolds, Peter H. 2004. *Ish.* Cambridge, MA: Candlewick Press.

Sarason, Seymour. 1982. *The Culture of the School and the Problem of Change.* Boston: Allyn and Bacon.

Sergiovanni, Tom. 2004. Address given at Principals as Curricular Leaders Conference, 20 October, Teachers College: New York.

Shaughnessy, Mina P. 1977. *Errors and Expectations: A Guide for the Teacher of Basic Writing.* New York: Oxford University Press.

Strunk, William, Jr., and E. B. White. 1979. *Elements of Style,* 3rd ed. New York: Macmillan Publishing.

Taylor, Sarah Picard. 2008. *A Quick Guide to Teaching Persuasive Writing*, in Workshop Help Desk Series. Portsmouth, NH: Heinemann.

Tyler, Cheryl, and Alison Porcelli. 2008. *A Quick Guide to Boosting English Acquisition in Choice Time*, in Workshop Help Desk Series. Portsmouth, NH: Heinemann.

Waber, Bernard. 1972. *Ira Sleeps Over*. Boston: Houghton Mifflin.

Willems, Mo. 2004. *Knuffle Bunny: A Cautionary Tale*. New York: Hyperion Books for Children.

Zinsser, William K. 2006. *On Writing Well: The Classic Guide to Writing Nonfiction*. New York: HarperCollins.

The WORKSHOP HELP DESK series

Pocket-sized professional development on topics of interest to you and your staff.

A QUICK GUIDE TO
Boosting English Acquisition in Choice Time, K–2
ALISON PORCELLI & CHERYL TYLER

Alison and Cheryl explain how choice-time workshops can be structured to help English language learners imagine, create, and explore language through play. They outline two units of study for choice-time workshops, the first using open-ended materials, the other using literature to inspire play.
978-0-325-02615-2 / $8.00

A QUICK GUIDE TO
Teaching Persuasive Writing, K–2
SARAH PICARD TAYLOR

Children have voices that need to be heard and ideas that need to be understood. Building on this premise Sarah describes why you should try a persuasive writing unit of study, describes two units of study for the primary classroom, and lists tips and ideas for helping students get their persuasive writing out into the world.
978-0-325-02597-1 / $8.00

A QUICK GUIDE TO
Reaching Struggling Writers, K–5
M. COLLEEN CRUZ

Colleen shows how to stop struggling with writers who struggle. You'll find effective support for students who say: I'm not a good writer; My hand hurts; I don't know how to spell; I don't have anything to write about; I never get to write anything I want to write; I'm done.
978-0-325-02595-7 / $8.00

A QUICK GUIDE TO
Making Your Teaching Stick, K–5
SHANNA SCHWARTZ

Recognizing that there is a vast difference between children getting it and children holding on to what they have learned, Shanna lays out the universal principles of "stickiness" and describes how they can be used to tweak your teaching for a more lasting impact on young writers.
978-0-325-02596-4 / $8.00